PENGUIN BOOKS

## Speaking for Ourselves

Alwyn 'Hop' Owen was born in Whangarei in 1926. He joined the New Zealand Broadcasting Corporation as a technician in the 1950s and became interested in radio documentary work while on the West Coast. He became a documentary producer in Wellington in 1964, later founding the 'Insight' documentary series in 1969 and the 'Spectrum' series with Jack Perkins in 1972.

Alwyn Owen has won a number of awards, including the Mobil Award in 1980, Best Entertainment Programme (in collaboration with Jack Perkins) in 1981, Broadcaster of the Year (the Bill Toft Award) in 1984, and Best Documentary and Best Entertainment Programme in the 1984 Mobil Radio Awards. He is married with a family of three.

Jack Perkins was born forty-four years ago in the Lancastrian town of Bolton and came to New Zealand at the age of eleven. He has a B.A. in political science from Victoria University, and is a well-known Wellington cricketer.

Of Jack Perkins's twenty-five years in radio, the last thirteen have been on the 'Spectrum' documentary series with Alwyn Owen. He won the 1978 Mobil Award for Best Factual Spoken Programme and the 1980 Mobil Award, with Owen, for Best Entertainment Programme. He is married with four children.

With best wishes -

Hugh Owen. & Jack Perkins.

# Speaking for Ourselves

Echoes from New Zealand's past from
the award-winning 'Spectrum' radio series

**Alwyn Owen and Jack Perkins**

PENGUIN BOOKS

Penguin Books (N.Z.) Ltd, 182-190 Wairau Road, Auckland 10, New Zealand
Penguin Books Ltd, Harmondsworth, Middlesex, England
Penguin Books, 40 West 23rd Street, New York, N.Y.10010, U.S.A.
Penguin Books Australia Ltd, Ringwood, Victoria, Australia
Penguin Books Canada Ltd, 2801 John Street, Markham, Ontario,
    Canada L3R 1B4

First published 1986

Designed by Richard King
Typeset by Typocrafters Ltd, Auckland
Printed in Hong Kong

*To all 'Spectrum' contributors – who, through their words,
have shared with warmth and generosity their life experiences*

# Contents

With best wishes to John, Rita
and Family.

Jack Perkins
&
Alwyn Owen.

# Foreword

'The only history worth reading', wrote John Ruskin, 'is that which is done and seen out of the mouths of the men who did and saw it.' Ruskin was exaggerating, of course. He was trying to force an unpopular view on British public opinion in the late nineteenth century. And to his 'men' we must add 'women'. But his general point stands, an eloquent antidote to the idea that history is made up wholly of stories about great men and great events, written by professional historians detached from their evidence. As this book shows, it is not so.

History consists of stories that create the texture of the past and give it meaning. They serve, as Robin Hyde once put it, 'to make all men of all generations and places truly intimate with one another'. Until recently, we have had access to far too few such stories in and about New Zealand. Professional historians have chosen, by and large, not to mine this lode. And we have come perilously close to losing that part of our history that was not political, military, administrative or contained in documents.

Alwyn Owen and Jack Perkins compiled this book without knowing they were doing so. As they write in their preface, they began the 'Spectrum' radio documentary series in 1972 with a brief to prepare thirteen programmes. Twelve years and five hundred documentaries later they are still at work, recording New Zealand stories in New Zealand voices, presenting New Zealand history out of the mouths of men and women who saw and made that history, building up the nearest thing we have to a national oral archive. Some of their interviewees, such as Whina Cooper, were public figures before 'Spectrum' caught up with them. Others, such as Nancy Sutherland and Peter Anyon, were well known in the districts in which they grew up or worked. The majority, however, were what would be called ordinary folk: Joe Gasparich in the Far North, George Davies in the Buller, Bob Edwards in the Hokonui, Florence Harsant at Waitahanui and Hahei, and others; but ordinary folk who had witnessed what subsequent generations would regard as extraordinary events: felling kauris and collecting gum, panning for gold, taking to the road and humping a swag, nursing victims through the epidemics that once ravaged Maori communities.

Astonishing as many of these stories do seem to a predominantly urban audience, protected and comforted by the technologies of the 1980s, they are the stuff of New Zealand's Maori, colonial and pioneering past. There is perhaps more breadth and depth of early twentieth-century New Zealand experience in this book than in any other single volume I have read. And it is spoken about in voices that began to talk when the country still had local and regional dialects, before the great cultural blenders of radio and television began to homogenise us. Ironic, then, that it was radio that first brought us these voices.

Broadcasts are transitory, however, even if the tapes on which they are based are not. The voices of 'Spectrum' interviewees initially catch the attention of listeners and then fade into the ether. They are difficult to recall, to investigate further, to enjoy again. Hence this book. Though inevitably they lose something in translation from oral to literary forms, the 'Spectrum' subjects nevertheless speak – and go on speaking – through these pages. Their sharp recollection of events, their eye for telling detail, their distinctive mannerisms, are all here still; they can be recalled simply by taking the volume off the shelf and thumbing its pages.

For me, an historian – and an historian primarily interested in oral history – the value of this book is enhanced by the authors' appendix on the methods of oral history. Owen and Perkins began with what A. H. Fox Strangways has defined as basic equipment for the oral historian: 'unfeigned sympathy, inexhaustible curiosity, lively gratitude, untiring patience and a scrupulous conscience.' All these were prerequisites for persuading their subjects to talk as candidly as they do. But to this intuitive base, the members of the 'Spectrum' team have added research skills, interviewing techniques and a high degree of technical competence in their use of recording equipment. Sound advice on all these matters can be found in the appendix, and it will help everybody, from the professional historian, to the student writing a thesis, to the amateur wanting simply to record a grandparent's recollections. Such information, set firmly in the context of New Zealand conditions and conventions, is not available from any other source at the time of writing.

I am happy to praise this book in the highest terms, to congratulate its subjects on their articulateness, and to commend Alwyn Owen and Jack Perkins for revealing and sharing with us the experience and eloquence of our fellow countrymen and countrywomen.

**Michael King**
Auckland, 1985

# Preface

In a certain sense, all men are historians.
— Thomas Carlyle. Essay: *On History*

The 'Spectrum' documentary series was launched by the then NZBC in early 1972, with an expected 'run' of thirteen programmes. The series was designed to contrast with the analytical, current-affairs documentaries produced by the 'Insight' unit, and accordingly the brief called for programmes with a high degree of human interest and a strong reflection of the New Zealand way of life. Thirteen years and more than 500 programmes later, 'Spectrum' still holds to this brief, and remarkably – for staff turnover in the electronic media is relatively high – we two, the unit's original producers, still run the series. The library of 'Spectrum' documentaries probes almost every facet of New Zealand social life, and has been described as a national resource.

A quarter of all 'Spectrum' programmes could be described as having an oral history content, and the chapters of this book are representative of this output. They cover half a century, from the 1900s to the 1950s – but this book is not a social history of that period. Rather, it is a collection of first-hand accounts of New Zealand life from people who recall with vivid intensity a particular experience or an episode in their lives: George Davies on the Howard goldfield during the Depression days; Albert Roberts, shipwrecked on Disappointment Island; Dr Peter Anyon in general practice in a West Coast mining township.

Most of the storytellers are in their seventies and eighties, a few in their nineties. Several of the contributors have died since the original programmes were recorded.

As producers of the series, and editors of this book, we make no claims to be oral historians, although inevitably, in the course of more than a decade of fieldwork recording for radio, skills and techniques have been developed which overlap those of the oral historian. Some of those techniques have been detailed in the appendix.

The original recordings were designed for radio, and in particular for a broadly based National Programme audience, and their value as oral history has always been a secondary consideration. Radio imposed its own criteria, and many of these would be quite unacceptable to the historian.

The initial selection of informants is a case in point. 'Spectrum' looks for people who have the ability to evoke a mood, a period, or an incident; who have the ability to articulate their thoughts and feelings – not necessarily in middle-class English, but in language that strikes directly at the listener. English is a superbly precise language, but precision in the speaker demands precision in the listener, a constant analysis of information. At another level, speech can bypass this filtration of ideas and communicate directly, and frequently at a very emotional level. This ability to communicate, to involve listeners, is a requirement for radio; it is not of course a criterion for the oral historian.

As well as the ability to communicate, the informant must have a good story to tell, and this requires rather more than an ability to recall events. In programmes of this nature, feelings are as important as facts; it is not merely events themselves that are interesting, but also the reactions and feelings they provoke. Thus Nancy Sutherland tells of childhood at French Pass, but more interesting than her anecdotes are the recollections of her feelings, related with such intensity – '. . . *bursting* with energy, *bursting* with aggression, *bursting* with hate . . .'

Some of the very qualities necessary for a radio programme of the 'Spectrum' type create problems for the editor who transcribes them to the written form. The degree of personality the programme requires is difficult to convey on the printed page, which deals poorly with the subtleties of spoken language. Stress, pauses, the hesitation before a telling answer, the sheer vitality of voice – or, at times, its weariness – are lost to the reader. If justification is required in the light of this, it lies in the fact that an element of personality *does* remain in the words themselves; that the stories are intrinsically interesting; and that in the printed form they do not suffer from the transience of the radio broadcast.

In editing material for this book, the interviewers' questions have been deleted, to maintain a narrative flow. Where possible, the original field-tapes have been used as source material rather than the finished documentary, with its necessary editing to meet the demands of shape and time. Care has been taken to retain meaning, speech patterns, rhythm, and idiom of the original speech. Some rearrangement of material has been necessary in several of the stories to preserve continuity – where, for example, an informant during the latter stages of the interview has suddenly recalled incidents or additional facts that supplement earlier information.

The original interviews which form the basis of this book were all recorded by us, with three exceptions: George Davies, Marjorie Lees and Joe Gasparich were interviewed by Laurie Swindell.

Invariably, interviews are preceded by research. In the 'Spectrum' unit this is undertaken by the producers themselves. Further research and cross-checking was undertaken when the programmes selected for this book were transcribed. In many cases, however, the intensely personal nature of some of the recollections made detailed verification impossible; in others, the events described will undoubtedly be clouded by the fallibility of memory, the faulty evaluation of data, or by sheer conviction, even in the face of facts.

Thus Albert Roberts, shipwrecked on Disappointment Island, saw his ship drive over the bones of a wooden vessel, wrecked at some previous time. Until his death, he was convinced that his ship drove over the remains of the *General Grant* – although all other evidence points to the fact that the *General Grant* was wrecked on the main Auckland Island, to the east of Disappointment. But that is his conviction. And he was there on the *Dundonald*; it's his story.

In a very real sense 'Spectrum' is an 'access' programme. It is about New Zealanders, by New Zealanders. It takes their stories, and broadcasts them to New Zealanders. This representative selection is in its way a tribute to all the many people who have contributed to the series; who have given freely and warmly of their time and experiences, and communicated the emotions, the triumphs, the sadness and often the wonder of their lives, through the microphone. To record their experiences, and often be party to their confidences, has been a rich and incomparable undertaking.

The Alexander Turnbull Library provided invaluable help when the original programmes were being researched, and their assistance in providing many of the photographs for this publication is gratefully acknowledged.

We should also like to make special mention of the ready support and encouragement we have received from Radio New Zealand during twelve years of 'Spectrum' and in the compilation of this book.

**Alwyn Owen**
**Jack Perkins**
Producers, 'Spectrum'
Wellington, 1985

# 1 Blue Ducks and Pay-dirt

George Davies recalls life on the Howard goldfield
in the Upper Buller during the Depression years.

*The Great Depression of the 1930s, and its accompanying wave of
unemployment, drove many workers away from the towns and cities
in search of a subsistence livelihood in the country. Some, remembering the goldfields where their fathers or grandfathers had worked,
struggled up half-forgotten creeks and gullies to reopen old workings,
or establish new ones.*

*The movement of unemployed to the goldfields was given impetus
by the Gold Subsidy Scheme, whereby the Government paid married
men thirty shillings and single men fifteen shillings a week to search
for gold. It was intended that the men retain the value of their gold
until it exceeded the subsidy; at this point the miner would have become
self-sufficient. In practice, however, few men earned more than the
value of their subsidy.*

*George Davies and his mates left the city for the Howard goldfield
of the Upper Buller. In 1932 the Mines Department fostered development of the Howard field, and by the winter of that year ninety men
were working the area.*

*Gold recovery was back-breaking work. The romantic image of the
prospector swirling his pan in a creek and discovering a fortune had
no reality on the Howard. It was, instead, heavy labour, which involved
clearing timber and large boulders from the claim, diverting a creek
perhaps, and certainly constructing head- and tail-races to bring water
to the face and dispose of the spoil. Only then could actual gold recovery
begin – if, indeed, gold were present.*

*For George Davies and his mates, there was an added element. On
seeing the first specks of gold lying between the riffles of the sluice-
box, they were exhilarated, but it was not simply because they were
'on gold'. Rather, it was the feeling that they had served an apprenticeship; that, in leaving the city and coming to the Howard as new
chums, they had found physical and mental skills previously unknown
to them, and become practitioners of a craft.*

George Davies – a 1930s
portrait
*Alan Scott*

We were digging a ditch on relief work at Lyall Bay during the 1930s
slump. There were three of us in our gang – me and Curly and Big
Mac – and the foreman came along and said, 'Look, if you blokes
jump in and out of that ditch a few times, you'll take more out on
your boots than you did on your shovels.'

Well, Curly, he was furious, and he said, 'Well, I'm leaving.'

Mac said, 'Where are you going?'

'Oh,' he said, 'that's OK. You'll see.'

Well, later on, Curly said, 'Any of you blokes want to come gold mining with me?'

We argued it out, and finally we were convinced, so we sold everything saleable and we hopped on the Nelson ferry, bound for a goldfield. When we were giving our notice in, the foreman suggested we buy the shovels. And Curly said, 'What do we want to buy the shovels for?'

'Well,' he said, 'you've got three shovels there. You've had them a fortnight. They're brand new. There's never been a bit of dirt on them.'

Curly's reply was a masterpiece. You couldn't sort of repeat what he said, but the foreman, he flushed and went off, and we departed in a blaze of glory, and that fixed him for all time.

We got talking on the boat, and, you know, we found out that none of us knew one single thing about gold mining. Eventually we arrived at a goldfield called the Howard. It's a sort of a river junction, and we were dumped out in an untidy heap on the roadside, and we had a week's food, a bit of money which we reckoned would last us a couple of months, a lot of enthusiasm, and no knowledge.

Anyhow, there was a little farmhouse up on the rise, and while Big Mac went off for further directions, Curly and I wandered down to the banks of a small stream. And Curly, you know, with all the aplomb of an old sourdough, he dipped some creek sand out into his gold-pan and commenced to try his hand. After a few swirls he said excitedly, 'This pan is full of gold, boy! We don't need to go any further. Our fortune is made!'

Well, I wasn't impressed, because as I said to Curly, if there was so much gold there, what was that little cocky doing farming a few chains away? Of course, Curly had a classic reply: 'Maybe he doesn't like gold mining.'

Anyhow, Big Mac arrived back with the farmer. He proved to be a kindly, understanding bloke, and he was a big help. He told us we couldn't get our gear up the creek, not by ourselves, and to take what we needed and he'd send up the rest in a few days. We were to ask for a bloke called Paddy, and he'd show us where there was a bit of ground we could work.

Well, that journey showed us how soft we were, crossing and recrossing the water; the packs weighed a ton, and every round stone we stood on rolled underfoot. Finally we met a bloke. Did he know Paddy? Yes, he did. Well, eventually we found Paddy, and he was making toast on a manuka fork that was about four feet long, and when I saw Paddy's fireplace I realised why he wanted that fork. It was about five feet wide and three feet deep, and it was filled with a red-hot mass of glowing embers.

Old Paddy was a pretty quiet chap, and he didn't give many explanations, but he showed us an area alongside the creek, and he told us how to mark it out and how to start in. So Curly of course said, 'This

Men on relief work during the
Depression of the 1930s
*Alexander Turnbull Library*

gold; I got a couple of panfuls down there while we were talking to
that cocky.'

Old Paddy said, 'Well, maybe you did – but what do you think I'm
doing in here? You might get ten bob a ton for that. It's mica.'

It was starting to dawn on us that we didn't know too much, and
we'd have to depend on Paddy and a lot of other people for a bit of
help.

We started in. Well, I never worked so hard in my life. We used
to stagger back to camp, and we were that bloomin' tired we couldn't
get a meal even, and we would mess around until finally somebody
would stagger up and put the billy on. We took turns in the drain,
and the work revolved around working a turn in the drain, and getting
wood to cover it to stop the sand and rocks from falling in on us. And
one bloke had to go ahead and clear the ground – and that meant cutting
down all the trees and getting everything out of the way.

Well, there were millions and millions of sandflies – especially in
the drain – and millions of blowflies. You know, those blowflies, they
would blow anything; hang a jersey on a tree and in half an hour it
would be white. Potatoes that were a bit damp, new blankets . . . We
had more or less got used to having porridge sprinkled with golden
syrup and sandflies, but blowflies – they were out. We shot some
rabbits, and had to skin them under water, to beat them.

Anyhow, Curly said he had a scheme that would beat them. 'Shove
the rabbits in a bag and pull 'em up a birch tree. That'll fix these cows.'

So we did that, and at teatime we pulled the bag down, and you know, the flies came out of it like a swarm of bees. So I said, 'Well, what's it going to be – maggoty rabbit, or scones?' We settled for the scones.

We had a pretty crook diet at this stage – a few spuds, some golden syrup, and bread, and for a variation we fried the bread in fat. Then one day we looked Paddy up and asked him how he dealt with the flies, and you know for the first time I saw a glint of humour in old Paddy's eye.

'Tell you what I do. Eat breakfast before it's light, don't eat again before teatime, and wait until it's dark before you cook it.'

Well, that fixed Curly.

Anyhow, Paddy relented and showed us how to make a safe from a muslin bag stretched over some wire hoops, with sticks across inside so that the meat hung without touching the side of the bag.

*       *       *

We kept on going like this from day to day – worked day and night – but we were not getting very far with that drain. You know, the people down there, they were pretty good to us, and I came to believe that poverty brings people closer together and promotes a bit of fellow feeling.

One of the blokes on the creek started a store up; he was called . . . well, let's say he was called Bob. But he had one eye, Bob, and it was a great place for nicknames. Well, Bob was known as 'The Bigot' straight away, because there was a famous Australian racehorse with

Gold mining in the Howard Valley. The bush cover has been cleared from the claim and the men are sluicing – washing the gold-bearing gravels into and through the sluice box.
*National Publicity Studios Collection, Alexander Turnbull Library*

one eye, and they reckoned old Bob looked a bit like him. Anyhow, he wasn't a bad bloke, Bob. He would give a lot of credit and, I tell you, I never saw anybody go out of that creek without giving Bob his money back, even if he had to borrow it from somebody else, or do a bit of work for Bob. Bob would get his money all right.

Well, there was one mob there they called 'The Animals' – I never found out why, but I got a pretty good idea. These blokes used to work at night, and they weren't averse to helping themselves to a bit of firewood on the way home. And there was one poor old bloke, he had problems getting wood. Well, they went home one night and, 'Oh, here's the old boy's wood. Give us an armful.' So they got an armful and chucked it on the fire. And about three minutes afterwards, she erupted. The camp oven disappeared, the windows were blown out, and the table was blown over.

Of course there was a devil of a row about this, and everybody wanted to know what was going on. The old chap, he was there, and he said, 'Well, I think it must have been the fairies.'

'What do you mean, the fairies?'

'Well, that's what you told me when I said somebody was pinching my wood. You said, "It must have been the fairies." So I reckon it must have been the fairies blew up your fireplace, eh?'

Well, of course the boys soon caught on to this, and there was a roar of laughter. The old boy had put detonators in his wood.

*        *        *

There was one old bloke there, he was known as Old Alf. Now Old Alf, he was a pretty mean man, and some poor fellow came into the creek looking for a bit of ground. Now Alf had worked a little bit of an island there and never got anything off it. So he said to this fellow, 'Well, there's a bit of ground there you can have for a fiver.'

Now Old Alf reckoned the ground wasn't worth fivepence, never mind about five quid! Well, this fellow started and he drilled a hole right on top of it. A fortnight later he took out five hundred pounds worth of gold from Old Alf's island, and Alf nearly died! And for a long time after that there was a notice on that island, and it had on it 'Alf's mistake'.

Being on the creek like that had its problems. We went to bed one night there and, boy, was it raining! It sounded just like somebody was turning a hose on that roof. We lay there and you could hear the old creek growling and roaring, and then we heard a knock on the door, so we hopped out and had a look. Paddy's there. He said, 'Look, there's a big tree down further up the creek, and we have got to do something about it. Now,' he said, 'it will turn the creek shortly, and you'll be in the creek and the creek will be in the dry.'

So we put our clothes on and hopped up, and here's this log, and it's a beauty. We all gathered round and it's teeming, and Paddy said, 'Well, somebody has to get out on that log and bore a hole in it with an auger, and they've got to put some gelignite in it, and we've got to blow it up.'

Well, everybody looked at everybody else, and no one was very happy about this lot. So Paddy said, 'Well, if somebody will go out and stick a hole in it with the auger, I'll take the geli out and shove her in the hole.'

And Curly says, 'I'll do it.'

Paddy looked at him. He said, 'You?'

'Yes, *me,* boy. Give me the auger, and I'll go out.'

Well, Curly climbed out on that log, and look, I wouldn't have gone out there for a hundred quid. It was just starting to roll, because the flood was half way up it, but old Curly, he climbed out, he screwed that hole in, and he came back, and everyone looked at him, because he was about the last bloke you would have picked.

Anyhow, Paddy, he got out; he shoved the geli in, lit the fuse and came back, and up she went. She blew clean in halves, and the old creek, she rushed down. And Paddy looked at Curly and he said, 'You know, Curly, you surprise me. I've got to have another look at you,' he said. 'I've changed me mind.'

'Oh,' says Curly, 'you've changed your mind, have you?'

'Yes, boy,' he says. 'I've put you amongst the men.'

                    *          *          *

We had a bit of a football team down there, and the toughest, roughest bloke in it was Big Andy. Now Andy was a big rawboned Scotsman with a big black spade beard, and he hardly talked to anyone – he was what you might call a bloke to himself. And you know, we went down that way one morning, and as we were passing Andy's place – well, you wouldn't believe it! There was a kitten there.

Well, nobody ever thought much about kittens or dogs on the creek, so we hopped in and said to Andy, 'Where did you get this kitten, Andy?'

'Oh,' he said, 'a bloke give it to me. But,' he says, 'it's a damned nuisance around the place. I don't want it.'

And Curly says, 'I'll have it.'

'Oh, no,' says Andy. 'Leave the kitten where it is. Leave the thing alone – it's all right where it is.'

Well, you know, that kitten got to be like a dog to Andy. It used to follow him down to his claim and sit on the bank and watch him work, and come home when he came home, and I began to realise that old Andy, he had a heart like a bit of butter. He was only tough on the outside.

Anyhow, one night I went down there to see him, and I walked in and he's sitting in the chair he'd made and he's got the kitten on his knee – and it's dead. And I looked at Andy, you know, and he looked at me, and he says, 'If you ever mention this outside, I'll kill you.'

And I said, 'What's wrong, Andy?'

'I stood on it.'

And you know, we used to go past there, and there was a little mound with stones round it and a little cross, and there's not one bloke in that creek game to say to Andy, 'What's in the mound, Andy?'

\*            \*            \*

Well, we finished the drain, and as they used to say on the creek, she was a blue duck – there was nothing there. Well, you know, this was the end for us. We were done. So we had a bit of a council of war, and as a first thing, we had to part with our rifle. We pawned it with The Bigot to get a few bob to sort of keep alive – and it was just keeping alive, and that's all – while we tried to find out what we were going to do.

We went round and saw a few blokes that we were pretty matey with, and one was old Wingey. Now Wingey was quite a character in his own way. First time we ever saw him was down at the foot of the creek when we were coming in, and he was dead drunk. He had a tin of potted meat in one hand and a bottle of whisky in the other, and he was having what he called his lunch. But he was so far gone, he said, 'Look, can you hop over to the farmer and ask him to sledge me home. I can't get home.'

So we went over to see old Cyril, and old Cyril's sledge was just a fork of a tree with a few bits of wire stretched between it. We loaded old Wingey on to it and, look, he looked like a trussed-up turkey, but we tied him on with ropes, put his bottle of whisky in his hand and got his gear on the sledge. Cyril hitched up the horse and away we went. We nearly died laughing.

Old Wingey didn't have any bright ideas for us, but one morning Paddy arrived, and he said, 'I've got a bit of news for you blokes. You're all going on the subsidy.'

'What's that?'

'Well, the Government's going to pay you all fifteen bob a week so long as you stay here and carry on mining. But you've got to sell your gold through the bank.'

Well, you know, that was like Father Christmas walking in on us.

After a few days, a bloke comes in to the creek, and he's got a list, and of course everybody gathered round to see whether their name was on the list. Well, ours was on, but some poor fellows there – there was three or four of them – their names were not on. There was nothing against them, just a mistake, but the look on their faces would have killed you when he folded up the list. And that was that.

Anyhow, we got the subsidy all right; in fact, we got a week's extra. We got the rifle back from The Bigot. We had another council of war, and we decided we were going to quit that creek and go over to the next one, and we might be lucky there.

\*            \*            \*

Well, today's the day, and we're off – going over to the other creek. And boy, we looked like camels when we went off. We had everything tied up and we could hardly move – but we were going to make it; we had all day. Anyhow, we went up the hill and across a big plateau, down the other side, and along a creek bed, and the first thing we saw was some blokes working claims. They were working a different way from the one we'd used on the other creek. These blokes were doing a sort of ground-sluicing, just bringing the water over the face and putting a box in to trap the gold. That was it – you were away laughing.

Anyhow, we went along this bit of a canyon sort of thing where these fellows were working, and we come to a track that went straight up the hill, and Big Mac said to me, 'Here, we have to go up there?'

'Yes,' I says. 'This is what Paddy was telling us about. This is what they call the "Gut-buster".'

Anyhow, we got up there all right. Our noses were just about touching the ground but we got to the top and we came out on to a big plateau. And here's this other place. It's like a town, with houses all around made of slabs and that sort of thing, and there's a fair-dinkum store there. We went over to that store and you wouldn't believe it – there's sausages, there's real bread, there's all kinds of things.

And Curly says, 'Right, this will do us, boy. Doesn't matter whether we get any gold or not, we got the subsidy. We'll live like kings here.'

So we pitched our tent there and went round and saw one or two blokes, and I said to one bloke, 'You've got a great set-up here, mate. How did you get all this?'

'Ah, well, he says, 'we got a pretty good committee here. We're always writing to the Minister or the Public Works or somebody, and telling them, "Right – instead of throwing rocks through shop windows, we're here trying to get a bit of gold to help the country out." He says, 'We tell them, "We're helping you – what about helping us?"' And he says, 'We're getting all kinds of things. We're going to get a school here soon. A lot of women and kids here, you know.'

Next day, after we got straightened out a bit, Big Mac says, 'Well, we gotta build a hut.'

'What do you want a hut for?'

'Well,' he says, 'I been talking to the storekeeper, and you know, he tells me she snows here in the winter. You could get three or four feet of it, and if you don't get a hut you'll die. You want a hut and about five hundred tons of firewood.'

'Aw,' I said, 'that's hard to believe.'

'Well, that's what he said. Have a look around here. Can you see any tents?'

He was right. There weren't any.

So – all right, we'll build a hut. Well, we didn't know how to build a hut, but one bloke, he wrote it down on a bit of paper what we had to get. So many hundred poles, so many hundred slabs, so many lumps for the bottom and so many lumps for the top, and we started off.

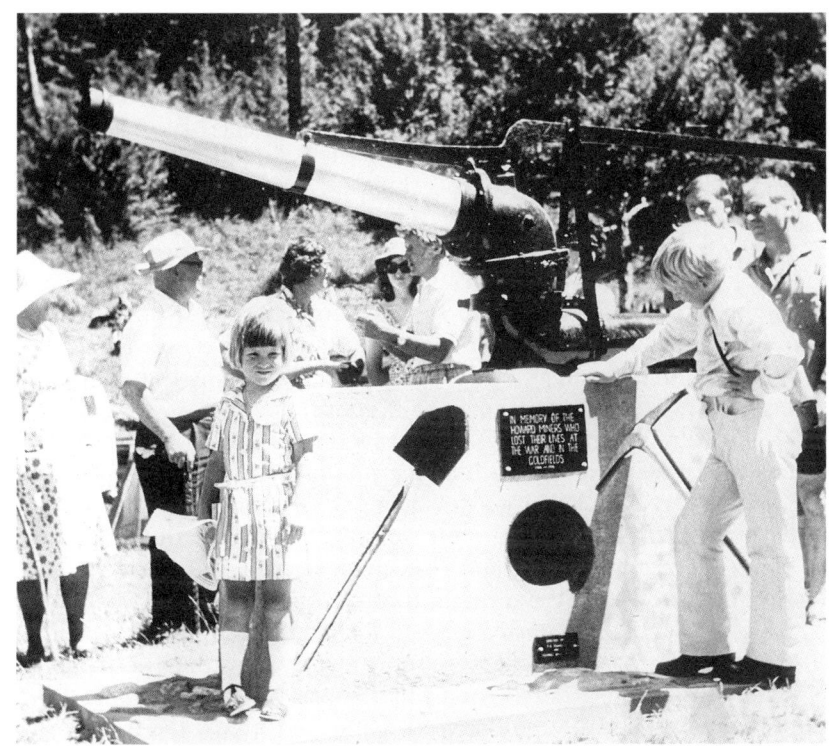

In January 1976, at the Howard reunion, this memorial was unveiled. It commemorates miners who lost their lives on the diggings or in war.
*Temple Sutherland*

Well, I never worked so hard in me life. We must have cut thousands of poles. We brought 'em all down and stacked them all in nice heaps, and we were proud of it. And we got the bloke over, and he had a look at them.

'Well, yes,' he said. 'About half of these are all right. The other half you can use for firewood.'

'What's wrong with them?'

'They're all curved.'

So, he shows us – you go round the base of a tree and you look straight up it from the bottom from several sides, and that way you can see if they're straight, or if they've got a curve on them.

Well, we're away again, and we were weeks getting that stuff, but eventually we got it, and we built a good hut too.

Well, we're all set up now, so we saw one or two blokes and asked them where we might get a bit of ground.

'Well,' they said, 'just go down the creek there and have a look. Anything that's not pegged, you can peg it. You're allowed to take a chain of creek frontage and five chain deep.'

So down we went. We thought it looked pretty easy to us, and we stuck some pegs in and started in. And we hadn't been going long before the stones showed up. There were some mighty big stones in that place – some of them were big as rooms in a house. So old Bob came down and had a look, and he said, 'Well, I'll have to blow them for you.'

So away we go and get gelignite and all the doings, come back and give it to Bob. He sets them up, and I never see so many stones in me life, all broken up into little bits. It took us four days to throw them away. But we got them away and started again, and we carved out quite a fair hunk of ground and put the water on, and put it through the box. And you know, after we'd put the water through, there was gold in the front of the box. Not a lot, but some gold.

Well, you know, that claim, it was all right. We were getting about four quid a week out of it. You know, we felt about nine feet tall when we saw that gold, because we'd made it. We were just a bunch of mugs that had come down from Wellington, and we'd made money.

We were on to gold.

First broadcast 29 April 1972

# 2 From 'The Land of Doing Without'

Davie Gunn, remembered by his son, Murray Gunn, of the Hollyford Valley.

*'The Land of Doing Without' was Davie Gunn's description of the Hollyford Valley he knew and loved. It was an accurate summing-up of the isolation of the valley leading down to Lake McKerrow and Martins Bay – and certainly it is a phrase that would have struck a responsive chord in the hearts of early settlers, sixty years before Davie Gunn took up his run there.*

*As gold returns declined in the late 1860s, the Otago Provincial Council contemplated development of the Province's hinterland. Despite an unfavourable survey report in 1867, a select committee decided the following year that a settlement at Martins Bay, on Otago's west coast, was a viable proposition. Nobody was more enthusiastic than the Provincial Superintendent, James McAndrew, who envisaged an Otago settled from coast to coast. The centre of the 40,000-hectare block, set on the shores of Lake McKerrow, was dubbed Jamestown by the settlers in his honour.*

*The project failed. It had been ill conceived and under financed. Settlers were inexperienced in heavy bushwork, and some of the best land was held by absentee owners and remained unworked. To the difficulty of breaking in heavy and often poor land was added the overriding problem of isolation. By 1879 the settlement had collapsed. A handful of settlers lingered on, and by buying or leasing grazing areas in the scattered river-valleys, managed to survive. At Martins Bay the McKenzies had a run and an isolated homestead, and this became part of an extensive 'temporary grazing lease' taken over by Davie Gunn.*

*Davie became an almost legendary figure in the Hollyford. He opened up the tracks and began guiding tramping parties through the district – partly to help finance the run, but largely, one suspects, to communicate his own love of the area. Bill Beattie, the well-known photographer for the* Weekly News, *first met him in 1937, and later described him in his book,* Bill Beattie's New Zealand *(Hodder & Stoughton, Auckland, 1970).*

> *Dave was average height, lean and wiry, with a sallow complexion. He was quiet by nature, likeable and friendly. But he didn't look the rugged type. I put this down, rightly or wrongly, to his diet. He lived in his huts in the Hollyford, eating out of tins, and I don't think he bothered about vegetables. I have seen many methods of handling horses; in all Dave's work I never saw a sign of cruelty or ill-temper, and that was pretty rare for a man coping with horses in that sort of country. No problem ever got him stuck, and I cannot remember even hearing him swear. No one would know more about the problems of mustering, for he had to try and find his stock scattered in miles of bush, and bring them out somehow or other to the road and rail at Mossburn.*

*Davie Gunn was held in quite extraordinary affection, not unmixed with a degree of awe, by a whole generation of trampers. Davie was the Hollyford, and it seemed fitting, if inexplicable, that he should die in the valley he had come to love so much.*

David John Gunn. This photograph was taken outside Deadman's Hut, Hollyford Valley, in 1938.

*Ruth McLintoch*

The bush had a hold over Dad, and you couldn't have dragged him out in the finish. I was just a year old when the family went to Oamaru as children to get an education. My mother always wanted to get a bit closer to the Hollyford, although she didn't do it, and the first recollection I had of my father was when I was about four or five and he came home as a terribly fit man, full of life and smiles and so on, bringing exotic things back like little gold nuggets in bottles and Maori axes and kea feathers. There was always something exciting about it when he came home. His clothes always smelt of smoke, because he left them in the old Deadman's Hut, where his suit got impregnated with smoke from the fire.

It all added a bit of glamour to his visits home, which only lasted for a fortnight at a time, twice a year. I didn't think it was anything unusual, because it went on all my childhood. At the same time, when he came home he started producing more and more photographs of the place. The scenery was so fantastic to him that everybody had to hear about it. His whole life seemed to be consumed by the Hollyford.

Thinking back, I'm not quite sure how my mother felt about all this. She never expressed an opinion as to its being unusual; she did not say it was exceptional, except that she would have liked to live nearer the Hollyford. She never got around to it actually, because us children had to be educated in Oamaru. We lived in a house belonging to a maiden aunt, and my father provided an allowance to keep the family going. Father had a struggle, of course, and he never did get out of the pioneering stage in the Hollyford, you might say.

Let's see if I can give you a picture of him, as I remember him. He was a quiet-spoken person, who would never get to swear. He had dark black hair. Short build – same build as I am, except that I am a bit stouter than he ever got, because he had such a strenuous life. He had a pale complexion, and he was very broad across the shoulders from lifting such heavy objects all the time – rocks, timber, throwing cattle around, and horses. He was quite slim in his legs though, for the amount of energy he could generate in them. He was a fairly serious man in lots of ways, because he had so much to cope with in this valley. He delighted in showing people around the valley, 'his' valley as his friends called it.

My father didn't collect many possessions; they were a burden to him, because he liked to be on the move. Comforts didn't interest him either because he thought they made you soft, and he called the Hollyford 'The Land of Doing Without', and didn't have any 'modern inconveniences'. For the same sort of reason, he fought shy of any sort of publicity. He reckoned radio and newspapers only conditioned people to accept things they wouldn't otherwise. He did take the odd ticket in Tatt's though, you know, because at the back of his mind was the thought that he would like good huts right through the Hollyford, and that might be a short-cut to it, after his cattle business was ruined in the Hollyford.

Apart from that, I don't think he thought much about money. In Deadman's Hut, which wasn't locked up properly, the season's takings were put in a biscuit tin, and it piled up to the top when the season was over. Some of the men he had working for him had access to that tin and could have grabbed handfuls of money, and it didn't seem to worry him. So long as there was enough money to pay the bills at the end of the year, he seemed content. Not being a businessman, he just didn't think along other lines.

Of course, Martins Bay had a history of sixty years of pioneering before ever my father went there. To give you a picture, the Hollyford is a glacial valley with Lake McKerrow near the seaward end. It is a dammed-up fiord. From the outlet of the lake, there's about four miles of river winding down to the coast at Martins Bay . . . and the Bay itself is about eighteen miles as the crow flies north of Milford Sound. They set up a settlement on Lake McKerrow in the 1870s, but I think it was the isolation killed it, in the same way it killed the Jackson Bay settlement further north.

Son Murray, with Dugald McScratch at the Hollyford camp, February 1982
*Murray Gunn Collection*

Well, the families drifted away, until only the McKenzies remained. Hugh and Malcolm, the McKenzie boys, stuck it out for more than fifty years at the Bay. They grew up in the bush – first-class bushmen, both of them. They had no real education, and growing up at Martins Bay, time didn't matter to them, because they never had to consult watches. They used to consult the sky and the state of the tide, but in time they began to let things slip, and by 1926 they hadn't bothered to muster their cattle for two years.

Civilisation must have had terrors for them, because they looked upon Queenstown as a city – it was about quarter the size then that it is now – and when they went there they walked single file around the streets, because they'd got used to walking single file on the bush tracks of the Hollyford.

One time, when Malcolm had eventually retired to Glenorchy, with a small job around Jack Wylie's house, he had trouble with his water-works and the locals got him flown down to the Frankton Hospital. Old Doctor Anderson was the doctor there, and he thought he would have him on, so he said to Malcolm, 'Ever had a woman, Mr McKenzie?'

Malcolm said, 'No, but my brother Hugh has. Twice!'

\*　　　\*　　　\*

To make an economic unit my father had to build these cattle up, and of course keep them under control, and open up a big area with tracks

Martins Bay, South Westland
*Alwyn Owen*

and huts, to give the cattle access to flats, and make it easier to drive them out. The early settlers had a terrible job getting cattle round the side of Lake McKerrow, and by going through the Pyke, with its much easier country, it saved a lot of extra work with them and got them out under easier conditions. The whole operation from start to finish took four months. In the later musters, leaving the road, it took six days travelling through the Pyke to get you and horses and dogs to Martins Bay. The horses would be heavily laden with stores, some of which were dropped at each hut. Sometimes you had trouble when the dogs got on to deer, and took off after them too.

There's a verse somebody – I don't know who it was – wrote about the muster. It goes something like this:

Davie's away to the mustering, down to the Bay again,
And four long months will pass before he's back in the haunts of men.
The horses are fresh; the dogs are keen, and eager to be away
To flush the scrub bulls out of the bush, to the yards at Martins Bay.
They'll lead the mob to the Hollyford banks, and wait for the slack of the tide:
Then they'll swim them across, and curse the stragglers that break on the other
    side.
They'll curse the sandflies and curse the rain, and they'll curse each wandering
    stray:
But 'I'll muster the mob 'til I'm seventy,' says Davie of Martins Bay.
They'll muster Big Bay and the Upper Pyke, and move on to Hidden Falls,
And the bush will echo the bark of the dogs, and the ring of the musterers' calls.
Then hurrah for the road, and Mossburn Town, a hundred miles
    away.
'Mustering's the life for a man!' says Davie of Martins Bay.

A good part of the mustering was done on foot in the bush, and this meant you had to have dogs that weren't trained to obey you too much, because they had to use their own initiative to save you from awkward situations. Well, this meant that when they saw deer, or smelt them, they were off like a shot, and you would have to wait maybe half a day for them to come back. That held up later musters.

Well, anyway, you got out to the coast and started at the south part of Martins Bay, collecting up a quiet herd of cows that would be used as a decoy mob. An inexperienced member of the party soon learnt to hold this mob on the edge of the bush while my father and his musterers sent the dogs out into the bush. The dogs did their finding job first, and as soon as loud barking was heard the musterers raced in to get their dogs to turn the cattle before they got too far away.

Davie on the track near the
Hollyford camp
*Ruth McLintoch*

It meant getting in there as fast as you could on foot, running through the bush, getting caught in bush lawyer and all sorts of things. After you got your cattle bailed up you then had the job of driving them back towards the decoy mob.

When the cattle were mustered on the flat on the south side of the Hollyford River, you moved on to the next step in the muster. It involved getting those cattle out of the home territory, which is the worst part of mustering. Once you'd moved them away from the area in which they'd grown up, they were much easier to handle.

There was a particularly difficult situation in getting them across the Hollyford because it was so deep and wide that they couldn't get a footing, and they had to swim. The technique was to wait for slack water, have the cattle up there at the crossing, and just force them through into the water with a wall of dogs and by shouting behind them. It took a long time to get them started and get them through there. I suppose it took about a day to get them across, and then you had to watch to see that they didn't come round and swim back again.

Once you got those cattle out of the home area, there was always a chap in front leading a horse. Now, in a mob of cattle there is always a leader, and it would get used to following the horse, and the rest of the cattle would be following the leader.

My father put a huge gate between two rocks at the northern headland of Martins Bay and he would force the cattle through there, and then go back for more and push them through until he had the whole mob through the gate.

The next stage would be right on to Big Bay, to the northern beach, where there was a hut and stockyards. By that time you would have to leave the cattle you'd brought from Martins Bay and muster the new area, do all the marking, and draft the ones you wanted, and move them on to the next stopping-over place, the Upper Pyke. Do the same there – same at Lake Alabaster and then Hidden Falls. It was just a matter of taking time not to force them, or else you just pushed them over a bank and they were killed. Through the bush you could only travel about eight miles a day, of course.

So that was the mustering, and the whole secret was to move them gently.

*　　　*　　　*

My father could move fast when he had to, though. There's a commemorative stone at Marian Corner to my father. It says something like this:

> This tablet was erected by the people of Southland to commemorate the magnificent journey made by David Gunn of Martins Bay to bring aid to the sufferers in the aeroplane accident at Big Bay on 30 December 1936. Mr Gunn made the journey from Big Bay to this point, a distance of 56 miles, over bush tracks, in 20 hours.

How this came about was like this. My father had just started to organise tramping trips around the tracks, and the famous pioneer pilot, Arthur Bradshaw, had started taking people into the back country. He hired a plane from the Southland Aero Club for these trips, and there was a Sister Buckingham on the plane on this occasion. They were supposed to land at Big Bay, where Sister Buckingham was joining my father's party to come out. Well, my father was waiting for the plane to land, but when it came in it got caught in a cross-wind, and dived into the sea.

Everybody rushed down there to help, and my father had to knock up a stretcher to get the injured people ashore. There was no shortage of flax, so he made up the stretcher using sticks and flax. I think there were four people on the plane besides the pilot. One of them was killed – Sutton Jones, a journalist. Sister Buckingham – she was a nursing sister at the Southland Hospital – had multiple fractures, and the others either had fractures or severe bruises. Arthur Bradshaw was pretty badly cut about the head.

The Hollyford Valley and peaks of the Darran Range
*Alwyn Owen*

Davie Gunn looks out across
Lake McKerrow
*Murray Gunn Collection*

There was a nurse in the party which was waiting for the plane, and she made them comfortable while my father set off for help. There was no means of communication, and it was normally a four-day tramp out to the road – that was at Marian Camp, the Public Works camp at the top of the Hollyford, and of course they had a phone there. My father set off after doing a full day's work; went round Big Bay to Martins Bay, rowed a dinghy up Lake McKerrow, then tramped through the bush to Marian Corner.

He was having a lot of pain rowing the boat because he'd cracked a rib a short while before, and he was lucky when he was rowing up the lake; it suddenly clicked into place. He got to the head of Lake McKerrow and spent several hours looking for a horse in the dark, to help him on the way out. Not that he rode it much, but he needed it to get through the deeper creek and river crossings. The last three miles, he had to abandon his horse and carry on through the bush to Marian Corner, where the Works camp was set up with a telephone. They sent two planes up from Invercargill to Big Bay, and flew out the injured people and the body of Sutton Jones.

*      *      *

But from 1936 on, guiding trampers through the Hollyford became more and more a way of life and business for my father. The cattle only occupied a portion of his time, so he became well known to hundreds of trampers and climbers and fishermen and scientists. They did the circuit with him, down the Hollyford, up the coast to Big Bay, and back down the Pyke. Later on he turned a lot of the work over to his guides. But he had a sort of charisma, you know, and you can get an idea of that from the old logbooks from his huts. There's one entry that reads:

> 27 January, 1953: Martins Bay
> When as my modest couch I sought
> At ten o'clock, I never thought
> That I should ever have the fun
> Of sleeping next to Davie Gunn.
> At 3 a.m. I found him there,
> The answer to a maiden's prayer.
>
> *– Ann Onymous*

Nothing could upset him. He could cope with anything. He delighted in meeting people in the most odd situations, and dropping whatever he was doing to be hospitable to them. He was an exceptional host, and he was a person – even though he was in the wrong, nobody took exception to him, because they knew he was so sincere – and he worked so hard that they accepted a lot from him that they wouldn't have taken from other people. Along with this, there was a lot of charm.

But he was a difficult man to work with, actually, and that's why I didn't come into the picture earlier on. To have survived in this area you had to be stubborn, and the stubbornness came out when you wanted to do something and he always found another way to do it. Even though it might be second best, he always found another way.

One time Jim Speden, who was his chief guide for four years, was with him when they got caught out in the dark riding down towards

An early guided party, ready for the track
*Murray Gunn Collection*

Hidden Falls. Part of the track had gone into the river, and Jim Speden was about a hundred yards or so ahead on horseback. He looked down in the darkness and saw no track ahead, so he calls out to my father, 'Track's gone into the river, Dave.'

'No it hasn't, Jim,' says my father.

'Yes it has.'

'No it hasn't,' says my father.

'Yes it has.'

'No it hasn't,' says my father.

So Jim edges his horse forward and they both fall into the river, and Jim calls back to my father, 'I'm in the water, Dave.'

'No, you're not,' says my father.

By this time my father had caught up and looked down the bank.

'Oh, you're in the water, Jim.'

\*　　　\*　　　\*

I came into the picture just as things were starting to get a bit more easy in the Hollyford. When my father first came over there, what with the stores only coming in twice a year, every scrap of string, paper and wire was saved. Tins were hung on shelves and so forth and the whole lot got dusty and dirty, but they had to be saved, because they

A party of descendants of Stewart Island pioneers at the Lower Pyke hut, August 1954. Davie invited them to the Hollyford and personally showed them around.
*Murray Gunn Collection*

might come in handy. When things were easier to get in the Hollyford, my father couldn't get over this habit, and he wouldn't allow anything to be thrown out. But when I took up the job permanently I decided that we had to get rid of some of this clutter, and tidy up the huts. First go I had was at the Lower Pyke. He wasn't around, but when he came back I could see he was most upset. He wouldn't tell anybody off, though. He just showed he was upset. Next morning the other chap with us wanted to get out to the end of the road before it rained, and my father said he would have to stay behind and tidy the hut up. It meant he would try to find everything I had thrown out, and put it back.

A short while later, when he was on his last muster, he was at Big Bay – just him and one man doing this muster, actually – and I had a real cleanup this time, going through that hut, getting rid of all the rubbish. This time I burnt the boxes and hid all the rubbish behind a sand dune where he wouldn't find it. He arrived back at the hut with his musterer, opened the door, turned and looked at this chap and said, 'This vandalism must cease!'

There was another kind of vandalism which he abhorred, and that was the kind of vandalism which involved folks breaking into supplies and leaving cupboard doors open for the mice to get in – and pots left dirty and rusty, and things grubby around the place. That's the only time he really swore. He'd arrived one time and found the Lower Pyke hut in a mess, and he grabbed a spirtle [porridge stirrer] and waved it in the air and beat it up and down and said, 'The buggers and the bastards! The buggers and the bastards!'

Jim Speden, his chief guide, felt the same way about sloppiness in the huts. Jim turned out some rather pointed bush verse and pinned it up on the wall of Deadman's Hut.

The Davie few people saw; in mufti, at home in Oamaru for a family wedding, February 1947
*Murray Gunn Collection*

> Before you go, there's one thing more:
> Have you checked the firewood store?
> Are you man, or are you mouse?
> Have you acted like a louse —
> Burnt up all, and carried none?
> Curses on you, more than one!
> Here's hoping that where next you dwell
> The fire's dead out; it rains like hell:
> The firewood's wet, the bush is soaking.
> Once again I'll say, here's hoping.

Jim Speden, you know, helped my father when he slipped sixty feet down a bluff one night, and somebody wrote a verse about that too:

> Davie Gunn lives way out west,
> A man of some renown,
> He sometimes drives a mob of steers
> Two hundred miles to town.
> He may fall somewhat heavy,
> But you cannot hold him down!

This happened because two of Davie's cattle-beasts had broken from one of the mobs coming out of the Hollyford above Deadman's Hut, and he went out this day to try and find it up on the slopes. He spent too long looking for the beasts and had to come back in the dark, over a bluff near the Hollyford River, near Deadman's Hut. He didn't climb high enough and fell about fifty or sixty feet down.

The only person around was Jim Speden, in Deadman's Hut, and he went looking for my father next morning, and heard him calling out. It was unfortunate that just at that time a cloudburst had hit the Hollyford and washed out the bridges for about three miles up the road, and it was hard to get help. But Jim helped my father down to the Deadman's Hut and went for the telephone at Marian, and the ambulance came right up from Invercargill, a distance of one hundred and sixty miles, to pick him up. They had to carry him on a stretcher three miles up the road, and he travelled all night in the ambulance to get to hospital.

He had several broken ribs and I am sure he had a broken neck, even though the hospital didn't admit it, because he couldn't move his neck for several months later, and he only talked in a whisper. He was injured about the face too. It knocked him around – knocked him back – more than anything else ever did, that accident. He seemed to age very quickly after that, but he did, with careful nursing, get his strength back again. I went down to see him one weekend when he was in hospital. They'd put him in a special room, and all his friends came to see him.

But really, I hardly looked on him as a father. I'd seen so little of him that I didn't know what it was to have a father basically, and when I came over here to work with him I had as much to do with the people he was guiding, and the guides, as I had with him. Often I'd be separated from my father, with one of these workmen or guides. I'd been spoilt by growing up in a house with two women and two sisters, and coming here was a big shock to me. I hated it for a start. I know it did me good, because I had been spoilt so much, and had to force myself to come back again.

I suppose I stuck it out because I liked to meet the people that came here; they were so friendly. Interesting people, too, all the time; well-educated people who could talk about different subjects. My father had mellowed with age, but I think really he only wanted me as an extra workman, and the future here held nothing for me. The deer had come in and spoilt the cattle side to an extent – to a very great extent actually – and he hadn't any money to do up the huts.

I'd been working in the County office, and I thought he was running the place on a thirty-three-and-a-third-year lease, but I found when I got there that he only had a year-to-year lease, which shocked me. He apparently wasn't worried about this, because he wasn't looking for money to develop the Hollyford area as a run. A long-term lease is necessary to do anything with a place like this. But I don't think he realised the position that he'd put me in.

He was having difficulty getting workmen in here, and things had gone back, and I think it was mainly because he'd lost heart. I put this down to old age, but I realise now that he must have been a very unhappy man when he died, although he didn't show it. I believe he did die pretty unhappy, but I had pulled out of the Hollyford by then too, because I couldn't see any future in it for me at that stage, after being here a year.

He died on a Christmas Day. Nudged his horse into the water to cross the Hollyford opposite the Little Homer Saddle, just as he'd done a thousand times before. He couldn't swim a stroke, you know – a lot of the bushmen couldn't. It was the normal fine weather with the river low, and he was taking stores down to get ready for the post-Christmas rush of people there. He had his musterer, Jack Jenkins, with him, and a boy, Warren Shaw, aged about twelve, and in cross-ing this rough ford with a bouldery bottom, Dick, the horse, stumbled. Normally the horses did often trip going through the ford, but this

Camp-oven cooking on the track
*Murray Gunn Collection*

Davie with Bess at Deadman's
Hut, April 1951
*Murray Gunn Collection*

time when Dick stumbled, he put his foot on a wet log, went to recover and just rolled on my father. The boy Shaw was swept off and down to the pool below. He swam a few strokes and went under, and my father's body disappeared. We didn't find my father's body, although we found the boy's in the river.

His friends put up a cairn near the junction of the Pyke and the Hollyford. Its inscription reads:

> In Memoriam – David John Gunn, aged 68 years.
> Runholder and Track Controller.
> Drowned in the Hollyford River, Christmas Day 1955.
> He lived with nature in this valley for 25
> years, and all who passed this way knew him
> as 'Davey, the Tramper's Friend'.

It was a big loss to most people. He seemed so indestructible. From a personal family attitude, my mother thought, well, it might have been a blessing in disguise because he had nothing to live for, with his cattle business ruined by deer infestation, no proper leases, and he had to face the family over promises of a future for me which he could not provide.

You won't find much left of what my father did here now, but it's in people's minds that he must have set an example to a lot of people not to think of money all the time.

He was quite happy with the simple things of life.

First broadcast 16 March 1974

# 3 Herea te Tangata ki te Whenua (Bind the People to the Land)

The extraordinary life of Dame Whina Cooper, who was born on the earthen floor of a kauta* and eighty years later awoke the conscience of a country.

*Whina Cooper first gained national prominence in 1951, when she was elected National President of the newly-formed Maori Women's Welfare League, a position she held until 1957. In the years that followed she worked extensively and tirelessly for the Maori community in Auckland, and established a Catholic community centre in the city. She named it Te Unga Waka, 'the landing-place of the canoes', as an indication that it was for the use of all Maoris, and not Catholics alone.*

*Whina has always possessed a superb sense of timing. In 1975 she very accurately assessed the groundswell of opinion on Maori land rights, and to publicise concern at the continuing acquisition of Maori land, she initiated and led the now-famous land march from Te Hapua, at the tip of the North Island, down to Wellington. Physically frail, but utterly indomitable in spirit, she captured the imagination of the whole country in a way that no other Maori woman has done since the time of Princess Te Puea. In doing so, she played a dominant part in the re-emergence of Maori identity, and in the struggle for the retention of land.*

*If Whina's name had been forgotten by the public at large until she re-emerged as a national figure in 1975, this was certainly not the case among the Maori people, particularly those of Tai Tokerau, the northern districts. Always a dynamic figure, even in her teenage years, she fought relentlessly for the land and its development, and for the advancement of her people. At her home in Panguru, on the Hokianga Harbour, she led the settlement as her father, Heremia Te Wake, had done before her. She set the pace in land development in the Hokianga; she was a storekeeper; she presided over the local branch of the Farmers' Union, forerunner of Federated Farmers, and she held a similar position with the local regional Rugby Union. She became adept at using the European 'system'. 'I'll work with any politician. I don't care what his politics are. If I can make him see the needs of our people, I'll work with him.'*

*Whina Cooper was honoured with the M.B.E. in 1953, the C.B.E. in 1974, and became a Dame of the British Empire in 1980.*

*This account of episodes in her long life – for Whina was born in 1895 – was recorded in 1978 in Ngunguru, where she was cultivating*

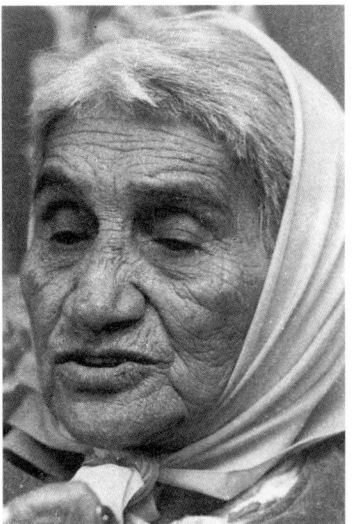

Whina Cooper
*Alwyn Owen*

---

*Kauta – a cooking house made from nikau and manuka

*quite extensive gardens. In accordance with Maori etiquette, the first introduction was made through a Maori friend, at the home of Whina's son in the Auckland suburb of Panmure. This was followed by a visit to Ngunguru at a later date. For a whole day there Whina spoke about her life, with lunch the only interruption. Recording followed the next day, and it too occupied a complete day.*

    *Whina's story conveys to a considerable degree the energy and ability of this remarkable woman. What cannot be so adequately expressed on the printed page is the other side to her character – her warmth, hospitality and charm.*

    *Her comment at the end of the recording session was typical.*

    *'What shall we call this programme, Whina?'*

    *'There is an old Maori saying: "Herea te tangata ki te whenua" – "Bind the people to the land."'*

It was my father that named me Joseph. I think I really should have been a boy, because I love men's conversation – more so than I do women's, because I don't mix with women talking about a pretty dress, or the fashion, or something to do with women. No, I would rather go to the men and talk about something like building or farming, or cows, or something to do with men's jobs. Oh, I like that. I love it.

    Well, when I was born, I was born at a place called Te Karaka, and this place is on the side of the Hokianga River, of course the first landing place of the first canoe of Kupe. Well this place, Te Karaka, is a very pretty place to live in. This is where I was born. There is a big bluegum there. I remember that bluegum and this house of ours. It was made of slabs and shingles and it had no floor, just the ground – it is beautiful you know, with mats and everything like that.

    Anyhow, it was dark, and I was born in there. And they call out, the midwives. One of them says, 'Oh, he is dead!' and my father jumped up with the holy water and baptised me – baptised me in the name Joseph. And then after all that, after a while I came to, and the others came along and saw that I was a girl. 'Oh, it's not a boy! It's a girl!' Oh, my father had a shock!

    What can he do? They can't baptise again – I am baptised already you see, as Joseph. So they put it Josephine, and they shortened that to 'Whina'.

    I was very close to my father. You know, I quite remember when I was a girl – a big girl – he used to piggyback me if we want to go somewhere. And I would say, 'Oh, I can't walk.' (I made it up.) 'I can't walk, Dad.' I said it in Maori, and he would bend down and get me on his back and piggy me all the way wherever we go. Oh, poor Dad, I am sure . . . this is how close he was to me.

    I am the favourite child, you know, and I learn how to talk and all that, going to school. The school was about six miles away, five to six miles from Te Karaka. At night he made a rule to blow out the light and start me with genealogy, teaching me all the tupuna – the ancestors – and he would want me to go over and over it all again. Oh, the trouble there! Oh, those tupuna got the hard names! I used to make such a lot of mistakes, and he would growl at me for making them. I never forget one tupuna, such a funny name — Tekenui. I say Ketenui; he say Tekenui; I say Ketenui. He was always wanting to correct me, of course. But then I got it, and lots of other hard names to pronounce.

It all had to be done in the dark. Perhaps it was because the mind won't be distracted all over the place, or something like that, you know.

My father was really interested in farming, and he told the people – not only me, but all the young people and everybody else – 'If you are looking for the money, the money is underneath those rushes (you know . . . tea tree, bush everywhere) – that's where the money is.'

So I ask him one day, 'Dad, you said there is a lot of money underneath the rushes?' (I thought there was real money under there, you see.) He said, 'If you dig it away, and the grass grow up, and the cow go there and eat the grass; if you milk and send the milk, and the cow is fat and you sell it, all that sort of thing, for beef – that's the money.'

He wanted me to go to school to learn more, but you see he had no money. But he was a man that believes in education. He wrote that in a book, you know, for his children when he dies. He has a book telling them what to do. That's the first thing he said, to go to school. Education is the thing we should be interested in, because we are going to live in the Pakeha world. You know, he wrote all this down. Anyhow, he had no money, and he said, 'Oh, I would like you to go for further education . . .'

Well, he heard that Sir James Carroll was going to a civic function in Dargaville, so he took a boat across the river and he went on horseback over to Dargaville to meet Sir James Carroll. He went up there, and he was talking to him, and he said, 'Oh, you know, I wish I had money. I would send my girl away to college.'

And Sir James Carroll said, 'Look – let me have your girl. Let your girl be my girl too, and I will pay for her education.'

So when he came back, he was so happy that he was going to send me, and he said, 'Well, you are going to college. You had better get ready.' He said, 'You have to go by boat.' Well, I didn't like that. I thought with all those waves out there I might get drowned! But never mind, it was my wish; I wanted to see what education I could get. Oh, never mind — go on this boat then.

I said to him, 'Is Auckland a big place?'

'Oh, yes,' he said.

I got on this boat – I think it was *Te Rimu* or the *Claymore* – it landed at Onehunga – and when we got to Auckland it was getting dark, and I saw all the lights come on everywhere. Oh, my eyes started to pop! My tears came down. Oh, what a big place! I thought Auckland

Heremia Te Wake, Whina's father. Aged fifty-seven when his daughter was born, he was a chief of the Ngati Manawa hapu of Kai Tutae and Te Rarawa tribes, a catechist in the Roman Catholic Church and a most capable leader, respected by Maori and European alike.
*Whina Cooper*

was only two or three houses, just a little bit bigger than Panguru. You know, you see pictures and all that, but when I saw all the lights and everything busy, I started to cry. All night I didn't sleep. I look out of the window. I see all the trams, and all the people going about. Oh, I can't see my Dad! Oh, we will be so far away! Oh, I don't know anybody, and all the people busy at night going to and fro on the streets – and this was the thing; I get frightened at nights, you know.

Anyway, the next day I go on another boat, for Napier, and at last we get to Hawke's Bay. First thing, when we were at the breakwater, some girls – Maori girls – came to meet me from the college. Oh, I was pleased, and my tears kept running down. I was really thrilled and delighted to see somebody Maori, you know.

And I remember my hat. Oh dear, I thought I looked so beautiful in my hat! This was a straight straw hat that was in fashion in those days, and what do you think I had on this straw? Poppies – beautiful red poppies. Oh, I wouldn't wear the blessed thing today! It was really terrible with all those red poppies on top. Well, we got to the college and they were pleased to see me and all that and the Sisters introduced me as the new girl just arrived, and I went and had a cup of tea and everything. And I caught all the girls trying this hat on – you know, in the workroom. They were laughing away, and oh, I'd thought it was beautiful, but after that, when they started yelling and laughing at it, I pulled all those blessed poppies off!

I was about six years at the convent. Six years. When my schooling was over, I just passed my Matriculation. That was the highest in those days.

*     *     *

I was twenty-one when I married, I think. Oh, what a life! He was Mr Gilbert, Richard Gilbert, from Ngunguru and he came over to Panguru. He was a great violinist – oh, he could play the violin! Of course all the girls in Panguru were after him, and a good-looking boy too, you know. I had no intention . . .

I had come back from school and I was working in the shop, and not yet thinking about a boyfriend or anything like that. But lots of talk at the settlement from all the girls wanting boys, you know, and I thought, well, I'll give it a go, too. So there was one night he was playing the violin with a lot of girls around, and I wrote a note and slipped it into his hand, and I put on it, 'Let me be the last.' Just, 'Let me be the last.' And I thought, well, I have a chance all right. And the other girls, you know, they got jealous, and I thought I had better ask my father, because I can't go – can't go any further – without asking my father. So I was working in the shop and he came in for tobacco, so I say, 'Dad?'

'Well?' (Oh, he is a very stern man.)

'Dad? Oh, I want that boy, Richard Gilbert.'

He said, 'You don't know him. He might give you a hiding. You

Richard Gilbert, Whina's first husband
*Whina Cooper*

don't know him. He's a stranger here, on a survey' – and all that.

I said, 'I think he is all right Dad. He's so good, you know.'

Anyway, I whakapatipati him – soft-soap him – and he said, 'Well, all right.'

And I think, 'Oh, that's good – what shall I do now?' So I went home that night and I told my mother that Dad said I could have this man and everything, and of course my mother had very little to say, because I am more of my father's girl, you see. And so I asked my father, 'Can I have the launch, Dad?'

'Why do you want the launch?'

I said, 'I want to go up to Rawene to get married.'

'Oh,' he said, 'all right, you can have the launch.'

So I can drive, you know, and I know how to drive the launch, and I got this boy on the boat and we went. And when we got to Rawene I went to a shopkeeper called Cooper, because I didn't have a ring – never had the money to buy one. So she asked me what I wanted, and I said, 'Look, I want to get married, so I want to borrow your ring.' She said, 'All right', so she took her ring off, one of those beautiful thick gold ones.

So I went up to the church, and the priest said to me, 'What's this? So quick. Aren't you going to have a celebration?'

'Oh,' I said, 'that's all fuss, that. Never mind about celebration.' (I knew we were going to be chased by the other girls, you know. They were waiting on another launch, and they were coming along behind.) Anyhow, we got married, and then the other people arrived, but it was too late; we were married.

I went back to Mrs Cooper with the ring, and she said, 'You can keep it.'

So that's the story of my marriage to Mr Gilbert. The old people in Panguru, they were up in arms you know. They didn't want me to marry him. They thought they would have a say before ever I married anyone – as if to say I would have to marry a prince or something like that. That was the way of the elders, you know.

Anyhow, I was married, and then after that I thought married life is a very funny life, and I said to my mother, 'Mum, I want to go back.'

But she said, 'No, no, no! You can't do that.'

But you know what married life is like at first start: you can't go to sleep. They wake you up all night! Hahahaha! I had to pray – this is true, God's honest – had to pray to God to give me the love, eh. You know, to make my marriage good. And I did. Oh, you have to read between the lines – you know, I can't tell you. You just guess yourself!

Anyhow, we had two nice children, one boy and one girl. We lived happily together and he became a supervisor, looking after the Panguru side – a lot of work. I was then very interested in farming, of course, so we joined in the Federated Farmers. I was President of the Federated Farmers in Panguru. Had seventy-two members. Got right into farming, and all that – see that every farm is clean. If you go there now you see tea tree and all sorts of rubbish on it . . . breaks my heart, you know, to see how it can go back. Anyway, we have to find the best way to get around the young people, to get them working, so we have a meeting, and say, 'Now so-and-so farm is not clean. Look – a lot of tea tree, lot of everything, and all rubbish. Right. We start with that farm. Clean it up with our teamwork. For nothing. No payment. The only thing, the owner of that farm got to kill a pig, or make a big hangi for dinner, and that's all.'

Everybody agreed, and in the morning of course I have to lead. That's action. Some people, they stand up and talk, talk, talk . . . all day, all week. No good – waste of time. Lead, not drive. Right, so I lead them like this, and oh, it is really good.

I was postmistress, and what else . . . good gracious me, I was a jack-of-all-trades. I don't know what else I didn't do. I had a business of my own, too. It was a shop and I had it for eighteen years. It was a great, great thing for me, and I learned a lot from being a storekeeper . . . about people, importing . . . all those sorts of things. I learned a lot being a shopkeeper, and for eighteen years they thought I was wonderful – you know, the agents and the travellers. They came around, and you know, I used to keep that shop beautiful. That's the shop what Andrewes got. It was my shop, and I sold it to them when I went to Auckland.

Why I give up the shop was first of all I got interested in land development work, and Sir Apirana Ngata said to me, 'It is getting dangerous.'

I said, 'What for, Api?'

'Oh, your husband being a supervisor now. They might think all you are interested in is getting money, you know.'

'Oh,' I said, 'that's easy – no trouble to me. I will finish up the shop, will close the shop. The people are the main thing.'

So I said to my husband, 'Oh, we had better close up the shop.' Beside that, you see, I had learned from the people – too many relations. Oh, if they only paid me back what they owe me! Whoof, I would be a millionaire. Relations! They come into the shop – want to buy the flour, you know. But I'm starting to get too big, and I am starting to refuse, and they know it. So they come into the shop and look at me, and they put their hand in their pocket. I say, 'What do you want?'

'Oh, I want a bag of flour.'

So I go to get a bag of flour ready, and they say, 'Can you put it down for the next time?'

Well, I think when they put their hand in their pocket they are going to pay, so that's why I go to get the bag of flour. You see, my people are getting cunning. You can't do much business amongst your own people. The best thing is to get them up to a standard where they can afford things – by farming – so I had better chuck up the shop and take up this farming development work amongst them and get them up to the standard where they can afford to buy whatever they want in the shops.

So I chuck it up, and went with Apirana, with his way of thinking. Got hold of all the nama, what they owe me – got the book and tore it up. I don't believe in summonsing my people. But oh, they owe me a lot of money. 'Never mind,' I said to God, 'never mind. My poor people.'

So I worked with Apirana Ngata. In fact, tell you the truth, no matter what government is in power, if its policy is good for the Maoris, I'm with them, to help any government . . . any policy that is good for the Maoris, I'm there to help. That's my motto. But development – that saved the Maoris in those days. It's a long story, because I was so interested in land at the time, but Panguru was covered with tea tree and rubbish . . . terrible. So we started clearing and fencing, but we did it in a way we call in Maori 'apu' – all together; work all together, you see, as a community.

Ngata's scheme provided the money for this. Oh yes, he got the money, but first of all I have to explain how we shared in this money. Ngata picked all the leaders of the North, all the Maori leaders from the Tokerau area. I think there was about sixty or eighty of us, and I was the only woman leader. Anyway, he took us all down to look at all those beautiful farms down Rotorua and right around to Te Kaha. And all these people were taking notes all the time, and he used to ask them, 'I saw you writing something in your notebooks – what is it?' And they used to tell him what they were writing – about the fences, the drains . . . everything.

I couldn't speak, because in Rotorua a woman cannot speak on the marae. All right. The day we left we went to the station to catch the train for the North, and he said, 'Whina! Now is your time! This marae

At the Whakarewarewa Native Land Development Conference. Whina is centre front. Hoani Te Heuheu is next to her (left), Apirana Ngata behind him (left) and William Cooper behind him (right). The men on the right are all chiefs of Tai Tokerau.
*Whina Cooper*

belongs to the Pakeha. I want to know what you have to say about this whole trip!'

Well, goodness, I didn't expect this, but I said to him – and quickly, 'Api, give me the money – and I'll beat you!' That's all I said.

In about three weeks he came to the Hokianga, and when he stood up to talk, he said, 'I'm here now, Whina, because of the few words you said in Rotorua on that station. I'm here, and here is my bank.' He pointed to one of the Tuhoe people with him. 'He holds the bank. Now, I want to know – how much do you want?'

Well, all right. I said to the people, 'Now is the time. Never mind about me, let me be the last. You people ask him how much you want in different areas in the North.'

So they all got up and said they want five thousand, three thousand, so many thousand, all over the North, and I never said anything because, you know, not right for me to be the first or anything like that. I be the last.

When everybody was served with money, then Api said, 'When are you going to have some, Whina?'

I said, 'If there's any left in the bag, I'll have those. If there's nothing, I'm happy.' That's what I said. But we had some. He gave . . . I don't know how many thousands he gave us to do the work. But he explained to us to tie our belt up.

'Tie your belt up. This is only a little bit to help with development. If there's five acres to be done, why don't you do the rest for nothing, because it's your own farm, and you're developing it for your own use and everything. So if it's fencing, do the same thing.'

All right, so we did. Oh, we went on and on, you know, and it's a great way of doing it, getting the young people together. But, you see, Maoris are difficult sometimes. You can't drive them; you have to lead them. I got to lead them, and make a lot of fun you know, so that they work. And they worked, oh they worked! Sometimes I would go away, and one used to go to the top of the hill and watch – you know, lookout. And he calls, 'She's gone!' and they all sit down. Everybody smoking, no work. All right. Soon as I come around, this lookout calls out, 'Here she comes!' and when I get there everybody is working. Of course, they only told me this afterwards.

*       *       *

There was a big enquiry into Api's handling of the development money, a big enquiry – a Royal Commission. But he had told us before then. He said, 'I want to plant the seed of development among the Maoris before I'm crucified, because I'm going to spend a lot of money, and they're going to get into me for spending it all.' And they did.

You know, we got word that there were two inspectors coming to Panguru. Before they came I had my books and everything ready. Everything ready – money and everything, in a safe, you know. We used to have to pay out to the ones who were working.

Well, we got these inspectors, and the first thing they say is, 'Well, we're here! We want to go and see such-and-such a place.' It might be where drainage had been done, or fencing.

'Yes. All right. We'll take you there.'

So when we get there they take a look, and they say, 'I thought it was only five acres, I can see now it's about ten acres.'

I said, 'Yes, because that's what Api said to us. He said, 'Tie your belt up; it's your own land, and if you can make it more than five acres, do it.' We had done extra without payment, you see. Just what I said, that we apu the work, and do it all together.

When this Royal Commission was held in the North here, it was held in Whangarei down near the railway there – the courthouse was down there in those days. We had selected witnesses to speak, so the lawyer put us in a room. I was there, and we were listening, and he was questioning them to see how these witnesses would answer. Of course, you know with me, instead of them answering – well, they were too long, you see – I answered all these questions the lawyer was passing across. He turned around and he said, 'Oh, that's the right witness. She's the one. Never mind about you fellas – she can go in the box.'

So I did. Well, I wasn't afraid before the Royal Commission. I answer all what I have to answer, but I laugh at our Pakeha field advisers asking for a drink of cold water while they were answering what happened in certain areas. They were uncomfortable. I wasn't, because I knew we had everything right. But still, never mind. I think that helped to pull Api out, you know – out of the mess.

It was a hard time then, because Richard Gilbert was very sick, and when Dr Smith saw him at the Panguru clinic he wasn't sure what the trouble was. Well, to cut it short of course, he died. He died of cancer. Oh, I did all sorts. Spent a lot of money, because he had to go to Auckland to the Mater Hospital. The best doctor in Auckland was at the Mater, and the best thing, he said, was to leave it alone. A miracle might happen and he would live. But of course he went like that – he just died.

*At the time of Richard Gilbert's death, Whina was seven months pregnant – not to her husband, but to William Cooper. Cooper was the senior land development officer for the Tai Tokerau district, and he and Whina had met at Ngata's Whakarewarewa conference that prefaced the 1932 tour of development schemes in the Rotorua and Bay of Plenty areas.*

*Cooper's own marriage was not a strong one, and his work took him away from home for long periods. Whina was attracted by his keen intellect, his personality, and the knowledge and expertise apparent in his work. The strain of caring for a sick husband was another factor in making the attachment seem almost inevitable.*

*On Richard Gilbert's death, Whina was free to re-marry, but there were two obstacles – William Cooper's own marriage, and the moral outrage she would surely face from the strongly Roman Catholic community of Panguru. Characteristically, she tackled both these obstacles head on.*

Land consolidation came on the scene. Apirana Ngata had the officers for this development work . . . all these consolidation officers. By Jove, I am interested in the land. I would like to catch hold of one of these officers. If I could marry one of them, well, we are set. But that one is married, that one is married, that one is married . . . they all have wives. All right, what am I to do?

All right – I started going around with one. Cooper. Showing him all the lands and everything at the North. Day after day, weeks went past, but he is a married man. Oh, I often go to his place. I often meet him, and his wife didn't welcome me very much, and of course she is quite right. And of course she can feel that her husband is a bit cold or something – I don't know. Oh, what a story to ask me!

I went straight, but it was good, really good. Because he said, 'I have a dream before, and I saw this woman in my dreams' – this is Cooper telling me – 'and you are the very woman that I saw in my dream.'

'Oh, well . . . you think so?' I said.

'Yes, you are the very woman, and I am falling in love with you.'

And I said, 'I am also falling in love with you, but what can I do when you have a wife?'

'We'll talk it over.'

'All right.'

'Are you prepared to come to my home and talk it over?'

I said, 'I'm prepared for anything. I'm not frightened. If that is the way, all right, I will go there.'

So we went and had a conference. Two of us – his wife and me.

So I told his wife, 'Look here, dear, your husband seems to suit me for the work that I am longing for somebody to help my people to do.' And I said, 'Well, I come straight to you now. Would you like your husband to be also my husband. I know it's a hard question for you to say "yes".'

She said, 'Oh, that's all right, because we have got no children to worry about. I can go back to my people. That's all right. Quite all right by me.'

Her husband turned round and said, 'Oh well, if you would say that, all right, you can have everything in this house. You can take every-thing.'

So he came to me with nothing but his suit and himself. And I took him. So it was an agreement – not a fight, not a anything – but it was agreed properly, because I told her that he is the man I want to have, because to help my people. Because of the land.

All right. What do we do now? I said, 'Look, I have to go back home.' I want to go back home, and I want to call a big meeting of my people, and he says, 'All right.' Somewhere along the line I wired my people, 'I want a big meeting tonight at the hall . . . I want all the people there.'

Well, they think, of course, being with a consolidation officer, must be a big take – you know, big business – about land and all that sort of thing, and they all gather. All right. I come down by myself. And I stood up to ask them. I said, 'Well, my people, now I am going to marry Cooper. I come to tell you all; to agree.'

My brother Pita jumped up to give me a big hiding. 'Oh,' he said, loud all over the hall, 'we put you up at the top of Panguru Mountain – Panguru that high – and now you are coming right down to the bottom, getting a married man' – all that sort of thing.

My committee – my women's committee – came round me – you know, protecting me from all these people.

And my brothers, oh, they were mad at me! See, they don't know that I have all arranged everything. And I was crying, you know. I said, 'I came to ask you people peacefully; would you let me go peace-fully?' And my committee was crying with me and I thought it was wonderful to come and tell the people, you see, but they were all up in arms, and saying, 'We had put you on top of this mountain. Now you have put yourself right down!'

In the finish it went smoothly. The committee started to talk and everything, and my people calmed down, you know . . . calmed down.

Cooper was working in Whangarei then, so we had to get a place in Whangarei, in Kamo. We had a house there and it's still standing there now. Anyhow, I started a new life, you see – Consolidation and

William Cooper as a young man
*Whina Cooper*

all that – but the whole of Tokerau, the North, was up in arms for me marrying this man. Of course, we weren't married yet, you know, just living together. Oh, they were up in arms. What was my answer? My answer was, 'Look we are nothing to the King of England.' (That was Edward the Eighth. He left his throne for that Mrs Somebody-or-other.) I said, 'What am I to that? Look at the King! Damn! What am I? It is the land, to you people. We got somebody now who can speak out for the land. We got somebody.'

Oh, then I got a child from him, and I used to go round and make fun with the people. I said, 'You know, I thought at first I got this man for the land, but he turned round . . . hello! Look what he did! Hahahaha! Gosh!'

Anyhow, I had four beautiful children; two boys and two girls, and they are in Auckland now. Well, that's Mr Cooper.

You know when I got married? When I came into Otiria. The people there, they begged and begged me to get married properly. I cried. I cried. I said I didn't want them to make a fuss, but they made a fuss and everything. So when we got married properly, then I went home to my people. And you know where we lived? At Te Karaka where I was born, in the little shanty near the beach. Smoke – oh, it was terrible! But we lived there. I said, 'We have to do penance.' So we did penance and, after that, both of us walked to the graveyard in Panguru, and I laid down before the grave of my father and mother and asked pardon for what I did; then we were happy. Then I had a home in Panguru, of course . . . then I come home to Panguru.

Of course, my husband is busy in his office in Whangarei, and I am home and had to do all the work, and he is busy getting money that way, and of course I am at home doing all the gardening and everything else. I think that is why I am suffering now with arthritis and rheumatic, of doing too much work. At nights, do you know, when the moon is shining, I am planting. Planting kumara . . . all sorts of things. I get the horses, get the sledge, start ploughing. And beside that, when we started the development, of course, I had to get the young people interested. I got so interested that with the bit of money I had from the shop I started buying the cattle, like Jersey – pedigree cattle, with all the pedigrees you know. But it didn't succeed, because the land is not really good; it is much too hilly for pedigrees. You want good flat country for that. That was a bad trial of mine, but still I made out of it on the cows – yearlings – that I sold. Those days very costly.

You know, all that land we cleared has gone back now. Why? No leadership. When you have no leadership the people will fall, never mind where it is. And that's written in the Bible. If you go by the Bible you won't go very far wrong. But it's the people that makes you a leader, if you're doing the right thing. It's not yourself saying, 'I'm just it. I'm going to become a leader.' No, it's the work that you do, and the people will then lift you up, without you knowing.

Of course the main thing is that pride of race, you know – because
if I never had that I don't think I'd be Whina. But that pride, that's
what I got. *I'm a Maori!* And I know the more I'm proud of my race,
the more the Pakeha take notice of me – you don't want to lower
yourself down, no! I see a Pakeha lower than myself, ugh! I got no
time for that Pakeha, because I know I'm not going to be pulled down
like him, and I walk away from him. I also walk away from the Pakeha
that I know has not the pride of a Pakeha.

Well, that's me. I believe in pride of race.

*       *       *

And you got to know that what you do is right. Tika – the right Maori
way of doing things. Like that time at Waitangi . . . oh, it was the
time of the centennial celebrations, you know, and they built that big
carved meetinghouse at Waitangi, and everybody is there for when
they open it. Sir Apirana is there, the Maori Battalion is there –
everybody there. I was there in charge of the catering.

All right. This house, it was opened by a tohunga from Omanaia,
Mohi Waitai, and they have to come in the early hours of the morning to karakia the sacred chants, and get all the gods of the forest to
go back to the forest, and all that sort of thing, to lift the tapu.

He had a big crowd down at the bottom; you know, down at the
bottom there is a marae. They came – the Ngapuhi people – they came
at about two o'clock in the morning, and I happened to be up at the
top near the meetinghouse. And I was dressed in a Maori cloak and
piupiu; oh, I was really dressed in Maori. And when they came I could
hear the thundering of the haka, getting nearer and nearer, and then
the tohunga had the ceremony of lifting the tapu. There were these
three ladies, of very high rank, you know, behind the tohunga, and
he was just about giving the key to these three women to open the door,
so I cut across from the corner of the house to the tohunga. Right
up to him. Instead of him giving the key to these three ladies, he gave
it to me instead. He gave me the key, and I opened the door.

You know, something forced me to do that. So I opened it and we
all went in then, and the tohunga called on some of the ministers from
the different denominations to say prayers. Well! They all asleep, you
see – tents everywhere. It was the early hours of the morning. So I
said, 'Oh, the Catholic is ready!' And a fellow alongside of me, he's
not the minister but he's a Catholic, so I make him a minister and
nudge him and say, 'Hey, say a prayer!' So he is the first to pray inside
the meetinghouse. Drive all the devils out! Anyhow, that finish.

Well, towards the daylight the news is going around: 'Whina opened
the house instead of these three women that was picked, and she wasn't
picked to open the house.' And they questioned the tohunga, see? 'Why
did you give that key to her?'

So he answered. He told them he couldn't hold that key. He couldn't
hold it – he had to give it over to me, for the simple reason that it

came to him straight away, the words of our great ancestor, Tamatea: 'Ka hoki nei ahau ki Panguru, ki Papata, ki te rakau tu patapata itu ki te hauauru – I return to Panguru, to Papata, to the tree that stands tall in the west wind.' He told them Hokianga was the nest of all the northern tribes because Kupe landed there, and Panguru was the sacred mountain. 'Te rakau tu patapata i tu ki te hauauru.' He saw me as that tree that stands tall in the west wind, and the ceremony had to return to me.

Well, you know, they've got to be satisfied with that, because Panguru, that's my mountain, and it's a true story of the great ancestor Tamatea.

After that, of course, the whole thing went on not very smoothly, because the Maoris are great people for nursing jealousy. Oh, dear, dear, me! There was this great big chief. He was looking after all the hangi, and all the people working behind, you know, getting everything ready, and he says he's going to go on strike! And some of the speakers are speaking in front of the carved meetinghouse, jumping up and down. Well, somebody came along with a hose, you know, and hosed them down. Oh, those old people ran away! They had to stop speaking then!

Anyhow, Api came along. He knew all about this trouble, and he said to me, 'Don't worry, Whina. I've got the Maori Battalion here. I'll get them to do the work. No worry.' So he called the commander in charge and got some of the men standing alongside the house and said, 'There you are. It's all over to you.'

I didn't know what to do with them, but I was blessed really to have inspiration in me and say, 'Oh, yes, I want six in the meetinghouse for doing up all the tables; six over here; six over there . . .' All like that, you know. Oh, I looked quite a big lady with all the soldiers, and I got really sparked up. Oh, it was good.

I ran the two places you see, the Treaty House and the meetinghouse, and dear, dear me! When it came to dinnertime, Bellamy's told me they would look after the Governor-General's table, because that was their job.

I said, 'Well, it's not your job here! We've got Maori girls here and they'll do the whole thing. We're looking after him here.'

'No,' they said, 'no, you can't do that, because we're supposed to do it.'

I said, 'Look, I'm telling you now, you'd better stand alongside the wall there with all your crowd. We're doing it.'

And we did. That's how everything ended up. Oh, everything went beautifully after that.

*William Cooper died suddenly in August 1949. Whina remained at Panguru for a further year, and then moved to Auckland early in 1951. Several factors influenced the decision – tensions between factions in Panguru, the need to provide secondary education for her second family, and an instinct that now was the time to work on a broader scale.*

I made up my mind I was going to Auckland. I just up and off to Auckland. Took my children up there . . . educated them, you know. On my own. My husband is dead. I have no husband, and I go up there. Thought I might strike a rich Pakeha. Hahahaha!

But no! I went up there, and the priest at Panguru don't want me to go. And the Bishop of Auckland, Bishop Liston – God have mercy on his soul – he wants me to go there, to be in Auckland. I said, 'My Lord, Father Wanders does not want me to come to Auckland.'

'Why not?'

'Because he said I was born to lead my own people. Not to lead the people of Auckland.'

The Bishop turned round and said to me, 'Tell him that there are more souls in Auckland than in Panguru for you to work with.'

So I told the priest . . . so I says, 'I'm off!'

When I got to Auckland I look at it, and the drift of Maoris into the town was coming and coming. I got there in 1951, and at that time a call went up by the Government for all women from different areas all over New Zealand to assemble in Wellington. Anyhow, cutting it short, they had to have a president for the whole of New Zealand – the Maori Women's Welfare League, to work the whole of New Zealand . . . plant the seed. And darned if they didn't pick me.

'Whina Cooper – anybody else?'

Nobody else. Only her.

Well, I started to think, straight away. I had tears in my eyes then, a few drops, thinking, Well, I never! Here I am now in position. Can I take it – can I take it? Too right I can! How can I take it . . . how can I? 'Please, Our Lady, help me to talk the right things to those mothers throughout New Zealand.' That's my prayer.

All right, off I went. Take my bag, everything – I'm off. Told my children everything, and started travelling. I forgot how many weeks – I think six weeks – I been away, right down to the South Island and everywhere. I kept talking to my children, as I go around meeting everybody, and do you know that I used to talk almost right up to daylight. They won't let me sit down, because I talk straight out – to the women, you know, and how to go about everything.

All right. I sat many evenings when I get back to Auckland. Freemans Bay was loaded with people, Maori people coming from the country to the city with nowhere else to go but just Freemans Bay, because they can find a little shack there . . . and about twenty of them in one room, and all that sort of thing. Well I never! No conveniences, no nothing; just a small room. And I worried about all those things. At night I get phone calls at my place, at one o'clock, two o'clock.

'Trouble, Mrs Cooper.'

'What is the trouble? Can I help?'

Whina and her first Maori
Women's Welfare League
executive. Mick Jones and
Rangi Royal stand at rear.
*Whina Cooper*

'Yes. Do you know they are having a party next door, and my children can't get to sleep. They are studying and they can't study. Drinking is going on.'

And, oh – I get to this place.

'Oh Nanny, Nanny!'

I said, 'Nanny, Nanny, be damn! Look at all these bottles and everything else. Look, if you don't look out I am going to cut your pension and welfare. Don't you know you are not in the country? Those people are your next-door neighbours and their children are studying school – education – education. And here you are, having a good time drinking' . . . all that sort of thing.

Then I go into the hotels. I see children playing outside, Maori children, and I ask them, 'Where's your mummy?'

'In there. In the hotel, drinking.'

I go inside. I go like this with my finger to them, to come out and have a talk. I say, 'You see the children out there? If you don't come out of the hotel now I will ask Welfare to take those children away.' I say, 'So you go home now!'

'All right, Mrs Cooper.'

'Take a taxi,' I say. 'Go on – get home!'

My other work is for the Maori Affairs in Auckland. I ask them, 'Why is it that the Maoris do not get houses? What's the reason?' –

because they are all bundled up in these places in Freemans Bay.

And they said, oh well, they only had about thirty applications. That's all – and there are hundreds there.

I asked the Maoris. We had meetings. I ask them why there are only so few applications. They say they ask other Maoris who try, and these other Maoris say, 'Oh, waste of time going up there. They are not interested in getting us houses.' So I roared up to Wellington. I don't go to Maori Affairs – damn Maori Affairs. I go straight to Parliament. Knocked on the Minister's door – that was Ernest Corbett – and they said, 'Come in.'

'Oh, is it you, Whina?'

'Yes.'

'This place got rules.'

I said, 'Never mind about the rules. I face trouble over here. I want you to fix it up. *This is more important than all the rules!* Look,' I said, 'I just want you to give me permission to survey the whole of Auckland – the Maori people that needs housing.'

He said to me, 'I have got an office in Auckland, the Maori Affairs. They are doing the job and they are getting paid for it, so why should you come in and ask me for permission?'

I said, 'To me, it is not fair up there – only thirty applications, and the Maoris are thousands in Auckland, wanting houses. I can prove

Whina and Tumanako Rewiti (left) conducting the Maori Women's Welfare League housing survey in Auckland
*Auckland Star*

it to you if you give me the right to survey the whole of Auckland.'

So he said, 'All right, I give you permission.'

'Right. Thank you very much.'

I'm out. That's all I want.

So he wired up to the Auckland office to help me – give all the papers to Mrs Cooper. Well, I got all the papers and then I took them over to my home. I had three typists – I took some of the Maori girls that I know can type. Got all the branches of the Maori Women's Welfare League in Auckland to have a meeting. Told them what to do . . . go street by street, do this, do that; come home, report back. Type everything. Took us a long time, because we had to knock at every blessed Pakeha place to find out if there is a Maori in there, and survey properly. But I was strong, very strong, in what I was doing.

Tell you who was another help – the Quakers. They said they would have everything ready for the branches, when they came back to report . . . and they did. They are good people, those – very helpful.

When I finished everything, I dragged myself up to Wellington with all the books and everything that had been surveyed – families, applications, everything – and took them to the Minister. Knock at the same door, and the same question. Show him so many people wanting houses . . . hundreds of people.

I got the houses. And that's how they live now in the suburbs and in Freemans Bay – good housing.

That was that. I enjoyed it.

*     *     *

But you know, it all comes back to leadership – leadership and the land. I never dreamed I would ever march for the land, but we did, of course, in 1975, when we came down all the way from Te Hapua to Wellington.

At that time, you know, I been thinking for a long time, 'What has happened to the leaders? Our great men are all gone. Apirana is gone; Maui Pomare is gone; Dr Buck is gone; Sir James Carroll is gone . . . every leader of ours in the Maoritanga is gone. And who is the one to lead? Land is going, land is going. Out of sixty-six million acres we have less than two million acres left. Good gracious, who is going to lead after these men? We'd better call a meeting and find out!

So quite a few of the interested ones gathered at my place in Auckland, and we talked about it, and everyone is interested.

'Well,' we say, 'this organisation – what shall we call it?'

So each one said something – 'We call it this,' and another said, 'We call it that,' and all the time I am sitting there, thinking. All of a sudden it come to me – call it 'matakite' . . . foresight, seeing into the future.

'Matakite,' I said, 'because we want to see ahead.'

Then we call a big meeting, and I said, 'Look, I don't want to be the leader to talk about this. I want a man. Who will come forward?'

They pointed. 'You! You lead!'

'Me? A woman? Oh, all right.'

So anyhow, lunch came, and I never enjoyed lunch very much because I am thinking all the time. Anyhow, I sat there, and I said, 'Look, we discussed this thing long enough. Eh, what about a march? Yes, I think I'll put it across to the people when dinner is over.'

I put it to them.

'What about a march? We march to Parliament?'

Oh, they all clapped.

'Yes! We march!'

So there you are. We started the march, all right – from Te Hapua.

Well, you know, it's a lot of organising, and without money it's hard . . . hard. You'd think the Maoris came to Auckland to get money, but they're the poorest people you can get. and you can't get out of them ten dollars; you can hardly get ten cents. Because they got money today all right, but tomorrow they haven't got it – that's how it goes. Anyway, we're off to Te Hapua and everything is organised and at our fingertips before we march, and when we leave Auckland it is raining and thundering.

Whina leads the land march through a North Island provincial centre. At left Cyril Chapman holds aloft the pouwhenua.
*Whina Cooper*

They said, 'Ooh, it is awful, going up to start our march!'

I said, 'Never mind. We're going to get the most beautiful day when we start our march!'

And we did. It was a most beautiful day when we marched out of Te Hapua.

But you know, I always have a crucifix above my bed, and I talk to it, because I have a belief. So during our land march I put my trust and everything into the Lord. That's why I say to the marchers, 'Let us make this a sacred march. The name Matakite means foresight. Well, God is the only one that can see the whole world. He's the Matakite. Him.'

Well I never forget our march. When I wanted to go across the Auckland Harbour Bridge, it was plastered all over the papers and everything, 'You're not going to come over this bridge!'

And the marchers said to me, 'Hey, look, Whina – we can't go over the bridge. What are we going to do?'

I said, 'Swim across. What's wrong with that?'

Oh dear! I said, 'No, you leave that to me.' So at Marsden Point I left the marchers and went up to the post office and telegrammed the Chairman of the Harbour Bridge. I said, 'Let us come on *our* – I didn't say 'your' – on *our* Harbour Bridge on this most historic march.'

And I soon got a reply. 'Come, Whina. Come across. The marchers can come over the bridge.'

Oh, they clapped with joy. 'Oh, you're good, Whina!' Thanked me. Oh, they couldn't thank me enough.

I said, 'Listen to me. You suffered yourselves all the way from Te Hapua. You're sore on your feet, and you tried to march even when you're sore. But even those pains are rewarded. You've been sore; you've been thirsty. But don't thank me, thank Him – because He knows.'

So anyhow, we went by the thousands then, and we shook that Harbour Bridge until it swayed when we marched across. I was in front, and I look down between the girders and all and I said, 'Oh God, I'm not Moses! If these people fall in the water, how can I divide the waters? Oh God, help me!'

Well, anyhow, I was pleased to get across. They divided all these people into sections, and I look behind me and see them all coming across behind.

So that's it. We use the bridge. Safely. Because I have a belief in the Lord, and He can do wonders; that's why He's hanging above my bed.

You know what the newspapers call me once? 'Fiery, forceful and fearless.' I don't know, maybe they're right what they say, because of the Lord's help, this way.

'Fearless': if I have anything to say – whether you're the King or the Governor or whoever you are – if I have something on my mind,

not for myself but for the people as a whole, I'm not afraid to express my feelings and my mind. I'm not afraid of it. There's no fear in that. Not when I'm thinking for somebody else and I know I got my facts right before I put it across. That's one thing – if I have an answer and I see I'm wrong, I soon tell you. Right away I submit to you. I surrender – I'm wrong. I soon tell you, straight.

And 'forceful'? Well, anything that I do I always like to go to the end of it, and force it through. If I know it's right, I force it through. I keep writing to the Governor-General or anyone . . . write, write, until I get the answer.

Then, 'fiery'. Yes, I am. You've got to be fiery. It's this way. You can't be all soft and pretend you're lovely . . . all that lot of fuss. Ugh! No, you got to be true in what you're speaking about, you know, and the people say, 'That woman is, oh crumbs, very fiery.'

But if people want to know how fiery I am, they got to see my heart. In there it's all love. For the people. I love my people, and I only wish, you know, I can do something for them while I'm alive.

First broadcast 28 August 1978

# 4 'I've Swung an Axe and Humped a Swag'

The recollections of Bob Edwards on bushmen and swaggies.

*Intensive farming in the late nineteenth century led to a demand for farm labour. The work was often temporary or seasonal, and many of the itinerants it attracted regularly crossed the Tasman.*

*By the 1900s, the casual worker, constantly on the move, had developed his own distinctive lifestyle and character – the age of the swagger had arrived. Swaggers were identified by their dress, their equipment, and by a marked streak of independence. The wit, shrewdness and eccentricities of some of these men-of-the-road have become immortalised in John A. Lee's stories of Shiner Slattery, most famous of all New Zealand swagmen. 'The Shiner' was exceptional in his sheer craftiness, but all the brethren of the road – by the very nature of their calling – were physically resilient, hard-working men, used to walking long distances as they followed their seasonal beat from farm to farm. Inevitably, some became seduced by the freedom of the life, and wandering, more than work, became an object in itself. These though were in the minority, and the average swagger only tramped the road when he moved from job to job.*

*The uneasy 1920s brought increasingly hard times, and many men who were restless by nature, and whose needs were small, abandoned the security of permanent work – or the search for it – for life on the road. Bob Edwards was such a person, fitted by early bushwork and a wandering nature for the life of an itinerant.*

*Much has been written of an anecdotal nature about the swagmen, but while stories of The Shiner, Russian Jack, Barney Whiterats and other men of the road are an essential part of our folklore, it should not be forgotten that this way of life depended on firm practical considerations, and on codes of conduct essential to their acceptance by farmers, and by others of their calling. Bob Edwards's account is unusual in that it describes the tools and techniques of the swagger in considerable detail. He has not followed the road for half a century, but his memory can still document the way of life of a breed of men now extinct.*

A swagger, c. 1900
*Alexander Turnbull Library*

The Old Dad used to do a lot of contracting. He would have a contract to get so many thousand posts or mine props, because mine props were in big demand at that time. Work wasn't all that plentiful, not work that paid a wage, and although the price per hundred for posts at stump or at the roadside – it was mostly at the stump in those days – was pretty small, irrespective of that, it was some cash at least that you could get your hands on.

The Old Man was a pretty softhearted sort of bloke really, and he would never turn down a fellow if he could possibly help it – he would always give a bloke a job. In a sense, 'giving him a job' doesn't quite give the right impression either, because what he really used to do was to cut up the contract according to the number of men that were immersed in it. All that he really kept out of it was his share and what it took to pay the store bill and to replace the tools of trade – the axes, the crosscut saws, the mauls and wedges. Those were the things that had to be maintained, plus the camp gear, of course.

Like most bushmen, his axe-work was a mighty necessary part of his makeup (and the Old Dad was a 'top hand'). If he wasn't a good man at the end of a saw – some blokes were 'jockeys', they rode it – well, he wouldn't last long in the bush as far as his work was concerned, so there were certain things you knew straight away – you weren't in a man's company for an hour before you pretty well knew the bloke you were dealing with. You only had to see his axe – how the handle fitted – for a kick-off.

As regards felling ability, take scarfing; when you scarf a tree you scarf it in the direction it is going to fall, and the bottom cut, the underswing of the cut, is level. Well, a good stump is a sort of a bushman's signature. A bushman who leaves a good stump, that's his signature, and you can tell what bushman fells a tree by the stump

A bushmen's camp, c. 1910
*McAllister Collection, Alexander Turnbull Library*

Land-clearers' camp, early
1900s
*Tesla Collection, Alexander Turnbull
Library*

he leaves. That's a thing that a bushman took pride in. The average
bushman, the man who gave himself to that life as part of his work,
well . . . he was part of his work. He often discussed problems with
himself. A Tassie bushman once said to me, 'I don't like that new bloke
the Old Man started. I been workin' across the gully from him and
he hasn't said a word to himself all day. Something bloody queer about
that joker.' The Tassie was dead serious; he figured that was about
as unsociable as a man could get.

But aside from that, these men had to meet up with all sorts of
requirements. When you went into a bush camp you were removed
from civilisation, you were living in a different world. You were living
in a world where a man's word mattered a hell of a lot, because if
he told you a certain area of bush contained a certain type of timber
that was required for the contract that you were filling, well you knew
that that timber would be there, and pretty well in the quantity he'd
described.

Further to that, it was a time when there was not a helluva lot of
money around, and you might have to spend your last quid in buying
an axe for that particular type of work. You couldn't afford to buy
an axe just for the sake of having one; it had to earn its keep. So in
every way, a bushman had to measure up as a man, and you had to
have a bloke you could take his word on, so that he would be a mate

that would stand by you if things went wrong, as they could in the bush. A bloke could have an accident, and he had to be capable of stitching up your skull if you were careless enough to take an overhead swing when there was a snag above you. Many a bloke got a serious cut in the leg or the foot, and his mate had to be a man that he could depend on. When you had a good mate you knew that his word was good and he measured up as a man right through. So all those things mattered. They mattered a hell of a lot, and those blokes were mighty particular about moral codes, too.

If you were dirty in a camp; if you were dirty with your clothes; if you allowed a dirty pair of socks to hang around in a camp – well, there's nothing more offensive. When a man is working hard he sweats a lot, so God help the man who wasn't clean about his personal habits and his clothing. When a thing was dirty, you didn't leave it and say 'Well, tomorrow will do.' You washed it there and then.

Apart from that even, as I say, their moral codes were fairly strict. I heard one helluva tough bushman, Charlie Moore – he and his brother Bill were the two greatest toilers I have ever seen, and Charlie's hand had been severed and he had a steel hook for his right one – I heard Charlie giving hell one evening to a bloke at Waione who was using some pretty foul language. Charlie got up and hauled him to his feet, and he said, 'Now you leave your dirty bloody language outside where you left your dirty boots! Don't bring your filthy tongue into the hut at all. This is no place for that.'

And that wasn't exceptional; that was quite a common attitude. And these were hard damned men. These were guys that didn't call a spade a spade, they called it a bloody shovel – but they had a moral code.

You didn't start throwing a woman's name around either, not inside the camp. You might do that out in the bush while you were working with the tools, and a few words would be bandied around about the last trip into town, and maybe a conquest that you'd enjoyed – but no names, and by hell you didn't carry it into camp. The camp was a place where you left your dirty stuff outside, and you kept yourself clean, because your food was in there and your bedding was in there.

The fair dinkum bushman was a bloke that . . . well, the storeman knew him, because the storeman was a helluva important man in a workingman's life at that time. There were some mighty people among those early storekeepers, real Christians because they grub-staked you, and hell, they didn't know whether you were going to make money or not. They just knew you had to have a chance, so they were damned good judges of character, and they knew the type of man. When a bushman walked into a country store and asked for credit they were damned good judges; they could sum a man up. And you know, somehow or other, as a man matured in that type of life, it showed. You could pick a man.

Booze was a thing that came into the bush on the rare occasions when a bloke could afford to buy something along that line – it might be twice in a year he could afford to buy a bottle of whisky. But they used to make concoctions of their own, and the most popular, I should say, was matai beer.

Now when you felled a big matai, that was the thing that showed me that all things are – well, maybe it was just a conception, and I could have been wrong perhaps – but it seemed to establish in my mind that all things are living things. When you felled a big matai, a really mature black pine – matai is the Maori name – you would see the main artery in the heart of the tree gushing out the life liquid. And as it gushed, it was a heartbeat, a definite heartbeat . . . you just stood, and watched that tree die, and somehow you felt guilty and sad.

It wasn't the sap; this was not related to that. It was a pure clear liquid, and it gushed out like the main artery gushing blood. But that used to be prized, and it would be caught in a billy. That was really something. It was beautiful and cool and sweet to drink as it was, but some of the blokes used to bung in maybe a handful of raisins and sugar, cork her up and let her ferment, and whether that fluid had any other properties in it or not I don't know, but you could get quite a potent drink from it.

Of course, down around Croydon, where I worked in the bush, that was the Hokonui country, and I could tell some stories about Hokonui whisky.

There was a family called McRae who started this still in the Hokonuis, and one of McRae's daughters married a bloke called Black. Now apparently the McRaes set the couple up in a shack down in the Lora Gorge. I think they paid him some sort of retainer, and it was understood that if the mounted police came through that area – because of course at that time they were looking for stills – Black was to get in contact and notify them of the fact.

Now I'm not going to say that I know how he was to do that, whether it was maybe by a signal fire, or whether he would simply ride through with the word – I guess the last would be the most probable. Anyhow, apparently Black pulled a doublecross on McRae, and when the traps came through – 'traps' being what the police were called at that time – Black did nothing about it. Apparently there must have been a row between Black and McRae's daughter, and the speculation was that she ended up sticking a knife in him. They found him, and he was knifed. I'm not sure whether or not she was proven guilty, but that was the Lora Gorge murder, and that was the reason it came about . . . that was how it came about.

Anyhow, getting back to McRae. The old Donald McRae, he used to come into the Old Man's camp, and he used to bring . . . I'm not sure what they call it – I was never very familiar with booze, and I just forget the type of bottle – I think it was a quart bottle, the whisky bottle at that time. But old Donald McRae, it was said he drank one of those a day. I remember the old bloke saying to the Old Man that somebody had told him about whisky being a danger and petrifying

RIGHT: H. S. Cordery, Collector of Customs and Inspector of Distilleries, and Detective Sergeant Hewitt, with an illicit whisky still seized at Ferndale, near Gore, in December 1913
*Mrs S. Perry Collection*

BELOW: A cache of Hokonui whisky, discovered at Awarua in December 1934
*Mrs S. Perry Collection*

the liver and all that sort of thing, and the old bloke said, 'Whisky? Look, I think the ideal death would be to be drooned in whisky!'

But as I say, he used to visit the Old Man, and at that time we had in the district the last man to have a price put on his head in that part of the country – a bloke called Ned Cosgrove. They reckoned Ned had held up the wagon that was taking the pay out to the different mills, and robbed it. But I don't reckon it was ever true. Ned Cosgrove was a bushman, and a bushman that was held in pretty great respect, and believe me, all the other bushmen made damned sure the police never caught up with him. He stayed at many camps in the bush through the Longwoods and up in the Croydon Range, and he gave the police a lot of fun for quite a long while.

But getting back to the Hokonui whisky. It found its way into all the local hotels, and it got there with the milk deliveries, in milk cans. All the milk was carried in cans in those days, and the milkman went from door to door and filled your billy from a can. How the whisky got into the milk cans, well only the McRaes could tell you that. They were born organisers, and they'd been at the game a hell of a time, and they'd evolved a way of getting it to the different pickup points. I've an idea they worked in with some of the local farmers. Maybe an extra can would be delivered to a certain cocky's place, and probably the cocky got a regular bottle of free whisky supplied to him for being a go-between. But that was the method of it. Incidentally, Hokonui was a colourless whisky. If there was any colouring it was added later, because as it came from the still, it was colourless – and she was a pretty potent drop of stuff.

I remember at one of the camps, the Old Man and a bushman named Billy Richardson had got into a heated argument, because we used to take a lot of bees at that time – take the honey, you know. You'd often find a hive in an old broadleaf. The heart was inclined to rot out in an old broadleaf, and the bees would swarm and hive in them, and we'd take the wild honey.

Anyhow, the Old Man had been skiting a lot about how he could take bees and suchlike, and how it was no trouble to him to take a swarm of bees, and of course it was only the whisky that was talking. This was late in the evening, and Richardson dared him.

He said, 'Well, there's a swarm on a kotukutuku by the track – how about taking them?' So the Old Man said, fair enough, he was game enough, so they said to me, 'Well, you light the lantern and bring it down, and stand by while we take this swarm of bees.'

Well, we went down there. The Old Man had a kerosene box above his head, and Bill was shaking the kotukutuku tree to try and drop the swarm down into it. The Old Man was sobering up by this time, and I think his nerve was going. He realised things weren't going to be too good once that swarm cut loose, and he wanted the job over quickly, so he told Bill to get stuck in and give her a fair dinkum shake. Bill did, too. He really whipped that tree around and he shook bees all over the Old Man. I realised things weren't going according to plan, so I threw the bloody light away, and got out of it. Well then, of course I wasn't too popular for leaving them in the dark with the bees, you see, and they made pretty sure they left it imprinted on my mind and on my backside that it had better not happen again.

But that's the sort of situation Hokonui whisky could lead you into. It was pretty widely known at that time. I guess all the football teams that visited in those days – all the country rugby clubs and so forth – I'd say that, when they visited, all their celebrating would be done on Hokonui whisky. And of course it would be a lot cheaper than the legal brands would be, so at that time the pocket might be able to run to a bottle of Hokonui now and again.

The Old Man really wasn't much of a businessman, and he got fouled up with one of his contracts. I don't know the ins and outs of it, but there was money he thought he'd paid when he hadn't in fact. I do know the honest squatter we were contracting for had gone broke. And when everything was sorted out, the Old Man came out of that contract without a zak to show for it. Well, I had been working with him on that one, and at the end of seven months' bushwork we didn't have a brass razoo. No money coming in . . . and we still had to honour the storekeeper who had grub-staked us.

*     *     *

Well, I took to the track. I came up north and swagged with a character that was well known on the track at that time. There was some great blokes around then – this was in the mid twenties. They were fellows that were on the track permanently, and they all had their beats. The East Coast of the North Island had a particular appeal, because it was a kinder coast as far as the weather was concerned, and that had its effect on the squatters as well. Good weather and good grass, and all that sort of thing, made for a generous squatter. Bob Anderson (his brother was a titled man), I swagged with him, and he was a great old character – a real swagger. I met Russian Jack on the road. I run into him a couple of times, but I never swagged with him. And of course I heard a thousand stories of The Shiner, and I'd say eighty per cent of them would be pretty true, too. He was quite a character, The Shiner, but of course I never run into him – he was before my time. But the one who took me in hand was Riverina Dick. Old Riverina Dick was well known around the East Coast, particularly in the Wairarapa area and southern Hawke's Bay – that was his stamping ground.

Different things brought people together to swag. There was I, on my Pat Malone, starting off on my first experience at humping a swag. Now these blokes like Riverina Dick, the established swagmen, they didn't seek company – the fair-dinkum swagman, he liked to be on his own – but they're prepared to take on an apprentice. This is a very real thing. They owe it as a duty to their fellow man to put him right – to show him the ropes, show him the track, tell him where the handouts are, and the squatters that treat a man as a man. But once that's done, and they consider you've had a fair go, they're not going to lead you by the hand for years. You serve your apprenticeship, and once it's finished, then you're on your own. So they're not blokes that seek company. Maybe just at odd times they like to share a smoke with a man, a yarn with a man – but when they hit the track they like to be on their own.

I don't really know why I was accepted; that would be Riverina Dick's story. Whether he'd shown other young blokes the trail or not, I don't

'Russian Jack', the last of the swaggers, photographed not far from Feilding, c. 1960
*Alexander Turnbull Library*

know, but I met him one night in a shack out from a place called Pongaroa, and we had a yarn, and I told him I'd been looking for work in the area and there was none around at the time – there wasn't a job to be had anywhere. He said to me, 'Well, I'm going through to the coast, and if you like you can roll up your bluey and come along with me.'

Well, fair enough. I accepted the invitation, and I had a fair idea of the requirements. I'd knocked around a bit and roughed it. I had a light bedroll, and it was good weather at the time, so I was down to what swaggies call a 'heatwave knot' – down to a very light bedroll. You do get a fairly good autumn in the north; it's really better than the summer, so you had roughly five months of good weather. So I swagged around the coast with Riverina.

I'll never forget, he said to me once, 'There's a sure handout along this particular track,' and we stopped at an old shack with a fairly high veranda, much after the style of the verandas on the Queensland side, where the termites are bad. Well, we sat on this veranda, and he said to the lady of the house – she was kindly looking and she seemed to be old, but remember I was pretty young at the time – and he said to her, 'Is there any chance of a feed, missus?'

She said, 'Yes, Dick, don't worry. There's a feed for you and your mate.'

Well, she came back with this big platter of scones, and old Dick got up and grabbed his hat, and he said, 'Oh, for God's sake, woman, not bloody scones again!'

I was upset by that, you know. For a start, I didn't swear in front of a lady, and that's a fact; I wouldn't think of it. That was the way it was. As I said, the bushmen had educated you that way. You didn't get this from any fancy crowd or society mob, this was the sort of thing instilled into you in the bush camps. You didn't swear in front of a woman, but you treated her with respect, and you also treated her hospitality with respect. So Dick had offended on both counts in my estimation . . . matter of fact, he dropped a hell of a lot in my estimation when he did that.

But I couldn't do that, so I stayed. For a start, I felt obliged to accept the hospitality that had been extended. It was a pretty generous sort of a gesture, because people didn't have a lot to give away. But after I'd had a couple of those scones, I knew why Dick had cut his strings, because, stone the crows, they were bloody frightful! And the after-effects were more serious than many of the drugs the doctors are heaving around nowadays – the side effects from them scones was drastic. For the next three or four days I fertilised forty per cent of the local flora. But they did cure my cold – I was too bloody scared to cough!

Old Dick, he was a great character, and he was looked on almost as a visitor that you could expect at certain periods. The different station owners he called on – the Armstrongs, the Hunters (of the big Hunter will case that went on for many years, longest on record I think – Sir Cyril Hunter and all those) – they would know him well.

But you know, a swagger wasn't a no-hoper like some people thought. It became a trade almost, and again, strangely enough, there were strict moral codes governing it, even though Riverina Dick wasn't the best example I could give you. Mind you, of course, there were certain words that were acceptable. Now 'bloody' was a word that was not really looked on as a swear word; 'bloody' was an acceptable part of your conversation.

Now where were we? Oh yes, that's right – the make-up of the average swaggy. Well, number one, he maintained a certain standard of dress. He didn't give a damn how patched or ragged his clothes were but, by hell, they had to be clean and he himself as well, whenever he got the chance, and . . . well, in this country the chance was always there, because you never had to go far from one waterhole to another, so you could always have a wash and clean your gear as well, and that was a thing a bloke always did. And another thing, too; the old polka-dot handkerchief was *the* handkerchief, and to be caught in possession of a filthy polka-dot handkerchief was a damn disgrace. It was a thing to be ashamed of, because these were the things that were important to him.

He had to be well equipped. When I say well equipped, first of all he had to have a good tea billy. A good tea billy was a very important thing. For a start, it had to be well blackened inside from having brewed a lot of tea, and heaven help the man who turned round and thought he was going to do a swaggy a good turn by giving him a new shiny billy, because he was losing a valued possession if he lost that fair-dinkum billy, because it takes a while to break a billy in.

And of course the advantage of a well-broken-in billy that carried a good heavy coat of tannin was the fact that when you had got to the stage when there was no flavour left in the leaf and it was ready for smoking, but no good for brewing, well, you could get a certain amount of flavour from out of the billy just on its own. You could boil up a restricted quantity of water and you could definitely get a flavour. You could get a taste of tea; it was there.

As I say, once the tea was finished for brewing, well, it was ready for smoking, and in many cases that was the swagger's tobacco. The billy was ninety-nine times out of a hundred an old 'cocky's joy' tin – the old golden syrup or treacle tin, because the seven-pound treacle tin was the ideal brewing billy. She was a beaut. She was really good, and it was a good billy because it didn't cost anything, and you could carry your pannikin inside it.

The pannikin was your manufacture, and it was generally made from . . . well either a two-and-a-half-pound syrup tin or a Highlander condensed milk tin made a heck of a good pannikin. You used it to drink the tea out of, of course, and you made it yourself. You made sure that the rim was well hammered down so as you wouldn't get your lip hung up on it, and then you made the handle. Now the handle was made by cutting another milk tin and folding it in about three folds, so that it made a strip about an inch wide. Then you made that into more or less the shape of a human ear – you bent it to a handle shape – and the top lobe would be folded down inside the tin you were drinking from, and the lower lobe would actually go underneath the tin and act as a grip. Now you could make that quite springy if you had three or four folds of tin, and you could take it off, wash the tin, and put the whole lot away inside your billy.

Another important part of the swaggy's equipment was his bedroll. Generally it was called a 'wagga'. Now the old wagga was popular in the wintertime – a bit heavy to carry, but it came into its own in the winter. The wagga rug was made out of the old one-striper sacks, and they're things that just aren't around these days. The old one-striper was the fair-dinkum chaff sack, because of course at that time oats and chaff were still used a lot for horsefeed. Later came the three-striper bag. It was a much shorter, smaller bag with a very much lighter weave, but the old heavy one-striper made a wonderful wagga.

The wagga originated over on the Aussie side, and generally to improve it you opened up two sacks, and this made a wonderful rug. Opening up two sacks gave you the complete length and width which was required for a good rug. Then, when you got the chance of getting your hands on some flour, you mixed up some flour-and-water paste, and you stuck a sheet of brown paper on to the wagga. Well, that sort of made the air stop going through it, and with that across you, you were as warm as pie and you didn't need anything else, not even a tent, because you could sleep out in the open, provided the weather was right.

If it was the wintertime or the spring, which is bad in New Zealand, well, you always had a barn to sleep in, or in many of the places you even got shearers' quarters to doss down in, and you were treated pretty well.

If they could have given you a job, they'd have done so, but they *couldn't* give you a job, those squatters. Damn it all, you could buy sheep on the hoof as low as sixpence a head. A shilling a head was almost the ruling price. They just didn't have the dough – there just wasn't any money around. But they were pretty damn good when it came to giving you a feed, and they didn't stop at that. Not every trip, but maybe every second or third trip, there would be a new pair of boots for the bloke that was on the track. There was always a plug of tobacco for him – there was always a plug of tobacco, and there was always a ration of tea and flour and sugar. That was more or less understood.

There was no pressure put on you, but it was an unwritten law that you didn't overstay your welcome. You maybe had a day, a night and a day, and then you were gone. If you were crook, then you could maybe lie around the station for a week, and you could go up to the cookhouse and get your tucker, but once you were physically capable of going on the road again, you were expected to go.

*     *     *

There were blokes at odd times that weren't a hundred per cent genuine swagmen. I wasn't. (And I cannot claim to have been a genuine bushman either. It just happens I done fifteen years of growing in bush camps. There were plenty my age on the track; most kids of working-class families were out fending for themselves at fourteen. Mainly, my adult life was spent at sea, or round the waterfronts or, at odd times, cane cutting in Queensland if I was 'on the beach'.) At all times I was prepared to work. I couldn't claim to be a genuine swagger.

You see, for a start, Riverina at that time would be a bloke in his fifties, I'd guess. To me he seemed old. Maybe because of hardship in those times, men seemed to age quicker, but a young bloke like me looked on him as a hell of an old joker, you know.

Riverina, incidentally, was a hard-looking bloke. The strange thing about him, he had neither eyelashes nor eyebrows, and that gave him a hell of a cold look. I've even heard fellows say, 'Well, Riverina is not far away from being a carpet snake' – because of course a snake has an eye like that, you know. Anyhow, he generally wore – and this was another thing pretty common with the swagger – he generally wore a good hat. Riverina always had a borsalino. How he come by it I wouldn't know, but a borsalino was looked on as a sort of prestige thing, you know. The brim was wider by far than the present-day brim, and it was one of the superior hats of the day. Definitely would be. A borsalino, stetson – these were the hats that had a bit of class about them. It was similar in style to a stetson, but with a slightly smaller brim, but it was a class hat.

Now that was the sort of thing a swagman prided himself on – his hat, a polka-dotted handkerchief, his boots. He had to have substantial boots because he had a lot of walking to do, so he didn't go in for any fancy footwear. In summertime, the average swagman would make his walking early in the morning till she got hot, round about maybe half past ten, and that would be time for him to pull up. Up until that time he'd probably have walked at a rate of around three miles an hour – that would be about his walking rate. Anyway, he'd pull up about half past ten, and he'd probably leave the rest of his walking until about four o'clock in the afternoon. Half past three, four o'clock he'd start, roll up, and get on the way.

He never measured distance. In a song I wrote, 'Restless Feet', I mentioned that: 'Never count the miles; measure not the load.' You didn't keep thinking about what you were carrying on your back or on your shoulder, and you didn't count the miles. The horizon was always there, and that's where you were headed anyway, and she was always in front of you, so it didn't matter. The miles didn't count. Destinations didn't matter – except, of course, there were certain points on the track that were vitally important to Riverina, where he knew there would definitely be a handout, where there was a good rest camp, or a good shack if the weather was bad.

*          *          *

As far as the hardships was concerned, you accepted them. You knew they had to come, and the bitter made the sweet mighty sweet. A few hardships were things you could look back on afterwards and laugh about . . . how you'd slept under a damned willow tree, maybe. Mind you, a willow tree could be a mighty handy sort of thing, because you generally find willows growing by a creek, and they have a habit of growing along before they grow up, and you might get a fairly substantial trunk that maybe travelled along for eight or nine feet before it finally shot up. Well, it didn't take a hell of a lot of work to develop that into a cover where you could crawl in and get a good night's sleep. I've used that many a time, and the average bloke on the track has used that sort of thing many a time. Or for that matter, even a good hedge. The majority of runholders generally put in a good windbreak of lawsonianas or something like that, and many times those provided us with a camp if we couldn't reach something better. But in the main you slept in barns and sheds.

This swaggers' hut was for many years a landmark at Weedons near Christchurch
*J. Henderson Collection, Alexander Turnbull Library*

No, I think the main hardships I suffered came simply from the desires of a young bloke. I don't mean just the physical ones. For instance, now, it would be the ambition of every young fellow of that time to have a navy-blue serge suit, which was the mark of . . . well, that was looked on as really something. You were somebody if you had that. And of course if you had that sort of thing you could hit the dance halls, because even in those outback places and even in those times, there was generally a dance somewhere.

People at that time didn't go to a dance simply because it was a break from their working-day life. They went there because it was a chance to be with people. A chance to feel the warmth of human companionship. A chance to share. People had nothing as far as money was concerned, but the women would knock up a few cakes, and if you were lucky there might be a few sausage rolls and that sort of thing. This was an opportunity to share with each other and have a bit of pleasure and human company. There were the odd times there was some booze, and generally there was a good scrap – you could just about bank on it that there would be a couple of good scraps.

It doesn't apply so much now, but in those days the women would be waiting for a dance, but the blokes would be gathered out the back, arguing the toss about who could swing an axe best, or who could ride a horse best. These were all things of the time. The people of the time were more dependent on each other. At the same time they were independent in their ways and each man wanted in some way to vindicate himself, to establish himself in the community. But when it came to human warmth and the desire for human relationship and the opportunity to share, these things mattered a hell of a lot. And really, that's what these functions were for.

Well, as I say, I wanted to participate in that sort of thing. But hell, a man couldn't participate, or you didn't feel you were entitled to, with maybe a torn wire-twist shirt or a bush singlet, a pair of dungarees or moleskin trousers, and rarely ever a pair of decent shoes. Hell's delight, for a man to own a pair of good shoes was really something. A pair of Blucher boots was the average footwear, and they were the cheapest you could buy. They went for around eight shillings. They got up to twelve shillings eventually, and then the blokes gave it away – they were getting too dear.

So these things a man wanted. Well, of course he maybe wanted to do a line with a sheila, and again he felt self-conscious, because he always felt that the bloke that was the best dressed had the best show, you see. Now these things at that time hit me a bit hard. Riverina was satisfied with the simple things of life, but it wasn't just that easy for me. Maybe this is where the break started to come from the genuine swagman to the bloke that didn't serve out his time, that didn't serve out his full apprenticeship. He was a failure as a swaggy. He became one of the orthodox members of society. He wanted to do an honest day's work for an honest day's pay, and have all the wants and all the avarice of the average bloke. I definitely became a victim of this.

I didn't realise that Riverina Dick hadn't only shown me the track that he travelled, and the handouts along the track, but he'd shown me something else as well really. But it didn't get through to me then. He'd shown me that this *was* life, that this is what it amounted to. All a man needed was shelter from the elements, food for his body to give him strength. The heavens were wide, God's scenery was free, and it was a man's duty to go and see it. And there's something in that, too. For a man to talk about his Maker and not want to see His works, well there's something wrong. There's something missing. That's where I think the swagman's philosophy was pretty sound.

And looking back on it all, those genuine swaggers like Riverina Dick, well, they earned, and were entitled to, a measure of respect. They didn't steal from anybody; they asked, they requested – but they thought it was their perfect right to do this sort of thing. They didn't pull the forelock or anything like that. They expected to be treated as human beings, and the mere fact that they were in a state of want wasn't necessarily of their own making. That was just circumstances again.

Most of them were thoroughly trustworthy blokes, the real swaggers; they weren't vagabonds or anything like that. People don't realise that. Some folk say, 'Well, the lazy cow doesn't want work. If you offered him a job he'd run a mile.' Now this was commonly said, and it wasn't actually true. You see, what drove a swaggy to the roads was that he was forced into it because of economic pressures, just the same as months of bushwork, with hardly a cracker coming from it, made me carry a swag. But once in this situation, the true swagman realised he'd gained a great measure of freedom. In a sense, he's found himself as an individual. So it became a way of life for him – a vocation, you might say.

*     *     *

Well, the whole damn world slipped into depression. It was coming in the twenties when butterfat prices dropped, and from then on she was downhill all the way. Being young and single, the Depression wasn't as bad for me and thousands of others in my age group. It must have been hell for the older men with families and poor devils that had dreams of owning a home and that sort of thing, because they were losing everything – they were losing everything. With us sort of blokes, well, we were back-country people, and that was a help.

Most of us worked a trap-line. You were trapping rabbits, and the old rabbit, well, he was a mighty important part of the economy at that time. What was known in those days as 'underground mutton', that was the average struggler's meat, and the average family depended on it. The demand for skins was not great unless the skin was good quality – winter hides might bring in as much as a zak each; sixpence a skin at that time. That's if you could find a buyer who wanted them, and had the dough to pay. As I say, trapping was quite common, and I worked a trap-line along with dozens of others, and as a way of supplementing the food supply. And also, there was a bit of living off the 'long acre'.

The long acre was the roadside, and maybe sometimes by accident you did cross a fence, but you seemed to think that if there was too many sheep wandering the long acre, one wouldn't be missed. In a way it was a criminal act, but many a man took one of those, and you sort of exonerated yourself by saying, 'What the hell!' A man was entitled to eat. So this was done fairly often. Not many blokes were actually ever jailed for this offence, because I think in a lot of cases the owners of the stock had no damn right to be grazing them on the long acre, so in a sense they were offenders as well. And in many cases, a lot of them did sympathise with the strugglers' circumstances. But then, as things grew worse, and a realisation started to come to men's minds that the Depression was manufactured, a tremendous resentment built up in people.

By this time I'd come to the city. I had some mates that were trying to get a few bob by hawking drapery, and they induced me to have a go at it too. That first brought me into contact with the major cities, and the people there were in a hell of a situation. We'd got a few quid – I don't remember how – but we'd got a few quid each, this mate of mine and I. Six or eight quid. At that time you could buy, through the wholesalers, socks at about ninepence, or cheap ties round about fourpence, women's lisle stockings, you could pick them up for around one and ninepence. Well, you knew that in the cities, where there was a little money at least, people needed these things. You also knew they were sympathetic towards a bloke that was trying to get along and knock out a few bob. But you had to have a pretty hard attitude. You had to have the sort of attitude that you wanted the money, the cash in your hand for the goods you had for sale, you see. Therefore you had to be a certain type of a bloke. Well, we didn't measure up, because I saw some damn sad cases of poor damn people that had no money, and I think the two of us ended up with empty suitcases and empty pockets. We ended up giving the damned stuff away. We weren't successful businessmen at all.

As I say, all this time feeling was mounting, and these things were bringing it home to me, too. I saw people who lived in luxury, and I saw people who had absolutely nothing, and that wasn't an exaggeration. In Auckland, I saw women begging on the streets, with baskets. And these were good people – these were good people, begging on the streets with baskets, just for food for their children. And that sort of thing really made a man think, because you began to wonder why. You *knew* there were sections of the community who were living in luxury, and they had servants, house servants, for a mere damn pittance, and if they did make a gesture they made damn sure everybody knew how kind they'd been.

Well, all these things began to make you wonder who was responsible, who was behind all this. You began to realise that you had a right to share in the things that were produced – you knew that any God's amount of stuff was being produced. There was no shortage of production. There was no shortage of manpower. But they were denied the right to work, and if you were denied the right to work you were denied the right to live as a human being. So as you moved into the real vicious crunch of the Depression, people were worked up to such an extent that they were prepared to go to any length whatever to obtain the things they'd been denied: the right to have a decent damn singlet; the right of the womenfolk to have underclothing that they wouldn't be ashamed to have seen hanging on the line, because that was a very real thing.

The flour bag provided the average poor people's family with their underclothes. The girls and womenfolk, their damned underclothes had to be made from flour bags. The flour bag was first-class linen, and through boiling, the brand could be removed. Mind you, everybody just wasn't that particular. It depended where you lived. If you lived in a settled community, you had to worry about it, but if you lived in the backblocks you didn't worry about it.

But that was a fact. The human dignity was just stripped off them. They weren't satisfied with just taking away the right to work, the right to a decent life; they weren't satisfied until they took the dignity away from them. Now that was a vicious system, and who was entirely responsible for it? . . . well, that would be going into a political discussion.

Maybe I was at the stage where I was over-emotional about these things, but then again, I don't really know, I reckon a man had every right to be emotional about it. But you were prepared to take drastic action. By that time you'd given away respect for the law, because you found the law was protecting only one thing – and that was privilege. So you became contemptuous of it.

Then again, you also made the mistake of blaming your fellow man to this extent, that you didn't realise that the guy that had a job or maybe took a job from you – maybe he offered to work for less than you would – was in exactly the same boat you were in. Now you immediately took out your resentment on the effect, and you didn't stop to think about the cause. The effect was there; it was right in front of you, so you struck at the effect.

I remember one time I was asked if I wanted to be in a decent stoush, and when that was put to you by blokes that were more or less your mates, well you'd have lowered the flag if you'd said no. So of course the answer was yes. I think from memory that we availed ourselves of a pick handle, or something in that line, each. Now this happened in Invercargill, and we got into this hullabaloo with some poor damned immigrants. What system they were brought out under, I don't know, but they were 'Homeys' – the word 'Pommy' wasn't in use then, and

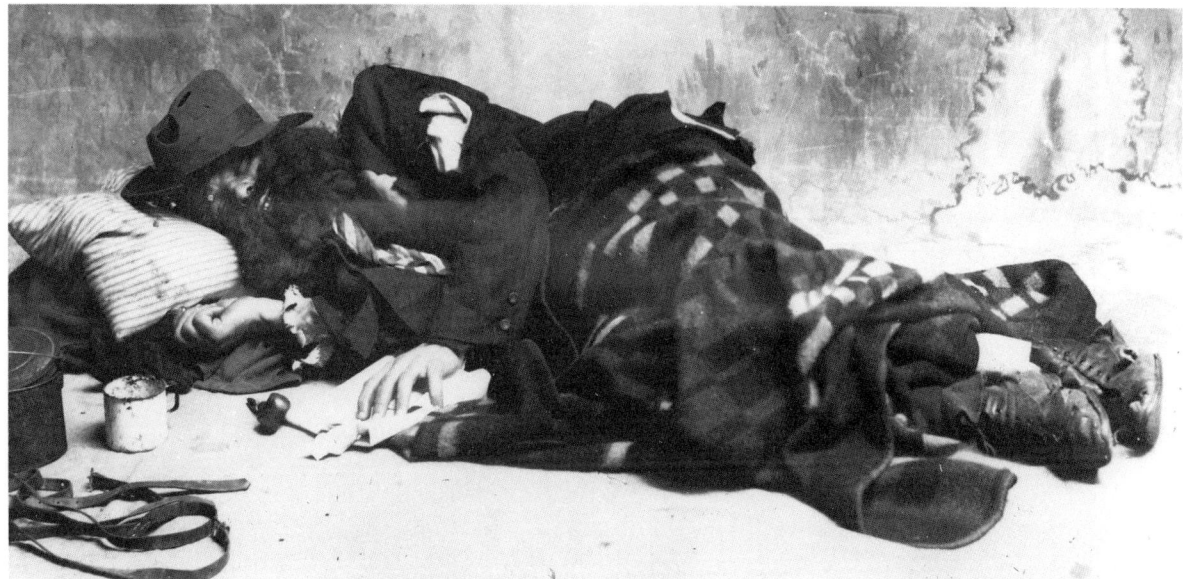

'The Swagger' (almost certainly a posed photograph)
*Tesla Collection, Alexander Turnbull Library*

we called them 'Homeys', and this was used in a derogatory manner . . . as if it was something contemptible, you know, when they were our human brothers when all was said and done. They were the victims of the same thing as we were – even more so. They had nothing, they had absolutely nothing. It looked to me, remembering and looking at them, as if some of their very manhood had been killed. They'd been left with nothing, poor devils, and they didn't have the physical strength to defend themselves, and here was I immersed in this. I was part of this, and I . . . I took part in it. But after a short time had passed, maybe only an hour, I began to be disgusted with the whole turnout, because it came to me that they weren't even capable of defending themselves; that they were in a hopeless condition. So I gave it away.

We accepted that they were a threat to our security – and what the hell did we have, when all's said and done? We had nothing, really, we had nothing. But of course from the married men's point of view – remember, I'm speaking from a single man's view – from a married man's point of view I suppose they did constitute a danger. They were a danger to his meagre economy – and again, he struck at the effect, not the cause. They were there in front of him, and they were a danger to his livelihood, to the poor paltry damn job he had; to the right to work – and barely the right to exist. But even this was threatened by them, so he struck out. Yet, when all's said and done, the poor devils were only the victims of the same system we were victims of.

Well, I swore that never again would I ever fall for that. I was ashamed of that. From that very moment to this, that's a hell of a black mark for me. It's a black mark, and I'm damned well ashamed of that. But that was an instance.

\*      \*      \*

So where does a man like Riverina Dick stack up against all this? It brings us back to this freedom of the swagger – to be your own man, and keep the System at arm's length.

That number I wrote – 'Restless Feet' – was really an expression of all that.

> Restless feet, itching for the road:
> Never count the miles; measure not the load.
> Oh, the heavens are wide; the scenery is free:
> Restless feet, don't you ever let up on me.
>
> Restless feet, life's a rocky road:
> Goin' to stub your toes, 'less you know that road.
> There's a promise we made; there's a rule we must obey:
> Restless feet, don't you get in temptation's way.
>
> Goin' to turn you loose on the open road,
> Underneath the open sky:
> Goin' to join the vagabond brotherhood
> And bid the blues goodbye.
>
> By a trickling stream my camp fires gleam
> As I wander high and low:
> The road is calling – guess I'll have to go.
> Roamin' on, round the distant bend,
> 'Till we reach the turn where the sunset ends . . .

## First broadcast 7 December 1975

# 5 The Wreck of the *Dundonald*

Albert Roberts's recollection of shipwreck, and nine months' sojourn as a castaway on the Auckland Islands.

*In the early hours of 7 March 1907, the big four-masted steel barque* Dundonald *was wrecked on Disappointment Island, in the Auckland group, two hundred miles south-south-west of Stewart Island. It was a shipwreck in the classic tradition, and the fifteen survivors endured seven months of hardship, including a sub-Antarctic winter, on Disappointment Island. At the end of that time, with remarkable ingenuity and courage, they built canvas boats and managed to cross the treacherous strip of water that separates Disappointment Island from the main island to the east. There, at Port Ross, they found a provision depot for shipwrecked mariners which had been established by the New Zealand Government. They were rescued by the Government steamer* Hinemoa *two months later.*

*Albert Roberts was the last survivor of the wreck of the* Dundonald. *Small and nuggety, he seemed indestructible, and was in fact in his nineties when he died, at a time when this book was being compiled. To him, there was little remarkable about his story. It was just one incident in his life, and he related it in a routine, unemotional fashion. 'It was taken as a matter of fact . . . that somebody had to suffer.'*

*This, Albert Roberts's story in his own words, is as fine a memorial as any seaman ever had.*

I joined the *Dundonald* in Cardiff as a deck boy, at the age of thirteen. We had to load coal, and then we sailed from Cardiff for Callao, with good weather all the way. We did have a bit of a dusting going round the Horn, but it was fair weather after that, and we were at Callao for about a month. Then we carried on in ballast, and the good weather continued all the time until we got to Sydney. But we made a wonderful trip; I don't think the trip had ever been made that fast – forty-five days. She was a fast ship, the *Dundonald*. Oh yes, she was a fast ship all right – and a big ship, too. Oh, by gum, a big four-masted barque. She carried 3,400 tons. And steel – solid steel. Nothing wooden about her, only the decks.

Well, we were in Sydney for about a month. We had loaded and everything, and we left on a Sunday, and there was a lot of arguments over it. The men didn't want to leave on a Sunday, because it's supposed to be unlucky – bad luck, you see. Anyway, the men protested, and there was a lot of chalk put on the doors about it – slogans and things – but we got out of there on a Sunday, and when we were about ten miles off the coast the tug let us go, and away we went.

The wind that we had was a head wind, and we were tacking all the time, so we caught a shark and brought him aboard and chopped his tail off and stuck it on the jib boom for to try and give us a fair wind. Seamen have got that silly idea of putting a shark's tail on the jib boom. But the wind was still ahead, and finally the captain decided that if the wind didn't change in the dogwatch – that's the four to six and six.to eight watch – we'd put about and go home the other way, Capetown via Australia. But the wind did change, so we carried on.

We had to head south for a start, before we ran our easting down across the Southern Ocean. Now down a bit west of south of New Zealand was the Auckland Islands, and we were supposed to pass forty miles to the north of them at midnight that night, but the Auckland Islands are forty miles out on the chart, and it's only of late years that the correct position has been shown.

So there we were in the dogwatch. I'd gone to bed about nine o'clock. I slept in the same cabin as the captain's son. He was a bit older than I was – I was the youngest aboard. Anyhow, about midnight I heard a lot of scrambling around above us – you know, on the deck – and then I heard somebody sing out, 'All hands on deck!', so it was the mate. I got out of bed and woke Johnny, the captain's son, and he

The barque *Dundonald,* coming up the Avon, England
*Alexander Turnbull Library*

turned to me and said, 'They don't want us, Albert. We're amongst the ice. We won't be any use up there.'

We went to sleep, and one of the fellows came down to call us and told us to get dressed, to put heavy clothes on and go on deck.

Well, when he'd gone, I saw the shadow of my mother at the door, with her finger up beckoning me. My mother. A picture of my mother. Now, I'm not a spiritualist or anything like that, but I really saw my mother.

Well, they came down a second time to see that we were up and coming along, so I can tell you it wasn't too long before we were on deck. The sailors were all working. We were working, pulling ropes, trying to do things, but we never had enough sail on to about-ship, and we tried to wear, but it was pretty well too late to do anything because we were right under the cliffs.

And it was dark – oh, God, it was dark, and misty too. We were aft, and the mate told us to go for'ard and get under the fo'c'sle head because by this time the yards were bumping up against the cliffs and bringing the rocks down on to the deck.

After that she started sinking, and we had to get out from off the foredeck and up on to the fo'c'sle head. She was sinking all the time, and when she eventually went down I made for one of the stays and hung on to that, and she was sinking and taking me down. So, of course, I let go then, but the sail was down in the water you see, and when I let go I got washed up against the fo'c'sle. I hung on to a rope, and all we could do then was scream. So one of the chaps, he got up on to the yard and bent over and pulled me up on to it. That's what saved me. When he pulled me up we went up to the t'gallant yard and stuck there all night, about eight or nine of us up there.

We couldn't launch the boats, you know. You're going to get the real story now. We *couldn't* launch the bloody boats. In those days all the boats' falls were unshackled and put underneath the lifeboats' canvas to keep dry, to preserve them – so we couldn't launch the boats; we hadn't any hope. Now that is the first time that this has come out.

Well, during the night, for the first half hour, we heard the fellows cursing and blinding and everything about the position they were in. There was no prayers said, I can tell you that. The poor old sailors there, they didn't take too kindly to it, none of us did in fact.

There were three men who got ashore from the jigger mast. You see, it was a funny thing – the ship broke and the masts went in different ways, in different angles. We never knew if anybody had got ashore until they started yelling in the morning and we yelled back at them. So they came up to where we were, as close as they could, and they were on the shore and we were on the yard on the sunken ship, and we chucked a rope to them and made our end fast on the t'gallant yard, and they made theirs fast on a rock. That's the way we got ashore.

When it got light, we saw a lot of bits of a wooden ship floating around, pieces of a wooden ship. We had gone in over the top of her, you see. Of course, ours was a steel ship, but the other one was a wooden ship, and I've always thought she must have been the *General Grant*. That's what I've always believed.

Well, when we got ashore, we mustered. The captain's son had stayed with the captain all the time, and the captain never left the poop. I never saw him after we left the poop, him or Johnny.

There were one, two . . . fifteen of us. We all got together then and we left the ship; we couldn't do anything down there. We went looking for the shipwreck depot that we knew was down on the Auckland Islands somewhere, and we searched the island, but we never found a darned thing. They put a depot down there for any castaways, you see, because it was on the track of the ships, for any sailors that got shipwrecked there. (There's no depot there now, they took it off, but they did put one down there, and a boat, on Disappointment Island, after we were rescued.)

Well, after we'd looked around we realised we weren't on the main Auckland Island. We realised that when we couldn't find the depot. It was only a small island – about two and a half miles.

We had to go without food that day. The second day we saw mollyhawks and albatrosses, all on the nest with their young ones, and of course we killed some of them, and ate their livers. We ate them raw. Raw livers, because we never had any fire or anything like that. Many a time I've had to howl, killing – my hands being that cold and useless – killing albatrosses. Many, many a time I was in tears at being so cruel, making a lingering death for them.

We'd been on the island about seven or eight days, and then one of the fellows found in his waistcoat pocket seven matches – wax matches. We all had matches, mind, but they were these blooming things – safety matches – no good at all; never good once they got wet. But anyhow, we started the fire going and then started to cook our food . . . and we kept that fire going.

The first fine day we had, the fellows that could swim took to the water to go down aft to the sunken ship and see if they could get some biscuits and stores or anything, but we couldn't get anything except some sail and rope. And we stuck there for seven or eight days, I think. We got sick, and we young fellows didn't like it there. The water was dirty – the blooming albatrosses bred over on that side you see, and there was all filth, and no clean water for drinking. So we saw the other fellows and told them we were going to find a place we could live on. So we shared the canvas out, and away we went.

We had a sick man on our hands – that was the mate. He was left behind. We couldn't do anything with him, we were too weak. That island was a volcanic island and there were three craters that went right down to the sea. We couldn't see it, but we could hear the sea roaring down there. And we used to take water to the mate, and raw food every day, but there was no hope for him, right from the beginning.

The fresh water we used to take, we carried it in a sou'wester – the oilskin hat we used to wear – and that's what we used to carry the water in all the time.

Well, anyhow, we went on the last day that we saw him. He was dead. He was in a kneeling position as if he was praying, and we did what he'd asked us to do there if he died; to just cover him up with sods and everything. Well, we done that. I gave the burial service over the mate. I gave the burial service to him. I just prayed, just, 'Our Father, which art in Heaven,' and to bless him. And as a kid, you know, hoped he would go to heaven, and everything like that. They stripped him of clothes because we was short of clothes, and put canvas over him, and covered him up with sods.

*        *        *

The part we went to live on was beautiful green grass and shrub, and we fixed up a tent. We were all sleeping in the tent, and on April Fools' Day there we got a gale of wind that night and it blew the tent away, and that made us then know that we had to have something different than a tent if we were going to put in a winter there. So that's when we started to build our huts.

The huts we built there were dug into the ground, into the side of a hill, dug in so that we put a foot or eighteen inches of shrub down in the bottom so as to keep us off the wet. Then we got the flax and plaited that – put that up against the wall. We were never up against any soil at all.

From what I remember, there were five of them. They were dry,

The huts on Disappointment Island in which *Dundonald* survivors lived for seven months
*Otago Witness*

and they were warm. Oh, they were warm all right, because before we went to bed at night-time, we walked up the hill – to the top of the hill – and then run down and then got straight in and shut the door, which was made of bird skins.

We never plucked the mollyhawks and albatrosses. We slit them and skinned them, and used the fatty side of the skin for washing ourselves and used the feathers as a towel, and by jingo, we had beautiful skin. We were living on the full birds at that time, and we had found out that we could catch a bird on the wing with a small stick.

We got strips of canvas about an inch and a half wide and sewed on 'Send help, Auckland Islands'. I stitched this on – this was properly stitched, mind – and we put them on albatross necks and the mollyhawks, and any bird we could get. 'Send help, Auckland Islands.' All the messages were that way. But we never got any response. They always ripped them off.

\*    \*    \*

All of us used to get our own food, mind, and a strange thing about it is that we never had a sick person on that island, only the mate. We all got very weak, and then after about a fortnight there we started to build up and never felt anything at all there – hard as nails.

Then there were the seals. The first seal we had was the fur seal, and we had to make ropes to go down the cliff to them, and there'd only be about four of us who'd go down there. But I had to go down there because I was the youngest and the smallest, you see. Because down on the beach there were all big boulders, and some of them would be five, six, and ten ton, and the seals made their dens in there. Well, I had to go in with a stick and poke them out – the young ones – poke them out, so that when they were coming out the fellows would knock them on the nose and kill them. Well, that's how we got our first seals.

A couple of weeks after, one of the fellows went down on his own and he came back in a hell of a fright. He swore that he'd seen a bear. We should have had more sense, anyhow, to expect bears down there in the Southern Hemisphere. Anyway, we went after this bear – went out to kill him – but we found out it was a sea lion. But after that, we could get as much seal as we wanted, and that gave us clothing and moccasins and everything. We found out with the moccasins that wearing them with the fur out, they would last us a fortnight. Otherwise, with the fur in and the skin outside, they would only last a day.

Then we found a vegetable on the island. Now I can't give you the name for that, but the root of it was just like a big cucumber and it was beautiful to eat. The root of it was white, and it was beautiful, and we cooked it same as a spud.

\*    \*    \*

We had two bonfires, on different points where you could see in different directions, and I used to go up to them in the night and say

A *Dundonald* survivor, George Ivemy, wearing a sealskin hat and boots
*Otago Witness*

my prayers, which I was always taught to do. Never mind. (Although I'm not a good fellow by any means now – I can swear with anybody and be nasty with anybody.) I used to ask to be rescued from the island, but I always had an idea there that I would be taken off. I was one of the ones that always said we'd get off. One or two of us had that idea, but some of the others . . . well, with a crowd, you always have somebody down in the dumps.

Anyhow, twice we lit those bonfires. Twice. But the ships came, and passed. The last ship that came was a little three-masted barque. He hoisted the ensign – British ensign – and it got dark. But I think he was heading between Disappointment Island and the main Auckland Island, and he may have hit them rocks, because we never heard anything more of him. He'd have come in the daylight – first thing in the morning – he'd have come round then. But he didn't come, and we always thought that during the night he'd hit the Sugarloaf Rocks in between us and the main island. Otherwise he'd have told somebody that he'd seen us; that's the first thing a ship will do. Of course, we got down in the dumps when we didn't see him again. But we take it that if he'd been alive and got anywhere, he'd have reported us.

Anyway, we decided we had to reach the main Auckland Island, so we started building our boats, which we done. Now these were canvas boats. They had to be canvas boats; that's all we could build. We had no timber – there was no timber down there for building a raft or anything. And no driftwood. All the wood we got was crippled wood – twisted wood; small twisted branches from a sort of scrubby tree. So we got these pieces, and we had to cut them, mind you, and we lashed them together and made a darn good job of it. Then we made a canvas cover. We knew exactly the length of canvas we would want, and the men could start sewing it up. And that's the way we did it.

We had to find ways of making oars, and then we hit on the idea of getting a forked stick and lashing canvas across the fork. We only just lashed it on, that's all, because it couldn't come off, being on the

The framework of one of the coracles in which the survivors reached the main Auckland Island. This unique boat was made from koromiko branches lashed together with pieces of rope and wire and covered with canvas.
*Otago Witness*

fork. And that's the way we went across. We made three of these things, and they looked like bathtubs. A Russian, Michael Poole, had seen them. Well, I'd seen 'em myself, but I never seen them made the way we made them.

When we were going, we got them sods and dug them out to make a fireplace. They took fire across, and the fuel for the fire was charcoal – half-burnt wood in little pieces, and that's the way they used to feed the fire – no blaze or anything like that. And of course there was plenty of bailing to be done, because the boats certainly leaked.

Well, the first boat got away, and they couldn't find the depot. They got across all right, and spent seven or eight days looking for it. We didn't know what had happened to them. We didn't . . . well, at that time we didn't think of anything, but it didn't make us very happy. But we'd started building the other two boats, and we launched them. I was in one, but the damned sea came and washed it away – I lost my seaboots and everything. But the third boat got across. They got across, and we got no signal from them, because when they got across they got into a heavy surf, and they lost everything. Mind you, it was a wonderful thing they did to make that crossing on that ocean there. You get as big a sea there as you'd get anywhere.

Well, anyhow, they came back about three or four days after, round the nor'west cape. We could see a boat coming on the water. Not the coracle. We didn't know what it was or who it was. And when we saw them we didn't know them, because they had all had a shave and a haircut and everything.

Well, they came, and they brought biscuits. (That's all they could bring, because the sealers had been down there and pinched all the stores . . . pinched all the stores. All the tobacco was gone, some of the biscuits, and all the tinned stuff, the tea and the coffee. We had beef tea all the time when we got to the depot.)

Anyhow, we went down to meet them there, and they'd had a shave and a haircut and everything. We didn't yell or wave our arms about. We were pleased, but we didn't do our nut. They told us they'd found the depot and had a cleanup, and put on fresh clothes that was in the stores there. And there was a boat at the depot as well, you see, and that was what they came back in.

They told us they were going to take us over in two lots. I was in the first lot, and when we got there they told us the directions where to go to the depot, and that's the way we went and found the depot – saw the notice up – DEPOT – and by jingo, weren't we glad when we got to that depot at six or seven o'clock that night. After a while the boat came in with the second load, and we got a big fire going. The depot was a bach, a big bach, and we got a fire going.

We'd been seven and a half months on Disappointment Island, and by jingo, I was glad to get across. But I'd had that idea all the time that we would find it and get there.

When we got into the depot there was a letter left for anybody that was shipwrecked, saying that the *Hinemoa* – that was the Government steamer – would be down in six months' time, and it gave the date that it was last there and left for New Zealand. Now that date was the sixth of March. We'd been shipwrecked just five or six hours after she had left!

Well, anyhow, in the depot there were blankets, and the only sad part of it was the food that had been stolen. But we had the biscuits, and the biscuits were in tins, put into galvanised – not galvanised, zinc – cases, and it was from these zinc pieces that we made a distress signal to send help to the Auckland Islands. We put it on a piece of wood, with a bit of a sail up. And it was picked up on the Campbell Islands and given to me – brought up years after – and given to me by the bosun of the *Hinemoa*.

There was an old gun at the depot that was used in Napoleon's days. The breech was broken off. We had to get wire, and every time we fired a shot we had to screw this wire up, because the thing was no good.

There was only clothes there for twelve, and I was one of the unfortunate ones that didn't get any, but I was happy – it never made me unhappy. I was warm, that was the main thing. And one good thing about it is that none of us got lousy, or anything like that. It's a funny thing, that. But we kept ourselves clean mind, though we never touched water; never had a bath for the whole time we were down there. But we were clean. We used to clean ourselves, as I'm saying, with a bird's skin – with the fatty part – and then use the feathers for a towel to wipe ourselves.

Well, we had to go and get food. There was no food there except the biscuits. On the main island we were introduced to the pig – and he could be a pretty nasty thing too – and quail. Crikey, we killed hundreds of quail down there. They were tasty, quail, you know; that was proper gentlemen's food. They're a flightless duck – that's a quail. There were plenty of rabbits there too, but I wouldn't eat them because they were the colours of different-coloured cats, and being a kid, I thought wild cats had been down there and they had crossed.

Then, apart from getting food, we built a wharf. We had to pull the boat ashore every night, and we thought it would be better to have a wharf so we could land the meat up there. Then we built a flagstaff alongside of it. We made a flag out of a sail and put 'Welcome' on it, cut out of an old piece of pants, the coloured letters and everything . . . I think it's still in the Christchurch Museum.

Well, anyhow, now about the *Hinemoa*'s coming. We were fast asleep one morning, and we heard a ship letting go her anchor – and by crikey, we nearly pushed the side of the bach out, trying to get out. The *Hinemoa*'s skipper couldn't get into the boat fast enough. You see, he knew somebody was there – there was a wharf and there was a flagstaff.

They gave us food – plenty of tinned stuff, and a little drop of cheer and stuff – but they had a scientific party aboard that they were taking

The jetty and flagstaff erected by the *Dundonald* men at Ross Harbour
*Otago Witness*

The grave of Jabez Peters, mate of the *Dundonald*
*Otago Witness*

south, so we had another fortnight to wait until they came back. And the scientific party sneaked a few bottles to us as well. Gosh, it was cheerful, I can tell you that! It was a godsend to us.

The captain disbelieved us at first. They reckoned it was impossible for anybody to land on Disappointment Island, but by crikey, we landed there all right. When they came back from that trip – they had to go down to the Campbells – we went around to Disappointment Island, and he went and had a look at the huts and picked up the mate's body and brought it over, and we gave him a reburial. And he told us there he'd left the Auckland Islands at five or six that night – the night we were shipwrecked. You see, they came down regular every six months, but it was nine months this time.

When we got back to Bluff we got a great reception. Oh, God, yes! The bands were down there collecting for us, and we got a good bit of money from them. But I'm very sorry to say – and it has hurt me for more than seventy years – that the Shipwreck Relief Society, the lousy devils, gave us two pounds. That's all they gave us, and we refused to take it. Fancy people landing, and not a damn thing on them, and being offered two pounds, a lousy two pounds!

So we got ten pounds from the Government, and no – the Government gave us all the clothes we wanted, but I got a special one from Sir Joseph Ward. The best sea-kit I ever had in my life, personally from Sir Joseph Ward – and don't go thinking, as some people would say, 'You must be a Mickey or something', because I'm not.

Now let me tell you this. On the day that we landed at Bluff, my mother, back in Cardiff, was getting the kids ready for Sunday school, and she saw me pass the window. Of course, they had given up all hopes of us, because they had never heard anything from the time we left Sydney. But she saw me pass the window. And she passed out – you know, she fainted. And the first words she said when she came

Albert Roberts with a memorial
plaque (mistakenly reading
'Alfred' Roberts) now in the
Wellington Harbour Board
Maritime Museum
*Evening Post*

Survivors of the *Dundonald* on board the *Hinemoa*. Albert Roberts is second from right in the back row.
*Otago Witness*

round was, 'Where's Albert?' and she said there that she'd seen me – she reckoned that I passed the window. Well, when my dad went down to the Exchange on the next day – that was the Monday – they said to him, 'Have you heard the latest, George?'

And he said, 'No.'

'Well,' they said, 'they picked up the *Dundonald*'s crowd, but not all of them.'

No names were given, only that some of the crew had been picked up, so of course my father got pretty active there in finding out. He found out that Monday night, before he'd gone to bed, that I was one of the survivors.

Well, today I'm the only survivor. There's none left except me. I'm the only survivor. But I think God was with me that night we was wrecked. And He was with me all the time, and that's the strongest memory I have. He was with the fellows there just the same – because I was with a tough lot, let me tell you that. I was with all nations.

It was just an episode. Yes. It was just taken as a matter of fact . . . that somebody had to suffer. It didn't stop me from following the sea. Oh, no, no, no! I've been to sea all the time . . . been to sea all the time.

First broadcast 10 February 1976

# 6 Two Wellington Childhoods

Marjorie Lees and George Davies recall childhood in Wellington, in the years immediately before the First World War.

*Marjorie Lees and George Davies have one thing in common – their childhood was spent in the Wellington of the 1900s. They walked the same streets, saw the same sights, witnessed the same events – the 1913 General Strike, the outbreak of the First World War – but because of their contrasting social backgrounds, they saw them through very different eyes.*

*Both informants were asked similar questions, and their combined responses shed light from diametrically opposed viewpoints on the way of life at that time. This 'double illumination' not only provides a vivid picture of the principal events of the period, but also underlines the sharp social divisions which characterised Wellington at that time.*

*Beyond the fact that Marjorie Lees and George Davies both lived in Wellington, and beyond the fact that they were distanced in wealth and social class, lies a common perception. Both saw life around them in intensely human, closely focussed terms, and with a simplicity and directness that are a common quality of childhood memory, regardless of background. Both – with childhood long behind them – have the ability to encapsulate in a brief phrase their conditions and feelings:*

George Davies: *'We weren't hard up – we were absolutely poverty-stricken.'*

Marjorie Lees: *'I was one of those miserable children brought up in a nursery.'*

*This, then, is their story.*

Marjorie Lees

## Marjorie Lees:

My father practised law, but he was not very interested in it. His uncle was the Chief Justice, and we rather lived in the shadow of Uncle James, and he was consulted about everything we did. He was very good to my father. He didn't actually adopt him, but he treated him like a son. When my parents were first married, they lived in a most attractive little cottage with a shingled roof, but after two years it was pulled down and Uncle James provided them with a new, large, hideous Edwardian mansion. He had an extraordinary theory that low ceilings were very unhealthy, so the house had enormously high ceilings, which meant a very large stairway, you see.

I lived in the nursery – I was one of those miserable children brought up in a nursery – and I never really went into my parents' room – the bedroom – without knocking at the door, and of course I never went

A childhood portrait
*Marjorie Lees*

Marjorie and her sister Trixie,
photographed when
bridesmaids to their Aunt
Eleanor
*Marjorie Lees*

anywhere near them when they were having meals, because you can't have children interrupting meals. And of course the drawing room was sacred too, because that was only used when Mother had visitors . . . her day 'at home', when all the ladies used to come and call, and so on and so on.

We were allowed into the library just before we went to bed, after we had been bathed and put into our dressing-gowns, when we went down and had a story read to us. And then I was sent up this terrifically high house and sent to bed, where I had to sleep in a room with Nan, who was my nurse. It was awfully lonely and quite frightening being sent up there by myself, because my sister was five years younger than I was, and I was very lonely.

And I was frightened. I was frightened all the time, of the most intangible things. I don't know what I was frightened of, but I was frightened.

I regarded my mother as a sort of fairy princess, because I thought she was very beautiful. She was very delicate, and she sort of went from one health diet theory to another. When she was well, she was very gay and went out to lots of parties, and when she was ill she sort of drooped about the place in lovely blue tea-gowns. And, of course, one of the horrifying things about the nurse was that, whenever I was naughty, she would say, 'If you worry your mother she will die, and you will have a stepmother.' You remember those ghastly fairy stories which we read in those days? Stepmothers were always cruel monsters, and I lived in absolute terror that my mother would die.

Opposite us there was a family of six children. They were considered suitable for me to play with, and I simply adored them. However, they left after a while, and that was the most shattering thing in my life. Then there was nobody on the hill. There were older people living on the other side of the street, and some other children close by, but Nan considered they weren't suitable for me to play with. Wicked old Nan was a frightful snob. I tried to play with one of the little girls when she came over, and I thought she was very nice, but I was told not to play with her any more. The next time she came I said, 'Oh well, I'm not allowed to play with you.'

'Why not?'

'Oh well, because they say you're common.'

She burst into tears and went home, and I felt dreadful about it. It really was wicked, wasn't it?

When I reached school age I went to Miss Faber's school, which is now Marsden, I think. It was a private school, and you see, Miss Faber had been at university with my mother and they were more or less great friends. I went there until . . . well, there was an unfortunate incident when my mother was away in the country and my father was angry with me about something, and I spent the whole day crying – you can, if you are a child. You can work yourself up into the most frightful state and get the most frightful headache. My father was most

This attractive little cottage
with the shingled roof in Bolton
Street, Wellington, was the
original home of Marjorie's
parents
*Marjorie Lees*

concerned about it, and he told my mother. I didn't tell Mother why
I cried. I said, 'Oh, you know, it was so hot in the school and there
was no air to breathe.' And I simply told them a lot of lies about it.
Mv mother had a quarrel with Miss Faber and I was taken away from
the school, and then I had a governess.

I had no pocket-money, but there was always Uncle James, who
lived with his housekeeper in this very large house down the hill
somewhat. It bounded our own, so that the grounds were really all
one, and I played in the garden. It was really a most magnificent garden
– not as a garden, but as a wilderness – and every morning I had to
take the paper down to Uncle James after my father had read it. Uncle
James would be in bed – he always had his breakfast in bed – and
every now and then he would say to me, 'Hand me my trousers.'

His trousers used to hang over the bedpost, so I would take them
over to him, and he would fumble in them and produce a gold sovereign
and say, 'There!'

I would take it home, and it was immediately taken away from me
and put into the moneybox, and I never saw it any more.

\*　　\*　　\*

One of the incidents which stands out very clearly in my childhood
was the 1913 General Strike. Almost as a matter of course, my father
was enrolled as a special constable, after the Massey Government asked
for assistance to help break the strike. I believe there was some sort
of rioting in which the strikers attacked the 'specials' after they had
been issued with batons and were marching down from the barracks.
There really was quite a nasty riot. The specials took refuge in Whitcombe and Tombs, and all the windows were smashed. My father came
back in a frightful state and said, 'This is the French Revolution all

over again, and you must be sent away to the country.' So we were all sent to the country, and I thought that was pretty poor, but the strike went on for a long time, so we were allowed to come back.

And do you remember, all the farmers came down with their horses and patrolled the wharves – they rode backwards and forwards all along the wharves. A tea place was set up for them in the Star Boating Club and I was allowed to go down and help my mother hand teas to them. I was about eleven or twelve, and I fell violently in love with Tiny Freyberg, of all people. I thought he was the most handsome and glorious man I had ever seen. He took no notice of me, but my little sister had curly hair and was very pretty, and he used to give her rides on his horse. I felt very miserable about that.

My father thought the men were absolutely wicked to strike. They were damaging the country, and they had no case at all as far as he was concerned. We took his opinion as a matter of course, and it never occurred to us to question it. I thought the strikers were evil people.

And apparently the specials rode about all through the town, especially through the slums where most of the waterside workers lived, and their wives emptied chamber-pots over them. Those were the tales you heard about – the wicked strikers, and so on.

A group of Miss Swainson's girls outside 20 Fitzherbert Terrace, c. 1901. Miss Swainson founded what is now Marsden School and Marjorie attended this institution approximately a decade later than the era of this photograph. Among the pupils above are Kathleen Beauchamp (Katherine Mansfield), second back row, seventh from left, and her sister Charlotte, front row at left.
*G. Moore Collection, Alexander Turnbull Library*

That was . . . 1913, wasn't it? Well, a year later the First World War broke out. They had a big clubhouse down the . . . oh, I can't remember. Anyway, it was one of the big dancehall places, and all the soldiers used to go there. My aunt used to help with the suppers and things and she said I could go too, and I would dance with the soldiers. I fell violently in love with one of them. I think he was a man of about forty. We had a place in Stokes Valley then, and he used to walk over from camp and see me on Sundays. This was in the school holidays. I remember the last day before going back to school, I was sitting talking to him, and my aunt came up in a great state and said, 'Marjorie, you have been sitting with that man all evening. Everyone is talking about you.'

I was dreadfully upset, and I went home. I was in floods of tears, and I thought, 'I'll never see him again.'

I never did either, because he was killed.

*     *     *

Six months after I left school, I was married. I really didn't want to get married much, because my heart was in the grave. I can remember my father stamping up and down out on the balcony, and saying, 'Marjorie, you're not very good-looking – thick ankles and one thing and another – and all the men have been killed off and probably if you don't take this chance to be married you will be left an old maid like your aunt.'

And I was so weak willed, I simply acquiesced. But I finally had my way and left him and went nursing in Christchurch.

Adelaide Road, Newton, photographed during the wharf strike of 1913
*S. C. Smith Collection, Alexander Turnbull Library*

George Davies
*Alan Scott*

## George Davies:

We had no income at all to speak of. I think our total income from all sources was about three dollars seventy-five a week – one pound seventeen and six in those days – from some sort of estate of Mum's father; and it went on for so long and then dropped to twelve and six a week, and then it disappeared.

Now there were five of us in that house. There was myself, two sisters, younger brother, and Mum, and she was what you would call a 'solo parent' today. Then Grandma came, and there were six of us. Our main object in life was just getting by – getting things to eat, and of course clothes for the girls; boys' clothes didn't matter so much.

The place we lived in had a fairly big bedroom where Mum and the girls slept. Then there was a little tiny bedroom – my brother was in there – and it had a bit of an annex, and that was my abode. We had one dressing-table, and that was in Mum and the girls' room, and everybody used it.

A coal stove, a wash-house, a shed with a copper and tubs – the damned tubs always leaked – a few mats on the floor . . . We had a kitchen table and a few chairs, and a couple of . . . well, we called them 'easy chairs', but they were anything but easy because the springs were half way through them. Still, they were seating accommodation. In the kitchen we had what we called a 'dresser'. Now that was a sort of cupboard with a shelf on top with cup-hooks on it. You hung everything on the cup-hooks, and the plates and so forth were pushed on the dresser. Not very hygienic, but everybody had those.

Bit of a fence at the back, and it always seemed to be leaning at a drunken angle, but I've got an idea that we used to push it over a bit, because we used to take the palings off for firewood.

And that would be about it, I think.

I often wondered, when I got a bit older and thought about it, what Mum must have been thinking about every day, because her life was just one long struggle – not to get anything over and above the ordinary, but just to get enough for us all. Looking back on it now, I feel we were too young to appreciate all her trouble. But we seemed to be quite happy and contented, except that one of my sisters had rather big ideas about what she was going to do and what she was going to be, and at this stage I realise what a good job it was that she had them, because we had all the ingredients for a king-sized inferiority complex in our house.

And poor old Grandma. She had no money, but Mum got paid so much for keeping her, and Grandma used to sit and crochet all day. Now she only had one lot of thread, or whatever it is they use for crocheting, and she would crochet, say, a dressing-table set, and then she would immediately pick it all to pieces, roll up the thread, and then crochet something else. And that's how Grandma's days went.

She only had one possession, which I think everyone would have

Newtown as George Davies
knew it before World War One –
Riddiford Street in 1910 (ABOVE)
and 1912 (BELOW)
*S. C. Smith Collection, Alexander
Turnbull Library*

been happy to have got, and that was a beautiful, heavily inlaid gold brooch. I got that way in the finish I could just about tell the state of our economy by whether Grandma had that brooch or not. If she didn't have the brooch it was in the pawnshop, and things weren't too good, but if she had the brooch, Mum was managing fairly well.

*          *          *

I had a few school friends, and we had a little gang – different little gangs – and sometimes we fought. But the ultimate wickedness as far as we were concerned was to rob an orchard somewhere, or go up to the Old Men's Home in Ohiro Road and get a few vegetables there, or pick some flowers. The old men would chase us with pitchforks. They used to terrify us, you know. If they saw us they raised a shout and we'd be off like a flight of starlings, right up and away from them altogether. But apart from that, oh well, we had the usual friends.

Sometimes the girls would bring girlfriends home, but not very often. We had a very small circle of acquaintances, very small indeed. It's the same today as it was then; if you've got dollar signs for eyes, well you're all right, and it doesn't matter what your character's like. If you haven't got money you haven't got friends, and that's all there is to it. We didn't really have any friends at all . . .

*          *          *

My first recollection of school would be going up to Brooklyn School, and I don't even remember which class I was in, but I do remember that at the end of the year they used to give out cards. It was a green card if you failed, a red card if you passed, and a white card for the top pupil in the class. Well, in this particular year, I can't think why, but I got the white card. I didn't know what it was for, but I took it home.

Mum glanced at it and of course she knew that a pass was a red card, so she concluded that the white one was a failure, and you know, she gave me a darned good hiding for that. And then the girls came home, and they told her this card was given to the top pupil in the class, and you know I lived in the glory of that for weeks and weeks because old Mum never forgave herself for making a mistake like that and belting me for something that didn't really happen.

There was a devil of a row about high school, because I didn't want to go there. I wanted to get out – it was only natural – and get a job and earn some money. My sisters pointed out to Mum that we were scraping the bottom of the barrel, and where was I going to get books from, and this, that and the other. Of course Mum got on her high horse and said, 'Well *you've* been to high school, and *he's* going too.' So that was it, and I went.

That's where the class-consciousness bit came in. Those boys were just a little bit better off than I was. My clothes were all patches, and there were innumerable fights – you know how cruel schoolboys can be – and they used to pick on my appearance and give me the works good and proper. I think the masters knew what was going on all right, but on reflection I think the best thing they could do was just to let me ride it out, and take no action at all.

But I was pretty good at cricket, and we had a cricket match and I won it for them. On the Monday in class the old master was unstinting in his praise for what I had done, and some of the boys pulled their horns in a little bit and gave me a little bit of respect – probably because there was something I could do, even if I couldn't dress properly.

There was no way we could go to Mum for money, but we had ways and means, you know, of getting a little pocket-money now and again. My brother and I would go mushrooming over the Brooklyn hills, and we would take the mushrooms to the old Chinaman, and he would give us a penny a pound for them. You would see them displayed for sale, but there was never any price ticket on them, so we never knew what he was selling them for.

And then we had a little 'billy-cart' – a box with a couple of wheels on it, and a shaft – and we used to go down to the wharf when the coal boats were coming in, and take a length of four-by-two with us. Now all the coal was unloaded from the boat into drays, and when the dray came out from Queen's Wharf, we would rush over and put this lump of four-by-two underneath the wheel and the old dray would bump over it, and enough coal would be shot off to fill the billy-cart.

Sometimes we would rush home with it, but people got pretty familiar

Unloading coal into drays on the Wellington wharves
*Wellington Harbour Board Maritime Museum*

RIGHT: Special constables in Customhouse Quay – men, mainly farmers, brought into Wellington by the Massey Government to help control the 1913 strike
*Alexander Turnbull Library*

BELOW: Strikers scattering as mounted 'specials' ('Massey's Cossacks') gallop up Featherston Street during the General Strike of 1913
*Alexander Turnbull Library*

with the procedure, and if they saw you rushing up the street with a billy-cart of coal, they would sing out, 'How much?', and you would put a price on it, and then be away down for another load.

Some of those dray drivers were pretty good, and they would push coal off behind them when they were going along, but the other blokes . . . many a time I've had a whip around my backside for running over with the piece of wood and the old boy's seen me and let go with the whip before ever I got there.

*          *          *

About this time we had the 1913 General Strike, and I remember it pretty well. My younger brother was going to school then and I was just on the verge of going out of primary school, and Mum warned us within an inch of our lives to keep away from the strike and not have anything to do with it, and to be straight home from school, but of course we kids had to go along Harper Street and have a look at what they were doing.

Every so often the farmers – the 'specials' – would line up in Buckle Street, all abreast on their horses, and at a given signal they would tear along Arthur Street like mad cavalry, scattering all the strikers. The strikers were all gathered in Arthur Street, and the farmers would disperse them and then reform at the top of Cuba Street and tear back. Now during this process, which was like Balaclava, the strikers provided themselves with a plentiful supply of road metal, and they used to let fly at these fellows on the way up and again on the way down, and there were quite a few of them hurt.

Well, we went down to have a look. I saw some chap thumping at the road with a fencepost, and I said, 'What are you doing?'

'Trying to get some rocks to throw at those jokers.'

'Well,' I said, 'I'll give you a hand.'

I had taken sides straight away, without knowing what it was all about. So I started humping up these things, and all of a sudden he sang out, 'Here they come!' I leaped over somebody's fence and then stood up to have a look, but unfortunately some fellow on the other side of the road had let fly at a special. He missed him, but he didn't miss me. I got the stone right on the top of my head, and I had to have about three stitches in it and a week off school. I got a hiding from Mum that I still remember, and I was told that when I got better I would have to go down to the police station, because a policeman wanted to see me. You know, I was so sick with fright I couldn't eat. People were frightened of policemen in those days. Little boys, if you mentioned policemen, that would curl them up straight away.

*          *          *

I can remember war being declared very well – that was the Great War, the First World War, of course. You know, all those fellows formed a procession that must have been a mile long, and they were four abreast. They were all marching down to Parliament Buildings to offer their services, and you know I was astounded – in the very front row was my old teacher from primary school. He really had the war fever.

Well, you know, I had four uncles, and they all volunteered to go away, and that was one Christmas I'll always remember, because all four of them came round. They were all in uniform and they were going to have Christmas dinner with us, and what was more important, they were going to provide it – and that really was something.

Well, you know, we had a fantastic time. There were all kinds of relations there. I don't know where they all came from, and I didn't even know half of them. The kids sat on the floor, and old Uncle Bert, well, of course, he was the life and soul of the party. He had a black bottle, and the more sips he took out of that bottle, the worse the stories got.

Anyhow, poor old Uncle Bert, that was the last time I ever saw him, but a little while after, there was a carrier arrived with a kennel and an old dog. It was Uncle Bert's old dog, and apparently he'd asked if I could look after it. Well, I swore that every butcher in the district would have to find meat for that dog, somehow or other. It had always been my ambition to have a dog, and although by standards now he was a pretty ragged old boy as I remember it, he was my dog – and that meant a terrible lot to me. Besides that, he'd been Uncle Bert's dog, and I sort of felt that old Uncle Bert had confidence that I'd look after it for him, and that did something for a kid, too.

Looking back on it all, we were a close-knit family, and little as we had, we had our home, and it was a loving home. We had a good mother, and she looked after us to the best of her ability.

We all know now, but at the time we didn't appreciate it properly, but I can honestly say that as far as we children were concerned, it didn't really get us down. As far as Mum was concerned, I wouldn't know; she was expert at hiding her feelings. She didn't know from day to day . . . she would have no idea what we were going to eat or when we were going to eat that day.

Well, no normal human being can carry on like that and not be affected. There must have been effects. But we didn't see them.

First broadcast 3 June 1972

# 7 Te Wa o te Parekura (The Year of the Pestilence)

Florence Harsant looks back on her early life in a Maori community beside Lake Taupo, and on the smallpox epidemic of 1913.

*Florence Harsant is one of the oldest persons represented in this book. She can look back on a long life of more than ninety years – but she is disinclined to do so. It is in the nature of this remarkable woman to be more interested in the concerns of the present. She was in her eighties when she taught herself to touch-type – a skill that became invaluable as her eyesight deteriorated – and she still writes articles for the newspapers that service her home area of Hahei, on the Coromandel Peninsula.*

Florence Harsant
*Alwyn Owen*

*It is typical of her personality that friends and neighbours knew little of her background until two 'Spectrum' documentaries told her life story. They were followed by a book,* They Called me Te Maari *(Whitcoulls, 1979), in which she detailed the incidents of her life. Further recognition came in 1981, when she was awarded the Queen's Service Medal for her work among the Maori people during the smallpox epidemic of 1913.*

*That work had its beginnings in 1905, when her schoolteacher father moved the family to Waitahanui, to open the first 'native school' in the settlement. Despite his objections, Florence rapidly became fluent in Maori. She also had very acute powers of observation, and more than seventy years later can still vividly recall the social life of a Maori settlement in the first decade of the century.*

*Her recollections of life in Waitahanui, and in the Maori settlements of the north, were set down in a manuscript which Florence Harsant sent to a friend, the author and historian Alison Drummond. Realising the potential of the subject for radio, Alison Drummond forwarded the manuscript to the 'Spectrum' unit, who used it as the basis for the two documentaries from which this account is transcribed.*

*The first programme was recorded in a car near Hahei Beach – Florence's own cottage was alive with the sounds of children at play, and an easterly wind whipping into the bay precluded recording in the open air. That first programme detailed some of the events of the 1913 smallpox epidemic. Subsequently, Florence Harsant revisited Waitahanui for the first time in many years, and there the second programme was recorded, as she relived the events of her childhood, and visited the three remaining elders whom she had known as children. She was welcomed on the marae, and accorded the honour of being the first woman permitted to speak there. Speech came slowly at first, as memory grappled with Maori words unused for many decades, then gradually, as she spoke, the old fluency returned.*

*Today, Florence Harsant lives at Hahei in the small cottage to which she came as a bride. Independence demands that she live alone, despite age and failing eyesight. She receives a constant stream of visitors – strangers as well as 'locals', because the cottage also houses a museum of artifacts collected by her late husband, and holds the local library, which she supervises.*

*Her dominant characteristic – warmth aside – must be courage. It is as evident today as it was in 1913, when as a girl of twenty-three she rode through the gumfields and isolated settlements of the North.*

My father was a schoolteacher, and in 1905 he moved from Taranaki to take charge of a newly built 'native school', as we called them then, at Waitahanui, on the north-east shore of Lake Taupo. In a way, it must have been a courageous decision for him. For my mother, it was a severance of ties with family and friends, because the central North Island was very isolated at that time, and we'd be living in a small community that was entirely Maori. She said very little, but looking back now, I realise she felt it very deeply. But for us children, it was just a great adventure.

We travelled by coastal ship to Onehunga, and then caught the train from Auckland to Rotorua. In those days Rotorua was very much a spa town, with people coming from all over the world . . . some of them to see the sights, yes, but just as many hoping for a cure for rheumatic complaints and the like. It was a very barren town then – barren in the sense that the hills around were covered in grey manuka scrub, very different from the forested hills today.

From Rotorua we took the coach to Taupo, still travelling through what was really a desert of scrub. Taupo was just a small settlement on the lake shore, with still quite a few reminders of its past as an Armed Constabulary base. Now here again we changed transport. The family and all our packing-cases were piled on the little lake steamer *Tongariro,* and Captain Ryan took us the short distance across to Waitahanui. Our furniture had gone ahead by waggon and was already in the house. All our goods were put off the ship and set down on the beach where the Maoris were waiting. There stood the house, up on a little rise, surrounded by dead tea tree, looking very uninviting . . . inhospitable . . . and we all walked slowly up.

My mother sat on the veranda, and she wept. She had suddenly realised how far away she was from her own people, and that she had to make a completely new life.

Father spoke no Maori, and the Waitahanui people had a very limited command of English. The women spoke almost none at all, but some of the men had a smattering, picked up mainly when they were away doing a bit of shearing perhaps, or fencing. That wasn't very often,

because you had to go quite a distance to find anything in the nature of good farming country, so really the settlement just worked on a day-to-day subsistence level. The settlement could only support a limited number of people, and in fact we knew that at times they practised infanticide just through plain necessity. My mother always took some clothes for a new baby, for the Maori women thought it bad luck to prepare clothes before birth. I went with her and we saw the little child but on going back the next day the baby was gone and the mother weeping. At that time there was no registration of births, marriages and deaths among the Maoris. No questions could be asked as no Maori would betray another – only the mother's tears told us.

The s.s. *Tongariro* (Captain Ryan) on Lake Taupo
*Florence Harsant*

They really were lake dwellers, the Waitahanui people. The lake was a great source of food for them. It was full of trout, and if there was a good blow and the lake got rough, inanga would be washed ashore, and they gathered them up in kits. The inanga was a little brown fish, rather bigger than a whitebait. Then you'd walk a little further and you might see several little heaps of koura, which are the small freshwater crayfish – so there was an amplitude of food for the Maoris in the lake itself.

Then they would come down to the lakeside to do their washing, and it was almost like seeing women washing clothes in the River Nile. The women would be in groups along the lake shore, all in their brightly coloured long dresses, and each with their pile of washing.

Everybody swam, of course; they were in the lake every day, swimming. They taught us to swim – the hard way, by swimming us out to deep water and letting us go, then swimming out of our reach. We had to swim or sink! Of course they watched us carefully. Everyone used the real old dugout canoes, and we learnt to handle them quite well ourselves. (You would find very few dinghies on the lake in those days.)

So you see, much of their life revolved around the lake. I remember one very curious occasion when they were expecting a football team to come from Tokaanu in the launch, but the lake came up very rough, and the young men were very disappointed at Waitahanui to miss out on their game. They stared out across those quite steep waves you get on Taupo, and said, 'Oh well, no football today!'

But one of the elders went down to the lake shore and said he knew some karakia – that's incantations – that were used years and years before. Mind you, he wasn't a tohunga, though they did have a more-or-less official tohunga at Waitahanui. This was an elder, a very old man. Well, he stood by the edge of the water, and he chanted away for a long, long time. All the people were watching the lake – watching the waves – and presently the wind began to subside. Then very slowly and almost imperceptibly, the sea began to calm, and presently it was calm enough for the launch to come over safely from Tokaanu. So the day was saved, and all credit was given to the old man for his incantations.

But here's the point, of course. Was it just a coincidence – or did his karakia in some way calm the lake? I can't say, but I do know that the Waitahanui people certainly believed in the power of his karakia.

The lakeside was very much a community area where the women, particularly, gathered to spend much of the day. They would sit there and do their weaving very often, weaving their flax mats, or beating the flax fibres to make the beautifully soft white muka for taniko weaving, or making feathered cloaks. There was always a lot of fun, and a lot of gossip as well, and in fact that's where I really learnt to speak Maori.

It was very common in those days that Maori was not allowed to be spoken inside the school grounds, because according to the educational ideas in force then, the quicker the Maori children learned English, the better it would be for them. My father wouldn't let me learn Maori either. It all had to be English.

I had a good ear though, and whenever I walked down to the lake the women would take me in hand and begin teaching me. Some of the words they taught me were rather . . . earthy, and they'd roar with laughter when I repeated them. I'd check them out with some of the older boys at school, and they'd say, 'No! Bad word, that. Don't you use that word!' But as time went on, I became very fluent in Maori.

\*       \*       \*

Away from the lake, the marae was the centre of activity. In those days we had to attend all the big tangi and meetings, and on Christmas Day they had a huge hangi, and of course we were all invited. There would be kiwi and pigeon, wild duck and trout, pork and puha, potatoes and kumara - a great feast, with plum pudding to follow. They used dogs to catch the kiwis. They were delicious, and quite a common thing at that time on a feast day. The flesh was quite dark, and very tender when it was cooked in a hangi. My mother cooked one once, but she couldn't get it to be as beautifully cooked as the Maoris did. Of course, when they made their hangi they used to put leaves from the bush – special leaves – in with the meat before it was covered over to be cooked, and that enhanced the flavour.

The old meetinghouse was made of raupo - one of the old-time wharenui – and you had to stoop quite a bit to get inside. It had an earthen floor and flax mats to walk on. At a tangi, of course, the body would be lying in state on the porch of the meetinghouse, and as we advanced there would be the karanga, calling us to come and weep for the dead – such a strange sensation to us when we first came, because we were quite unused to the Maori tangi. It used to send a shiver down my spine listening to it. Sometimes the body would lie there a week before the funeral, to allow time for relatives in outlying districts to come and pay homage to the dead. And after a tangi, the Maoris would be poor for quite a while, because it would have taken so much food to feed all the many visitors who came.

I always felt sorry for the widows at those early tangi. It was considered quite the wrong thing for a widow to comb her hair, or change her frock, or wash. She attended to the calls of nature, and that was about all. She just had to sit there and weep, and to do anything like tidying herself up was supposed to imply that she wasn't very sorry that her husband had gone. But there was such a genuine shedding of tears that you felt that really death was a big loss to them all.

As well as tangi, the marae was the scene of weddings, but not weddings in the sense that we know them nowadays. In those days they had what was known as the 'Maori wedding', which was not legal to the Pakeha, but was a binding thing among the Maori people themselves.

A young couple would decide that they wanted to become man and wife, and they would have to tell their parents they wanted this. Well, at night-time everyone would congregate in the meetinghouse and the couple's parents would discuss matters between them: whether they thought it was favourable or not; whether they gave their consent or not. And presently the girl would be asked, 'Do you want to marry this man?' – or I suppose, properly speaking, 'Do you want to sleep with this man?' She would shyly answer, 'Yes', and they would put the same question to the boy. And when he'd answered, there would be a great amount of talk and laughter and rejoicing, because now they had taken one another in front of all their people. They had in

Florence Harsant and Tai
Rawhiti, a childhood
companion, reunited at
Waitahanui
*Alwyn Owen*

fact become man and wife, and they were bedded down in the
meetinghouse in front of everybody as a married couple.

After everyone had settled down and everything was quiet, you'd
see the mother of the girl quietly slip along to where the couple were
sleeping, and she would lift up the rug that covered them, and if she
found that they were lying there skin to skin she would walk away
with a smile on her face, knowing that everything was well, that they
loved one another, because according to the old Maori love songs, to
love one another, their skins must touch.

I remember one arranged marriage – or near-marriage, really. I'd
become friendly with a young girl called Ruta – the Maori form of
Ruth. Her parents were somewhere down Wanganui way, and she'd
been placed in the care of an uncle and aunt in the settlement. They
arranged a marriage with a middle-aged Arawa man from the Rotorua
district, and as an exchange they would get quite a nice little parcel
of land. Well, the man came down from Rotorua and Ruta wouldn't
have anything to do with him, and the aunt and uncle were furious.
When she was asked in the meetinghouse if she'd have him, she just
gave a flat, 'No!' Well, the uncle and aunt gave her a good thrashing
to make her change her mind, and locked her up in a whare.

I'd gone to sleep that night, and I woke up when I heard someone
tapping at my window. Ruta had managed to push the raupo aside
and get out of the whare, then she'd waded down the Waitahanui
Stream so that she wouldn't leave any tracks, and she'd come to the
schoolhouse. Well, I let her in and got her a change of clothes, and
then told my father. He didn't want to hear about it. He wasn't happy

at all. I can see his point of view. He had to live with these people, and he didn't want to get involved in any feuds. He told me that the whole thing was in my hands.

Well, I hid Ruta under the bed. The aunt and uncle searched the whole settlement, and then they came to me. Had I seen Ruta? So I told them yes, I'd seen her a couple of days ago down at the lake shore gathering koura. They went away. They weren't very happy, and they were very suspicious, and they kept a pretty close watch on the schoolhouse.

Well, they started enquiring about Ruta in the villages round about, but nobody had seen her. The next day I managed to slip out to our post office and get to a telephone, and telephone the constable in Taupo, and he came out on the pretext of a fishing trip. Ruta showed him her bruises, and he went off to talk to the uncle – and while he was talking to her, the aunt slipped out and came up to the schoolhouse. She called me all the Pakeha liars on the face of the earth, and worked herself up into such a rage that she danced a haka in front of me. Just then the constable came back, and told her that, if there was any more of her nonsense, she would land up in Mount Eden, and that put an end to her display quite quickly.

Ruta was sent down the Wanganui to her parents – and here's the sequel. A few years later, when I was travelling Maori Organiser for the Women's Christian Temperance Union, I went down the Wanganui . . . and met Ruta. She was very happily married to a Pakeha man, and had a young child with her. She wanted to give me the child, because that was Maori custom. I had helped her, and this was repayment on her part. I explained that, as a travelling organiser, there was no way I could look after a young child properly – and her eyes just flooded with tears of relief. It was a terrible thing for a mother to have to offer, but that was the Maori way, and she accepted it.

Old habits died hard, and in some ways the taking-up of Pakeha ways really was a mixed blessing. There was one very elderly woman in the pa, and she was tattooed from her head to her feet. This was most unusual, but it was a sign that she was really of very high birth. She was the widow of a great fighting chief who belonged to Waita-hanui, but who worked a lot with Te Kooti in the times of war, and she disliked the Pakeha very much. She said that with the coming of the Pakeha, the Maori men were no longer any good. Before the white man came, they used to work the soil, and hunt to bring food home to the marae, or they'd be out on the warpath, fighting. But she said now, with the coming of the Pakeha, there was the waipiro – the drink – and tobacco, and all the evils the Pakeha had brought them, and the men had become very lazy, and left all the work to the women. And she would rock backwards and forwards, and moan, 'Aue! Aue!'

No, she didn't like the Pakeha. They had spoilt her people.

The Maoris at that time lived in whares, and they were just like the meetinghouse scaled down, with raupo walls and thatch, and an earthen

Florence Woodhead, organiser
for the WCTU – a 1913 portrait
*Florence Harsant*

floor covered with beautiful flax mats on which they used to sit or sleep. The houses were quite small, and always composed of just the one room, with wide overhanging eaves to make a porch. In the centre of the whare would be a hollow, and the men would go out and get manuka and cut it up, and burn it into quite big embers. They would carry these in and put them in the hole, and that gave warmth to the whares in wintertime.

They were quite waterproof. They were beautifully cool in the summertime, and really quite warm in the winter. The cooking, of necessity, had to be done outside, and if it was fine, well, they would all eat outside. When we first went there the food would all be dished out in a large tin milk-pan, and everyone would just sit around and eat with their fingers. When they all got around like that, somehow they were always happy, with everyone talking and laughing as they ate, enjoying the food. And really it is a fact that to pick out choice morsels from a dish and eat them with your fingers . . . is a surprisingly enjoyable way to eat.

*         *         *

I had three years at Waitahanui. I suppose I wanted to stretch my wings a little at the end of that time. I could speak Maori fluently, so I moved to the Mission House at Whakarewarewa, a Church of England mission, and I worked there for a couple of years until I had to leave to look after my mother, who had fallen ill. This time my parents were living at Otamatea, and while I was there I was approached by the Women's Christian Temperance Union, and I agreed to become a travelling organiser for them, and work amongst the Maoris.

There was a real need for temperance work just before the Great War. The Maoris were drinking very heavily – the women as well as the men – and there was a terrible amount of neglect as far as their children were concerned. Most of the drinking, I think, was done up on the gumfields, where the Maoris used to take their gum to the Austrians to sell it. That's the Dalmations, of course – we called them 'Austrians' in those days, instead of Dalmations. The Austrians used to sell them their wine, which I'm quite sure was doped. And while I was in that area, I wasn't allowed to travel alone. It wasn't considered safe, because the Maoris were in such a drunken state. Even the women were so drunk that they would be riding on horseback, with a child perhaps, and if the child dropped off the horse, they would just carry on. They didn't know what they were doing.

The settlements in the North were very different from Waitahanui. The people were all closely housed together in mostly wooden houses – you didn't see many raupo ones – and they were spotlessly clean. They had flax mats on the floor, and you never entered a house without taking your shoes off; that was an unheard-of thing to do. They had their kumara and potato patches, and they all had pigs, which they killed off for meat. Most of the settlements were near a river, where they could get eels – or fish, if they were by the sea. They used to make their own bread, which was almost unleavened, and cooked in camp ovens. All the cooking was done in camp ovens. So you see, they were almost self-supporting.

Every morning and evening they had prayers. Somebody would bang on a tin or a cowbell and the whole settlement would come together to say prayers and sing hymns, and it was only then that they would get back to their normal work. It was an education to see how the missionaries had brought these people to live in such a way. It was no hardship for everyone to come to the service; they just automatically came, young and old. And the old people's word was law – they ruled the whole settlement, and what they said had to be done. Not like today.

At the other extreme, you might say, you had the publicans. They weren't very pleased with me at all, because the Maori bushmen used to spend all their money in the hotels over the weekend. All their earnings used to go to the publican, and anyone who came trying to do anything as far as temperance was concerned was looked on as being their enemy.

I arrived at one place after dark on a very stormy night. I didn't know where to go, so I went to the hotel to stay. By the time I reached there I was dripping wet, so I took off my coat and a maid took it to the kitchen to dry it for me while I ordered a meal and sat down. I was having my meal when the hotelkeeper came in, and he noticed my badge – a little white ribbon on my jacket – and he said, 'Ummm . . . I see you belong to those temperance people.'

'Yes,' I said, 'I'm the Maori organiser.'

'Oh well,' he said, 'you can leave. I'm not having you staying here with the idea of taking away my living. The Maoris are my good customers.'

So I finished my meal, and he told the girl to bring my coat, and picked up my luggage. And I said, 'What are you going to do with that?'

'I'm going to put it out. You'll have to leave. You're not staying here.'

'Well,' I said, 'do you happen to know Constable Wallace at Kawakawa? He's told me that if I'm ever in any sort of trouble I only need to get in touch with him, and he'll help me. First thing tomorrow morning I'll ring him up and tell him that you tried to put me out of your hotel.'

The change in atmosphere was quite funny, because no sooner had I told him this than he was all over me. He took my luggage up to my room and was really very nice. He was terrified that I would report him to this Constable Wallace – and in fact I heard later that he'd been warned he'd have his licence taken away if he wasn't careful.

But the Maoris would come in at the end of each week to hand their pay cheques to him, and then they would drink until he told them they'd cut out their money. To my mind, there was no possibility that they could have drunk the whole value of their cheques, but he kept the

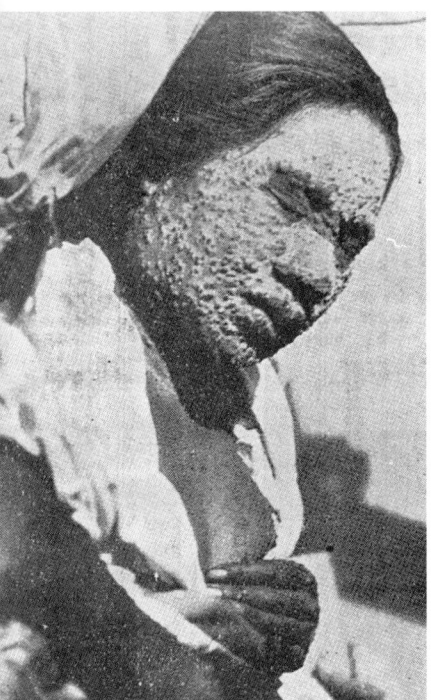

Smallpox victims of the 1913 epidemic
*New Zealand Free Lance*

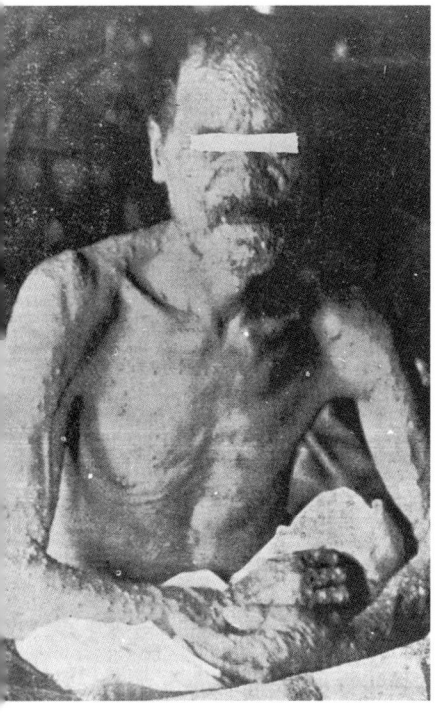

lot. They would go back with no money, and of course that was the lever I had with the Maori women, because I would explain to them what really happened to their husbands' cheques. So the Maori women saw my point, and they were keen on joining the Temperance Union.

I went to one place where they were having a very large tangi. There were hundreds of Maoris, and there were also two Mormon elders. Evidently over in Utah there were quite a few Maoris, and they had taught these elders to speak the Maori language before they came to this great gathering, so this was their opportunity. One of them prayed for the gift of tongues, and then suddenly burst forth into the Maori language. Well, the Maoris made much of this, and they made much of the two Mormon elders. When one of them became very ill they looked after him and nursed him and crowded round to see him. What they didn't know was that the illness was smallpox, and as the Maoris returned home from the tangi, they spread the smallpox virus throughout the North. It turned out that one of the elders had been exposed to smallpox on his journey out.

Now a lot of the details I didn't learn until later years. From what I've since found out, the same ship also carried smallpox to Australia, and it was recognised there straight away. But the North Auckland district was very isolated at that time – they used to call it 'the Roadless North' – and nobody quite knew what was going on. I believe . . . I think a doctor in Whangarei was very alarmed, but the medical authorities in Auckland didn't realise the extent of the epidemic, and for a long while they thought it was a very serious form of chickenpox.

As I travelled through the northern settlements I came across pa after pa that had smallpox in it. Some of the patients were so terribly ill that they couldn't wear trousers because of the pustules on their bodies. They couldn't wear anything on their feet. They were practically covered with smallpox from head to foot. Whole families went down with it, and there was no medical officer amongst them – no one at all – so they just did what they could for each other.

They had their own native ointments which they put on the scabs – which did no good at all – and finally the victims would die. In some cases, where the whole family had died in a house, the Maoris were so frightened of the disease that they burnt the house with the bodies in it, because they were afraid to have a tangi.

I arrived at one place late at night in pouring rain, and the only accommodation I could find was in a house full of the smallpox. I was invited in, and I had to make a quick choice – stay there, or stay out in the rain all night. I decided to go inside.

A Maori made me a cup of tea and gave me some bread, which I was afraid to eat. I had some chocolate in my travelling-box, so I ate that and drank the tea without putting my lips to the cup. Blankets were brought out of the room where the sick people were, but I wrapped myself up in whatever garments I had with me and slept on the floor rather than in the bed. In the morning I got ready to leave, but it was a question of whether I would get transport on the launch or not. The Maori said that if it was known I had spent the night in an infected house, I wouldn't be allowed on the launch, and would have to stay indefinitely.

So after I had put my riding-skirt on, he took me out and splashed me with mud, to make it look as if I had only just arrived. I went down to the landing at the beach, and when the launch came in I asked the launchman if he would take me to Whangarei, and he said, 'Yes.' He said it looked as though I'd had a very muddy ride, and I said yes, the roads weren't in a very good state.

Well, I boarded the launch, and when I got to Whangarei I went straight up to the hospital, and reported that in the Whangaruru settlement every household had smallpox, and there was nobody there to look after them. They sent a launch back there immediately. I reported all the places I'd been to where there was smallpox – the full extent of it was quite unknown at that stage.

I'm getting ahead of myself really. You see, by this time the health authorities had realised they were dealing with a smallpox outbreak, but they didn't realise its extent. Auckland was riddled with it, and so was the Waikato, but those areas were accessible. The North wasn't, but they set up field hospitals and vaccination clinics at places like Kawakawa and Kaikohe, and the doctors and nurses did a wonderful job.

Ready for the road, 1914 – Florence riding Beauty and leading Satan
*Florence Harsant*

I had been vaccinated on my way through the North, but the injection didn't take. I carried on, though, because I got into districts where I didn't know the illness was present, and when I'd got so far, I couldn't turn back. I wouldn't have been received by the people behind me, so I just had to keep going until I reached Whangaruru, where I could catch the launch to Whangarei.

In one place I went to, the storekeeper told me he knew the Maoris had smallpox, and he made them stand well away from his store and shout out to him what they wanted, and then he would tell them how much it was. He had a bottle out on a post – a jar of disinfectant – and the Maoris had to put their coins in it, then he would tie their groceries on to the end of a long pole, and poke it out at them.

The same thing happened when they took their horses to a stable. In one place the stableman refused to give them a head-stall; he threw the chaff on the ground, and the horses had to eat it off the ground. Two Maori women were very incensed, and threw their money on the ground – if it was good enough for the horses to eat off the ground, it was good enough for the man to pick up the money off the ground.

They were not encouraged . . . the white people simply discouraged them from coming anywhere near them if it was possible, but of course the storekeepers had to give them stores, or they would have starved. As it was, some of them were desperately short of food. They'd eaten all their pigs, and the white people wouldn't employ even healthy Maoris, so money was very very scarce. I heard later that the same thing happened in the Waikato, and in some places they couldn't even post a letter or uplift their pensions from the post office. There was a lot more fear than compassion on the part of the white people. They didn't ask whether the Maoris were being looked after or anything else. They were just left to fend for themselves.

Well, I was re-innoculated at the Whangarei Hospital, but unfortunately for me it took so badly that I was ill for a long time. I wanted to go home to the Kaipara Harbour. I sent word to tell my parents I was coming, but I was sent a telegram to say I wouldn't be allowed to land, because they didn't want the infection there. And so I stayed at a Maori minister's home in the Waikato to convalesce, and from then on I left the smallpox behind and went south to Gisborne to travel the East Coast.

First broadcast 20 November 1974

# 8 A Matter of Principle

Duncan McCormack, a pacifist during the First World War, describes his experiences in New Zealand as a conscientious objector.

*Duncan McCormack arrived in New Zealand from his native Scotland in 1913, a year when this country was in a state of political turmoil. For some time, growing unemployment had led to increasing industrial strife, and this climaxed in the great General Strike of 1913. It was a time when socialism was being preached on the street corners, when future leaders of the Labour Party were speaking from their soapboxes in Auckland's Quay Street. A time when socialism held real meaning and promise for millions of workers, who believed that capitalism could – and would – be replaced by a more just and humane system, and a worldwide brotherhood of labour.*

*Capitalism, with its attendant exploitation, depression, and repression of the working classes, was seen as the world's ultimate evil . . . and in the outbreak of war in 1914 the socialists saw only confirmation of their views. War was a direct result of the contradictions inherent in the capitalist system. What quarrel had the workers of the Allies with their German counterparts? Both groups were being manipulated – why then should worker fight against worker?*

*A philosophy of socialist pacifism was hard to adhere to in wartime, however, especially against the weight of an enormously energetic propaganda machine. In peace, many of the tenets of socialism sat easily alongside those of Christianity – particularly those which preached non-violence and pacifism, but the Church in war was faced with exactly the same problems as the socialists were, and as part of the Establishment, organised religion was clear where its duties lay.*

*Within the Church, and within the socialist movement, there were those committed to pacifism regardless of pressure. Even while enlistment was voluntary, this view was held at considerable personal cost. When conscription was introduced in 1916, it led to open confrontation with authority.*

*Duncan McCormack's story is that of a socialist objector whose religious principles – initially at least – only reinforced his convictions.*

Duncan McCormack
*Alwyn Owen*

Resistance to authority was definitely in my mind when war broke out. It was in my mind from the beginning. I definitely decided that I would not go to the war. I would take any consequences whatever . . . because we objectors were prepared to pay any price, and that wasn't just a negative attitude – it was very positive.

This was a matter of political attitudes, and church affiliations came into it a bit . . . well, I don't know if 'affiliations' is quite right; we were just church members. I did take seriously some of the teachings and the precepts, and Christianity was supposed to be concerned with love – 'Do good to those who hate you' and 'Love your enemies' and so forth, and that seemed to make good meaningful sense, and I think it had an influence on my feelings when war broke out. But even so, when war broke out just a year after arriving in the country, it was fairly explosive – it was a situation that I had never contemplated.

Politically . . . well, remember that at that time I was only in my twentieth year, and I had not had much political experience, but when I arrived in New Zealand in 1913 I did hear Fraser and Semple. Meetings were held in Auckland in Quay Street, outside the Roller Flour Mill, and speakers literally stood on a soapbox in those days. Sometimes they had a proper rostrum, but it was more often a soapbox; it depended upon the occasion. One of the great speakers was Oscar McBrine. He was a waterside worker, and he was an official in the Labour Movement. He was regarded as one of their best speakers. There was the influence of Oscar McBrine, Peter Fraser, Bob Semple and Fred Way. Fred was one of the finest Labour spokesmen of that day. From them I got the earliest beginnings of my political knowledge, I would say.

The NZ Socialist Party membership card of Oscar McBrine, an early Labour Movement orator well known throughout the country
*Alexander Turnbull Library*

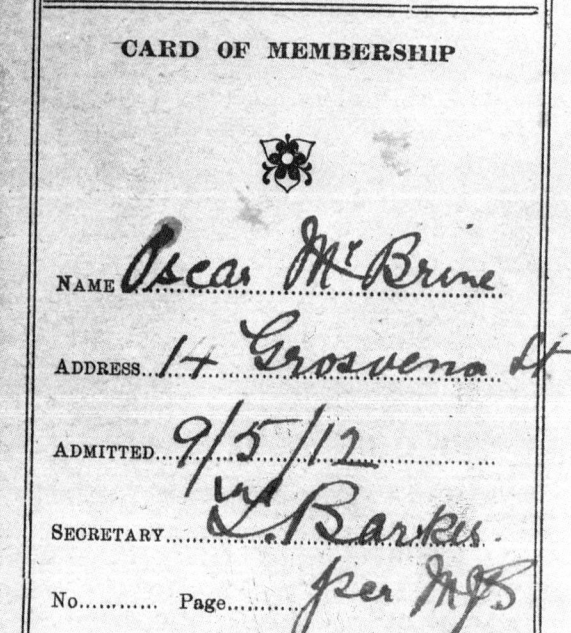

**OBJECT**

The inauguration in New Zealand of an Industrial Commonwealth founded upon the Socialisation of Land, Machinery and Capital.

**METHOD**

(1.) The education of the community in the principles of Socialism.

(2.) The Industrial and Political organisation of the Workers.

(3.) The independent representation of Socialist principals on all elective bodies.

**N.Z. SOCIALIST PARTY**
(AUCKLAND BRANCH.)

**CARD OF MEMBERSHIP**

NAME  *Oscar McBrine*

ADDRESS  *14 Grosvenor St*

ADMITTED  *9/5/12*

SECRETARY  *L. Barkes.*

No............  Page............  *per M.J.S*

G, T. Langley, Printer, 22-24 Pitt Street Auckland.

Socialism preached a pacifist creed. It did; it was very anti-war. In fact, when war broke out, the Labour Movement was very much against it. It was contrary to the tenets and ideals of socialism, because the workers in each country are told that they're fighting for their hearth and home, and they can't all be fighting for their hearth and home and then go away ten thousand miles to fight. That's not fighting for their hearth and home.

So we did get a knowledge of the background of the war. We knew that Europe was riddled with secret agreements, and we knew there was nothing in the motivation of the war that should induce any working man to go and fight in it. I got that amount of knowledge. And of course that, combined with the influence of Tolstoy, Bernard Shaw, and the Fabians, all had a strong bearing on my attitude to the war when it broke out.

Of course, propaganda went into gear straight away. Warmongering became the great feature, and even the churches had a very bad reputation in the war, because I suppose they're beholden to the Government on matters of rate exemption and so forth, and it's natural they would be behind the Government in a war – and they sure were! They were almost totally behind the Government. That was when I came into conflict with the Church. And of course I left the Church,

A group of early Labour 'evangelisers': far left, James Black, author of the 'Black pamphlet' which gained great notoriety and helped undo Sir Joseph Ward; kneeling centre, Michael Joseph Savage; standing next, R. F. Way, a street-corner orator and later a Labour candidate; standing next, F. N. Bartram, Labour MP 1919–25; kneeling far right, Scott Bennett, an orator who filled Auckland theatres on Sunday nights for years.
*John A. Lee Collection, Alexander Turnbull Library*

and . . . you might say, I was dismissed from it . . . because we were considered to be traitors to the country . . . shirkers and cowards . . . and the churches had become recruiting platforms for the war. I was actually a Sunday-school teacher at the time, and when we were arrested, the Church just simply forgot us. We were never inquired about; no inquiries were ever made about us when we got into prison. That was the finish of Sunday schools and churches as far as I was concerned, because when I got into prison I came in touch with very enlightened people, and I heard many discussions, and my whole attitude to churches changed.

It was voluntary enlistment up to 1916, and during that time propaganda was very much against young men who wouldn't enlist, especially if they were single men. They were insulted, and white feathers were sent through the post. I didn't get any white feathers, but I got an envelope containing an empty epsom salts packet, and written on the back of the packet it said, 'If you can't go to the front, go to the rear.' That was the kind of insults that were being put around at the time.

This sort of thing came from outsiders, not workmates; there was no difficulty at all with workmates, because men working in industry just had no time for the war at all. There was a large body of anti-war feeling.

They compiled a register of men – eligible men – in 1915, and then in 1916 the Conscription Act was brought in, so I knew it was inevitable that I would come into conflict with authority. I can't recall which ballot I was in. It was not the first one...but we got our call-up orders. I just went on with my work and completely ignored it, knowing, of course, that I would be arrested in due course.

*       *       *

Two military policemen came to the house one day, and they did allow me a little time to dress, and take a few necessary things. In that respect they were a little better than some, because some of them didn't even do that. In fact they . . . I know one man who was arrested on a flax mill, and he was just dragged into camp in his flax-working clothes – unshaven and so forth. They wouldn't allow him to dress. But I will say that these chaps were decent enough not to do that.

We lived in Dominion Road at the time, and when I was arrested I was taken to Fort Cautley at Devonport. When I was marched through the streets of Auckland, walking between the two 'Red Caps', I felt very uncomfortable, but I think they felt just as uncomfortable. They wouldn't walk along Queen Street. They didn't like the exposure to the public any more than I did, so they went through High Street. At that time Whitcombe and Tombs was being built, and there was a rush of workers to the hoarding of the building, and the military police were jeered and booed, but I received a little cheering. It was the only time in my life I'd ever been cheered by a group of people. The only time.

Well, from Fort Cautley at Devonport, I was taken up by these military police to the Rutland Street Barracks, which was the military headquarters in Auckland at that time. I was marched in before a Major Price. He'd already been away to the war and come back injured, and I noticed he had several fingers off his hands.

I was brought in between two sergeants, and standing right behind me was a sergeant-major. Well, I wore a cap at that time, and I'd walked in there with my cap on my head, and the sergeant-major behind me grabbed the cap and threw it away to the far corner of the room. That was the last I saw of that cap. I was there to be insulted and browbeaten, which I was, in the form of questioning. Can't recall the questions, but I was adamant about my attitude. The questioning didn't last long, and I was marched away again, and back to Fort Cautley.

After a fortnight in Fort Cautley I was taken by a military policeman in civilian clothes to Trentham Camp near Wellington – taken there by rail. When I arrived in Trentham I was immediately taken to Hut 21, and that was the first time I ever came into contact with other conscientious objectors. It was quite a long hut – may have held about twenty or even thirty conscientious objectors – and of course there was a lot of jollification in meeting others. I quite enjoyed Hut 21.

You could say I was a conscientious objector for mixed political and religious reasons I suppose – philosophical reasons really, because some of my religious ideas were a little tattered, although I believed in the Christian attitude of love to others, and so on, but it was ninety per cent political belief. When I went to prison later on, they made an attempt to classify us, and you might have read in the book *Armageddon or Calvary* – that was written by Harry Holland, who was the great Labour leader of that time – he tells about this classification. It was rather absurd, because two men came to the prison and interrogated each one, and from this interrogation they classified us, according to whether we were religiously or politically motivated – the sheep and goats as it were. The intention of this was to disenfranchise the political ones for ten years after the war!

Of course, the religious ones were not the greatest offenders. The ones who were branded as dangerous were the political ones. They were more enlightened politically, and they took an interest in politics and economics, and they could analyse the war situation better. The Christian objectors were not people who would analyse the situation at all. I came to respect the political ones more, because after all, religious objection more or less derives from commanded morality, and commanded morality is a rather negative thing; it's just 'thou shalt not do this, and thou shalt not do that'. But that attitude was not the attitude of socialist objectors.

Well, the outcome of this led up to my first sentence, which was imposed by the Camp Commandant, Colonel Potter. But that was just a try-on. Before that, I was ordered to take my kit. Now the procedure was to take you to the supply building where the uniforms were held – the stores – and the kit was laid out on the floor, and you were escorted

William McCormack, Duncan's brother. The loss of Willy in the disappearance of a 'coffin ship', over-insured and under-maintained, lent additional weight to Duncan's socialist convictions.
*Duncan McCormack*

there by two sergeants. A lieutenant came in and ordered you to take the kit, naming you according to your military designation – 'Private so-and-so, number so-and-so, this is your kit. I order you to take this kit.' And whatever you said in reply, he would note; he noted it down on paper.

I just point-blank refused to have anything to do with it. I know that what some of the fellows said was unprintable, particularly so with the political objectors. But I did point-blank refuse to take the kit, and I said, 'I'm not a soldier. I don't recognise myself as one, and I refuse to take the kit.' I think that was all I said. It was a very brief proceeding, and we were just marched in and marched out.

After that I was taken before the Camp Commandant and questioned. I think that procedure was to see . . . to test out how determined you were to maintain your stand. But we were all quite positive in our attitude. We didn't ever consider taking a passive role – stretcher-bearing, or anything like that. We considered it would have been very little different to being a soldier, and being in some fighting capacity. It was never suggested that I do stretcher-bearing, and I never thought about it.

The questions were along the lines of, 'What would you do if the Germans came and raped your sister?' Well, the Germans were a long way off and it was most unlikely that such a thing would happen, and that was the answer to that. But that was the sort of thing they put up. It was a propaganda question.

Of course, at that time the whole country was riddled with propaganda. People were told, for example, that the reason for going to fight ten thousand miles away in Europe was because the Germans were cutting the hands and feet off Belgian children. The Germans had invaded and were making their way through Belgium, and they were supposed to be throwing babies in the air and catching them on the points of their bayonets. Well, very few people believed that, but there were always a few people who would believe anything.

Anyway, as I said, I went before the Camp Commandant, and the whole thing was pretty brief. The moment he discovered you were not likely to give in, he just ordered a month's imprisonment on half rations. And that was the first sentence I got.

I served that month on half rations in the Alexandra Barracks in Wellington. The Alexandra Barracks stood where the Dominion Museum is now. It's on a rise; a crown in Buckle Street. I suppose it was a form of punishment, but as part of the sentence we had to pull a great heavy roller up and down the shingled yard, for no purpose whatsoever other than just exercise, and probably punishment. The roller was so big that not all hands could hold the pulling handle. So they tied ropes to it, and there was a string of men – perhaps about fifteen men – pulling that roller up and down the shingled yard. An exercise in futility would be the best way to describe it.

Well, the month soon went, and the military police were waiting, and we were escorted back to Hut 21, and there we were until the first court-martial.

The proceedings were the same. Evidence was taken that you refused to take the kit, and instead of coming before the Camp Commandant you came before a full-dress court-martial, which was rather awe-inspiring, I might say. But it was farcical as far as justice as concerned, because the sentences were already determined by the War Cabinet under the Conscription Act. Parliament determined on the sentence of eleven months' hard labour.

I can't say I felt worried about it – I can't remember being worried at all. It was really just the kind of thing I'd expected, and others had been sentenced before me. I'd anticipated what it would be, and I'd got quite reconciled to the consequences.

*     *     *

Now part of my time was served in civilian jails, but the bulk of the time was really spent on the prison farm at Paparua. First of all I was escorted to Point Halswell Prison in Wellington. The procedure there was that you would be divested of all your clothing, get in a hot bath, your fingerprints were taken, and you were given your prison clothes. The prison clothes, of course, were designed to humiliate, with broad arrows all over them. The garments were really very ugly.

I can't recall how long I was there . . . it's a long, long time ago. It may have been a week; it might have been two . . . but from there I was taken to the Terrace Jail in Wellington. Now this was a very grim building, and of course is long since demolished. I went there a few years ago to see the remains, and . . . nothing is there.

It was in the Terrace Jail that I met Peter Fraser. Conscription was passed in December 1916, and then those who spoke against conscription, like Semple, Fraser, Tom Brindle and John Thorn – they were all well-known Labour identities of the day – they were charged with sedition, and were tried before a magistrate and given a twelve months' imprisonment sentence. They were not sentenced to hard labour. They spent most of their time studying in the prison yard. Peter Fraser used to go out with an armful of books, and one of those books, I happen to know, was by Karl Marx.

I found opportunity to speak with Fraser – it was quite accidental really. He was an older man – by twelve years. Any conversation had to be swift and to the point, as it was against regulations, so it was just, 'Hello, what are you in for?'

'Oh, I'm a conscientious objector.'

'Good on you, lad. Stick to it, lad. You'll get our support.'

That was all my conversation with Fraser, because you must not be seen talking to another prisoner.

That jail term wasn't an experience that Fraser looked back on with any affection, because of course he became Prime Minister of the Labour Government, and the experience of actually administering a government changed a lot of his ideas. From being a rebel and, you might say, a revolutionary, he came to be an entirely different person. He came to be an administrator of government, and as a prime minister he had to take a very much modified attitude.

When I met him again in the Second World War, he'd already been to England, and gone through all the procedures of meeting the King, and doing what a prime minister would do. And the occasion of our meeting was rather surprising. I was waiting to see if I could get into a play which was being performed, an anti-fascist play called *Till the Day I Die.* I hadn't booked a seat, so I was waiting at the door to see if I could get in. A limousine drove up, and the chauffeur got out and opened the door, and in walked Peter Fraser, the Prime Minister. He walked straight up to me and looked me in the eye, and he said, 'Ah, we've met before. Where have we met?' – and shook hands.

I said, 'We met in the Terrace Jail in Wellington.'

Wartime socialist cartoons from issues of *Maoriland Worker*: 8 March 1916, captioned 'The one shall give – the other lend' (RIGHT), and 16 June 1915 (OPPOSITE)
*Alexander Turnbull Library*

It was like a bombshell to him. He just turned on his heel and walked inside the building, without another word. I think a skeleton came out of his cupboard, that's just about what it amounted to, because his prison days he wanted to forget – and something came up which reminded him of them, and I think that is why he reacted as he did.

*　　　*　　　*

I had it easy compared to some. You'll remember that fourteen objectors were bundled off to France, and Archy Baxter tells about that in his book *We Will Not Cease*. We heard about it very soon after it happened, because there was an outcry about it. These men were

# FAT AND THE PROFITS

**FAT: HIS WORK.**

Higher Rents.
Higher prices for Bread.
Higher prices for Butter.
Higher prices for Flour.
Higher prices for Everything.

CAPITALIST

PROFIT SCREW

THE CAPITALIST:—"You go to the war, Tommy; I'll look after your wife and family."
—With acknowledgments to "Edinburgh Socialist."

shanghaied from the Terrace Jail and taken in the middle of the night and put on a troopship. It came to our knowledge through our visitors bringing in the information. But there was such an outcry about it that it was never repeated. It was only that one isolated case, when these fourteen men were put on a troopship and taken to France. On return one, Mark Briggs, was nominated to the Upper House by Labour members as a mark of respect and sat in it till it was abolished in 1951.

Well, as I say, we were put in the Terrace Jail for a time, and the problem then was for the authorities to place all the conscientious objectors somewhere and accommodate them. Some were sent to prison camps for tree-planting – I think the places were Waimarino . . . Kaingaroa . . . those are the names I remember. But after that we didn't see anything of one another until we got to our respective prisons or camps.

The one I happened to get to was Paparua Prison, outside of Christchurch. It was a prison farm, and we had farmers in our ranks, and they knew that farm was only fit to run five hundred sheep, not fifteen hundred. And of course it was a joke about hearing the sheep's bones rattling in the night, and about them having to lick the moss off the stones to get a feed. It was hopelessly overstocked.

Oh, I should have mentioned that on the way to Paparua Prison I was transferred from the Terrace Jail in Wellington to the Lyttelton Prison. While I was there I worked in the quarry gang, and we were marched each day to the Port Hills. Straight up the middle of the main street, under a warder with a rifle.

I'd never worked in a quarry in my life, and I was rather terrified when I had to hold a gad for a big navvy who was swinging a fourteen-pound hammer. That hammer had to come right down on top of that gad – they call it a 'gad', I think – and I had to hold that very steady, or I could have had my hands bashed with a fourteen-pound hammer. That rather terrified me.

In the prison yard there were flagstones with a number on each and a crowsfoot mark, where the bodies of executed men who'd been hanged in that prison were buried.

When I first arrived there, on my first day in Lyttelton Prison, I was rather bewildered. I'd never been there before. A man passed behind me and tapped me on the shoulder, and whispered in my ear, 'You're one of us. You'll have milk in your tea while you're here.'

And he just vanished. I afterwards found out that this was Tim Armstrong. How he knew that I was one of them I don't know, but then word goes round very mysteriously in prison. And sure enough, we got milk in our tea. Of course, men got no milk according to prison regulations. (I think women did get a little, but men didn't get any milk.) I found out afterwards that Armstrong had known the prison warder who brought the milk in the Waihi strike. And when all the other prisoners in this wing were locked up, those left were Armstrong, O'Brien, O'Rourke, myself, and another conscientious objector called

Albert Church – these five. And then, when every other man was locked up, Armstrong would come round with the bottle of milk, and we had milk in our tea, which was a horrible mixture of half tea and half burnt breadcrumbs.

After the sentence had been served at Paparua Prison, two military police were waiting at the prison door. I was handed over to them, taken back to Hut 21 at Trentham Camp.

It was the same procedure all over again: ordered to take the kit . . . another refusal . . . another court-martial . . . but this time the sentence was two years' hard labour – as determined by the War Cabinet. It was not determined by any consideration of justice.

We did have some lighter moments in prison. We had concerts, and right around the cell house we'd give an item. Of course, some would be too shy to give an item, but we always had a few characters there who could sing and talk and play the comedian and so forth. One chap we had – Anderson was his name – he was a spiritualist, and he used to tell us that he never stayed in his cell overnight; his spirit left his body and went home. He was quite a good singer, and always sang 'Just a Song at Twilight'.

We had one prisoner called Paddy – I can't recall his surname at the moment – but he was Paddy, and he was a very outspoken Sinn Feiner. He was actually a conscientious objector, but for very different reasons from others. For example, he would have fought in any way *against* England, but he wouldn't fight in any war on the side of England. He used to stand every night at his cell door before being locked up – whether the warders liked it or not – with his fist clenched, and yell at the top of his voice:

> Ireland was Ireland, when England was a pup,
> And Ireland will be Ireland still,
> When England's buggered up!

Every night it was a ritual with Paddy.

\*     \*     \*

Now I'd been given that two years' sentence at the end of 1917, and the war ended a year later, on 11 November 1918. That didn't cut my sentence short immediately; it dragged on. Men were released just in ones and twos. The news of the end of the war was very welcome to us, because we knew that we would be released – it was only a matter of time. But naturally, we were anxious to get back to our relatives.

Of course, the end of the war coincided with the great flu epidemic. Some of our chaps got flu. I didn't get it, as it so happened, but some of our chaps were very ill with the flu epidemic. Some were so ill that, in order to give them the needed attention, our cell doors were left open, so that they could attend to one another. And that was a very great experience, to be freed from spending a night in your own individual cell. When we were in this period of the flu epidemic and given our liberty within the wing to walk up and down, at the end of the passageway there was a door – a single door – and the top panel of that door was open to the air. It was just covered with expanded metal. To look out there and see the stars was really a treat. I hadn't seen stars for maybe six months or eight months, and to look out of that window at the sky and see the stars was something to be remembered for ever.

Well, in my case, I served the whole two years of my sentence, and once again, there were two military police waiting for me. We were not discharged from the prison. We were still regarded as soldiers. The military police were there again, and we were taken to the military barracks in Christchurch and we were discharged from there and given a soldier's discharge, and paid our wretched sum of money which was prison pay. It was so little I can't remember how much I got, but I think it was about a ha'penny a day we were paid.

So, I was free at last. Oh, it felt wonderful!

There was no bitterness from other people that I encountered after I was released. None at all. I didn't encounter any feeling against me in the building industry. No. In fact I think it was rather the reverse. There had been men that had been away to the war and had come back, and I know that one man in a group once said to me, 'My God, I wish I'd had the guts to do what you did!'

My views did change though, between the wars. Your views must change if you're progressive at all. Lots of things had happened, and I think there can be different types of wars, you know. In my country, in Scotland, there were wars fought for freedom, and a tradition was built up of fighting for freedom. If I'd been of the right age, I'd probably have fought in the Second World War. All war is bad but all wars are not equally bad. It was a war against fascism, wasn't it? It was a different kind of war. The quality of the war was different. But . . . I might not have recognised that in the beginning. I don't know – it's very hard to say.

But I certainly would not have held rigidly to the same views that I held, because the First World War after all was not a war to fight for hearth and home, as we were told. We were lied to. It was really a war for the redistribution of the spoils of colonialism. And we came to recognise that. Might I quote a verse written after the First World War:

> Ten million men went forth to fight
> When forty statesmen said 'twas right.
> They fought and bled ten million strong
> To prove the forty statesmen wrong.
> Had forty statesmen fought instead
> Their lie'd have cost but forty dead.
>
> – *Anon*

First broadcast 14 July 1979

# 9 The Sea Before, the Bush Behind

Ted Ashby's memories of the bush farm that was his home, and of the scows that serviced it.

*Ted Ashby's account of life at Orere, on the western shore of the Firth of Thames, is an example of 'location recording', in which a location is used to trigger the memory, and provide a frame of reference.*

*In radio, such a frame of reference is invaluable. In the sound of the sea, the crunch of boots upon rock, the mewing of gulls, it draws the listener into the story, and gives the interviewer visual and aural pointers. Ted Ashby's walk up the hill to the old family graveyard, and his recollections there, have an immediacy and atmosphere that would not be conveyed to the listener were the stories simply related in a living room.*

*The printed word cannot capture this atmosphere or immediacy, but the major benefit remains; familiarity with a well-remembered location has stimulated an emotional response, and coloured thought- and word-patterns, and these do translate to the printed page. Even in transcription, Ted Ashby's story becomes not so much the telling of a tale as the reliving of earlier experiences.*

*Ted Ashby's two loves are the bush and the sea – and in particular the scows, bred to their work of servicing and developing the North, and in that development, finding their own demise. He has published two books:* Blackie *(Reed, 1978), a novel with a bushman as its central character, and* Phantom Fleet *(Reed, 1976), a detailed and affectionate history of the scows he knew so well.*

Ted Ashby
*Alwyn Owen*

Somewhere about 1898 or 1899 my father bought the block of land where we're sitting now. He'd sold a couple of rafts of timber and knocked up a bit of money and he arranged to get a house built here; that's the old house you see up above the beach there now. He arranged with a friend of his, Billy Spencer, who had the cutter *Matakana,* to take him up to Auckland, and they shipped all the material for the house in one cutter-load and brought it down here, and unloaded it on to this beach.

It's a flat sandy beach – a beautiful beach – and there's only one fault about it. It's open to nor'nor'west, or nor'east, or easterly winds, and you can get a very nasty sea coming in here. But the old boatmen were pretty good predictors of weather, and they knew when to come on an open beach and when to lie off an open beach.

Anyway, he brought all the timber down for the house – the timber, bricks and everything – and Dad engaged a builder by the name of Billy Mann, and with the help of my father in his spare time, and my elder brothers, they built the old house you see up there on the hill.

They shifted in there in March 1900, and this was a big event for the Ashby family. It was the first time that my mother had ever had a permanent place to live, somewhere that nobody could push her out of, or charge her rent. She had a stake in the ground. It gave the family a totally different outlook really, because instead of being nomad itinerant bushmen shifting from job to job, they could set down permanent roots. Not only that, they had a house that had a stove in it and paper on the walls instead of just pages out of the *Weekly News*. It had coloured wallpaper on the walls.

The stove had a wetback and a hot-water system, and my mother and sisters thought it was just something out of another world. It had come to life, like Cinderella and the pumpkin and glass slipper thing. It had happened, and there it was.

Well, I was born about 1902, and altogether with little Emmy, who died young, there were fifteen of us. The rest of us lived to be quite mature aged people. Not only did we live on, but we lived on as part of an involved little family, the fourteen of us, for years and years and years, until it almost seemed that we were invulnerable. We were a tribe, or a hapu as the Maoris would call us. And for years and years we would all pull our chairs under the table there, all sixteen of us; the fourteen brothers and sisters and my father and mother . . . and any swaggers who happened to be around.

The house at Orere, c. 1902. In the foreground can be seen the bullock yard.
*Ted Ashby*

The Ashby family, c. 1903. Ted Ashby is the babe in arms on the left.
*Ted Ashby*

The thing you have to try and realise is that at that time the house was sitting there in the bush. At the back was bush; in front was the water. There were no roads, only odd bullock tracks going nowhere, where you'd hauled out the timber. No roads leading anywhere. You either walked or rode around the coast, or you had to go by boat. There were a lot of fishermen with boats, and odd cutters and ketches and scows running around, and these sea people got to be our friends. They were our means of communication, as well as our providing them with a living by giving them timber to freight. And they kept us alive by giving us the essentials and keeping us in touch with civilisation.

The whole of the attitude then was geared towards survival – a thing that we don't realise today. Everything was planning ahead for survival, whether you grew spuds, or kumaras, or whether you put a bit of an orchard in; whether you shot wild cattle or wild pigs, it was all part of food, the supply of food. Everything was looked at through those eyes. The merit went to the chap who got the biggest pig or who got all the fish, or who shot the most pigeons.

I can give an instance of my brother Bill and I, on a Sunday, shooting forty-one pigeons – and I don't know where the hell the conservationists were at the time. But we shot forty-one pigeons one Sunday, and my brothers Alf and Fred shot forty-three the following Sunday and beat us by two, and consequently their mana went up and our mana went down. But you can imagine the food there was in forty-odd pigeons. It fed the family for half a week, and the same with the catches of fish. There was plenty of fish around. You had to have multiple quantities of food, and everything really was planning ahead for survival.

Right up until about 1910 there was no other Pakeha landowners settled on this coast. There was the odd Pakeha-Maori, and I don't know what their position was exactly, but they seemed to be tolerated by the Maoris to give it a go, dig gum and sort of live off the land. There were several of them here, and the only other people were surveyors sent down to survey blocks of land, or, later on, the roads . . . surveyors and bushmen. The bushmen would come down to take jobs cutting firewood or working bush for different companies, and they always had to land at our place, because we had the only boat landing. They would stay overnight and then take their tents into the bush and pitch them, or build nikau whares. But they were only a nomad crowd, because they would just stay there until the job was done, and then they would flit away again. Consequently we had no permanent neighbours right up until about 1910.

You see, there were so many things tied up with this way of life that it was a totally different civilisation, you might call it. I can never remember actually learning to ride, only sitting on top of a saddle in front of my dad or some of my brothers or sisters. When I was too small to hold a gun I can recall as a kid being allowed to pull the trigger of a rifle to have a shot . . . that sort of thing. And I can't remember ever learning to swim. I was lucky in that by the time I reached the age of five we had a school, but the older brothers never got to school – only a night school we had later on in the old house there.

*          *          *

We got our income every year from chopping firewood in the summertime and hauling it out and stacking it on the beach here, before shipping it away in the winter. That was a sure breadline, and every year there was a big demand for that. Before there was a ready supply of electricity the demand was for tea-tree firewood, and so we built up a constant trade. Every year there would be hundreds of tons of firewood go off the beach here, and I think we had a closer association with the boatmen and bushmen than we really did with the farmers. There was a fraternity there; same with the fishermen. This placed us in a very different position to lots of farmers. Really, the bulk of farmers who bought land were either businessmen, or farmers, or men with money to invest, and they came from a totally different social circle. We came more in the same social circle as the fishermen and scowmen, and we spoke the same language. We farmed, but we were never farmers – we were a dead loss as cockies, and we used to

LEFT: Waggoning firewood at Orere, c. 1902
*Ted Ashby*

BELOW: The *Tuahine* heads the fleet at an Auckland regatta. This scow freighted thousands of tons of firewood from the Ashby property at Orere.
*NZ Herald*

milk cows and never had any sheep for many, many years. Sort of had a contempt for sheep, although we would milk cows. But our interest was working in the bush and catching a fish, riding a horse, or something like that.

And the sea was the highway, and this beach was our terminus . . . the landing. All that a landing meant really was that there was a stretch of sand or shingle with not too many boulders, where you could bring a boat in without getting it smashed to pieces. You had to have somebody there with a boat, and people who were used to open-boat work, specially on a beach like this that is open to the strong nor'east and easterly gales. You get a helluva nasty sea in here on occasions, and consequently the men who grew up with these boats had to be experienced surfboatmen.

Everything that came in, whether it was for bushmen coming to pack their camps back a mile or so, or surveyors coming in to pitch tents and things, all had to come on to this beach, and come ashore in that open boat, from perhaps a regular steamer or from a scow or cutter or something. The only way they could come ashore was by that open boat, and consequently this landing got to be known, because it was the only place that there was always an open boat there and a crew, irrespective of weather.

We had a big surfboat, about eighteen feet long, and generally about two, or sometimes three, of us would crew it. But that boat didn't only have to bring ashore stores of flour and tucker, potatoes and things, because when the farm got to be developed a bit, it had to bring ashore manure and all that stuff. You'd have your horses and sledges down there to meet it, to cart it ashore and store it, and you'd have to make two or three trips sometimes in the open boat to bring enough manure ashore. Sometimes you had quite a big team – horses and men – to take the stuff up from the boat when you came in, especially if there was a big sea running.

So that's what a landing was. Later on, when the place got more civilised, the scows and cutters and ketches used to come in to Orere because they could go aground there sheltered, and the teams come straight down alongside them . . . and the same thing applied on the beach here in fine weather. You see, there was the firewood and timber. I've seen this flat covered with kauri logs. I've seen ship timbers – big ship timbers – piled up there, waiting for shipment. Now those couldn't go by open boat. Those had to be loaded in the cutters and ketches in the early days. In the latter years the scows would come in after the high tide had passed its peak a couple of hours so that when they were loaded they had enough floatage at the next high tide to float off. If you loaded them at the top of the tide, they wouldn't float off at the next one, because of the weight of the cargo.

There's no doubt about it, those scows were a main factor in developing the North. The scow evolved to suit local conditions. I think it's pretty well alike in all countries; they develop the type of vessel necessary for the conditions and the weather. With our shallow-bar rivers and tidal streams, and having to load on open beaches like this, the cutters weren't a success. They were deep-bodied vessels with a keel, and directly they went aground they laid over on one side, which made it very awkward to load or unload cargo.

Another thing, they were all hold vessels, and consequently you couldn't stow stuff like ship timbers or cattle or bulk timber . . . they were just about impossible. Well, that's where the scow proved such a success. I think the name was a carryover from the Dutch, and the design was a development of the type of vessel used on the Great Lakes in North America. I think that's where the model really came from that started the old scows off. Well, with the cooperation of the owners and skippers and builders, they slowly evolved the New Zealand scow – the Auckland scow – which proved the only really adequate method of water transport for our type of work. You could drive bullocks up a ramp on to a scow's deck; you could turn around and lift the wagon aboard, and you could stick it all on the deck – with a hold boat you couldn't do any of that. They were there because they were sensible.

I have a strong affection for them. I can't help it. Same as I have for a bullock. I have a warm feeling for a bullock. It's not natural, it's a silly thing – a grown-up person shouldn't have that sort of feeling – but I have a feeling for a bullock that I would like to go and get every working bullock left in New Zealand and cut feed for him. I think we owe that much to them, on account of the rough treatment they got. Ah, but today you wouldn't have to chop many leaves for them! There's only about one team left, I think. There might be a few with waggoners up north, but I don't think they've ever known the real rigours of working in a muddy gully up to their bellies in mud in the wintertime. I don't think they've ever experienced that.

So I feel the same way about the scows ... a silly, sentimental feeling, but there it is – I can't help it. I've written verse about them, and it's no great shakes as poetry perhaps, but it sums up my feelings:

LANDFALL

There are stormclouds out to seaward
And the scud is flying free.
The weather cap sits low on Moehau.
There are whitecaps out to leeward
With a sullen, angry sea,
As the first gusts hit the overladen scow.

They are clewing up the tops'ls
As the sheets are eased away
And the helmsman breaks her off a point or two.
He is trying for the shelter
At the head of Omaha Bay,
Out past the danger rocks of Takatu.

He fights to hold a compass course
Against the wheel's kicks,
The sea-murk closing in with every squall.
He is fighting for a landfall –
Just some point to get a fix –
Before the early darkness smothers all.

There's a noise like tearing canvas
And the black clouds roll and spread,
And lightning briefly rips the weather sky.
The thunderclap that follows
Is too close overhead,
And is echoed by the seabirds' plaintive cry.

They know they've run their distance
As the skipper checks the log:
Through salt-rimmed eyes this lookout stares ahead.
Then for a precious moment
Through a lifting of the fog
He sees the old bald dome of Rodney Head.

It's there for just a moment
Till the fog shuts in again,
But with his shout the skipper snaps a sight.
From off his chin is dripping
The fog-dew and the rain
But he no longer fears the closing-in of night.

He alters course a point to port
And drives on up the bay.
The wake shows white astern on every crest.
The sails and deck are soaking wet
With driving rain and spray
But there's a lifting of the clouds towards the west.

They raise the leading beacon
And stand on to take the bar.
It's plain sailing as they pass it, down to lee.
They jibe the main boom over
With a timber-shaking jar –
Then they're round the point upon a tranquil sea.

The skipper heaves a grateful sigh
And steps down from the wheel.
He hears the cable chatter through the hawse.
He knows a deep contentment –
Something landsmen never feel –
An emperor, above his country's laws.

And that's the way it was . . . you really did feel like that. You see
– well, I suppose it was inevitable, looking back – I became a scowman.
We'd been working kauri up in the Solomons, my brother Fred and
I, and we'd come back pretty crook with malaria. Malaria is a horrible thing, and always, per usual, Orere was the cure-all for everything.
We were reared here together; we had been closeted together; we had
laughed together; we had played together, and we were a complete

OPPOSITE: The main boom
comes over on the scow *Rangi*
*Cliff Hawkins Collection*

fraternity. Every time we had been crook in the past, Orere always made us better, they nursed us, looked after us, fed us, and the whole family gathered round. So our one ambition, when we got really crook, was to get back to Orere. Well, we did finally get back here and we were pretty sick for about ten or twelve months with malaria, but it gradually faded away, and then we had to look around and find something to do. We had no trade or anything; we were only bushmen and bush cockies, so my brother and I drifted to the Auckland waterfront and the scowmen, and we got into scows that way.

I had to set to work and learn from the bottom up, but I happened to get hold of a helluva good skipper, and he helped me a lot. We gradually went from one boat to another and got more efficient at the game, and . . . oh, I don't know how long I was on the scows – scows and tugs and barges. Altogether about fifteen years, something like that I think.

*          *          *

You know, a scow was an abortion of a thing, really. As far as orthodox shipbuilding goes, a scow wasn't a vessel; a scow was a flat-bottomed monstrosity – flat on the bottom and flat on the deck, with a V-bow on it and a long run aft, and then rigged like a schooner or a ketch.

The first scows that were built had lee-boards to hold them on the wind, like a Dutch barge – that's where the idea came from. But it wasn't practical here, with the offshore work. The thumping of the boards was too tough, so they finally put centreboards in them. The first one was built up at Leigh in 1873 and built for a fellow called John Spencer by a shipbuilder there called Meikeljohn. That was the first scow, and she was only about sixty feet long, schooner-rigged, with lee-boards and bluff ends. But she proved such a success that they quickly evolved from that until finally not only did they build a seaworthy vessel, but they built a vessel that would really sail as well; a good safe sea vessel.

Those ships did trips across the Tasman, those big scows, and they acquitted themselves well. As far as I know, they never lost a scow on the Tasman run. And as far as working the bar harbours, the shallow coastal rivers and the open roads, and laying on the beaches, no vessel could take the part of the scow. And sail! They could sail as good as any of the Auckland schooners in the finish, and they proved that in the regattas.

The trouble was, there was never enough money put into the maintaining of them, and they were just treated like bullocks, and they weren't given a fair go. They sowed the seeds of their own destruction finally. You see, when the roads started to be pushed through, all the materials for the roads, the metal and wood for the bridges, and the steel girders and things, had to be freighted by scow, but when the roads were finished, the scows could no longer compete with the trucks, so the scows were left to rot. All the primary work that had been done by the scows was taken over by the trucks, because they could deliver stuff straight to the door of the person who required the material.

You have to realise that, on the stock and the cattle scows, the skipper and the crew had to be as good as a good back-country farmer; they had to know how to handle cattle. On the log scows they had to be as good as a bushman, because they had to know how to jack timber and how to load timber and how to stow timber. And when it came to handling sand and stuff, they had to be straight-out shifting men, with wheelbarrows and shovels, and all that type of work.

You had to be a versatile animal to be a proficient scowman. You had to be able to look after stock if they got down or got sick or anything, and you had to be a shipwright – you had to be able to plug up a leak if a scow started to leak. You could go down inside and caulk up the leaks, because it was not like a hold boat. In a deck scow you

The *Rangi,* deep laden with rimu logs, coming up the Waitemata Harbour
*NZ Herald*

can go down below and she's all open, and you can see the water tumbling in, and you can set to work and somehow block it up. So you had to be a very versatile animal to be a good scowman – you had to practically be about six tradesmen in one.

*     *     *

When it came to loading shingle, you would bring your scow in on the shingle beach and load her there broadside-on, about two hours after high water. You'd put your deck-planks out and your spreader planks and bring your wheelbarrows ashore, and shovel shingle into those barrows. And day or night, you had to go along those nine-inch spreader planks and from there up that fourteen-inch deck plank with one foot on and one off – alternately, you see; there wasn't room for two feet on that plank. And you had to be able to do that night and day and block that blasted deck up before the tide beat you. It was hard, it was really hard going, shingle-pushing, especially on a hard beach.

And the scowmen were able men all right, no doubt about that. Like the bushmen, they were hand-picked, sort of . . . they hand-picked themselves, you could say. There was no room for a no-good on a scow, nor was there in the bush. You had to be a pretty efficient animal, otherwise you were just ruled out.

Most people had nicknames then. 'Bill the Liar', for instance – well, that pretty well explains itself, doesn't it! I think he was a Norwegian – Bill Larsen was his name – but he was a great cavalier, Bill. I came into the scows as a bit of a kid, and somebody told him who I was, and he said, 'Are you Ted Ashby?'

And I said, 'Yes, I'm Ted Ashby.'

And he said, 'You're down at Orere, and your father's a big bushman?'

I said, 'Yes. Who are you?'

And he said, 'I'm Bill the Liar.'

That explained everything; he was known as 'Bill the Liar'.

I don't know where Lemonade Fred got his name from – he was another Norwegian, Fred Nordlin, and a very steady, good scowman, too. Jibboom Jack got his name because I think he stuck to the jib boom when the scow went into Castle Rock down the Bay of Plenty or something – and he got the name of Jibboom Jack. But most of them had nicknames, you know.

*     *     *

They were great men – great workers. But it gets right back, you know . . . different workers, different jobs. For the person with a bit of imagination and a sort of appreciation of nature, the feeling of being in full charge of a big scow was . . . well, as I say, you were sort of an emperor above your country's laws. I mean, you're in charge of this ship; you are in charge of the whole lot – just yourself. It's your

OPPOSITE: The versatility of the scow – *Rangi,* perfectly at home in a small tidal creek
*Tudor Collins*

own ingenuity and your own experience that you are relying upon, and your mates in their bunks are relying on, for you to do the right thing, and I think this gives you a feeling . . . a sort of proud feeling almost; a feeling of efficiency.

Here is this big lumbering scow, and you look up there and see these sails all drawing beautifully and you give a bit of a push – just perhaps a couple of spokes of the wheel – and you stick it back on the becket perhaps, and you see the ship come right on the dead course, and you know that you've done it. You know that this thing is responding to your little hand, and the vessel responds just like a well-trained dog or a well-trained bullock . . . and it gives you a sort of feeling of power, in a way. Not vicious power, but pleasurable power – controlled power – that you're complete master of what this huge thing is doing. It gives you a feeling of achievement. You forget about the storms, you forget about the tough times, expecially if it's a fine night – moonlight maybe – and the breeze is singing in the rigging and everything's drawing well, and you can leave the wheel for a while and just watch the lining-up of the mast on a star, or something. I think it is those moments that come through now and again on special trips that make you come back again and again . . .

*     *     *

You see this little graveyard on the headland here? My father and mother are buried here, and my elder sister and her husband. There's another grave, too – a little unnamed girl that our people gave permission to be buried here. I always come up here whenever I visit Orere. I don't know whether there's any sense in it, or whether it's just a nostalgic attachment, you know.

My father died in 1944, about twenty years after my mother's death, and he kept his faculties very vividly right up until the night before he died. We all got home – the whole fourteen of us got home – the night before he died, and although it was a sad occasion, it was a sort of joyous reunion as well, because I don't think we realised how close he was to dying.

I remember he was lying in bed and I went in to see him about nine o'clock, and he said, 'I'll tell you a yarn, Ted.'

I said to him, 'You aren't going to die.'

'No,' he said, 'I know I'm dying.' And he said, 'I must tell you this yarn about the bull.'

I think what really brought it to his mind was him with his family around him there, sort of setting a parallel for the story.

Well, according to his yarn, there was a farmer in Texas who reared this huge shorthorn bull, and it was going to be the best bull in the world. He was going to breed big cattle and sell them for oversized yearlings. But when the bull grew up, he found that it wasn't fertile; it couldn't produce any offspring. So to recoup his losses, he decided to take his bull round the sideshows, and exhibit it at so much a time

OPPOSITE: The scow *Ranger*, laden with shingle, making home 'wing and wing'
*Auckland Public Library*

for anybody who wanted to see the biggest bull in the world – it had grown to a three-year-old by this time.

Well, he had this bull at a sideshow one day and an old cockie came up to him on a stick and said, 'What's this about this being the biggest bull in the world?'

And the owner said, 'Well, it weighs so-and-so, and it's so-and-so high and so-and-so long, and it's definitely the biggest bull in the world.'

This old cockie said, 'Look, I'd like to have a look at that bull, but I can't afford the five dollars you're charging to get in. I'm a retired farmer myself, and I've never had a bull anywhere near as big as that. Been too busy rearing a large family, I guess. But I would like to take a look at that bull.'

'No,' said the owner, 'if I let you in, I'd have to let everybody in.'

'Well,' said the cockie, 'I reared a big family and I've worked hard all my life, and I haven't got long to live. Surely you'll let me see the bull, just for a generous gesture at the finish?'

The owner said, 'Well, how many kids did you raise, anyway?'

'I raised eighteen.'

'Well,' said the owner, 'here's five dollars. Go in and let the bull have a look at you!'

Dad told me that yarn about nine o'clock at night, and about six o'clock next morning he was dead.

*    *    *

You know, sometimes I think I've got too many memories . . . too many. They haunt you when you get older. I didn't think memories ever would. I didn't think happy memories could haunt you . . . didn't think happy memories could depress you. It's your moments in the past. You can never relive them or recapture them, that's what haunts you, and unless you fight back strong you can very easily get depressed with happy memories. People say that happy memories arc good, and it's only the miserable memories . . . but that's not right. If you could recall those incidents; if you could relive them; if you could just have a talk with those people that have passed, it would ease the situation. But I think all memories are depressing things, and it's their very remoteness and the fact that they are beyond recall that makes them almost unbearable sometimes.

I have a sort of nostalgic verse – just an emotional thing for the family really, with no poetic or literary merit . . . just for the family, and this graveyard:

ORERE: YEARS AFTER

There's a stretch of sand and shingle, there are rocks washed by the tide,
A creek runs crystal clear to the sea.
There's a graveyard on the clifftop, with a straggling fence beside,
Near a waterfall that tumbles endlessly.

There are strangers on our beaches, there are cars parked on the shore,
Transistors can be heard both night and day,
And in place of soft-voiced cattle, I can hear their fiendish rattle,
As outboard motors streak across the bay.

I listen for the echoes of the axe strokes from the hill,
The bullocks with their old Kentucky bells.
How I'd like to sense once more, from the stockyard on the shore,
The sound of barking dogs, the branding smells.

I could walk up 'neath the tree groves to the old house on the hill,
With the kitchen windows wide to meet the day,
Where oft I'd see my mother stand, with a flour bag in her hand,
To lift a batch of 'Boy's Cake' from a tray.

The old house hasn't changed much, though the big wood stove has gone,
And no more I'll see clean chaff sacks on the floor,
Smell the drying clothes, feel the mud between my toes,
Nor will sister 'Lalla' greet me at the door.

They are gone, but not forgotten, those scenes from yesteryears,
But their memories are with us here to stay,
And oft too vividly it seems, they wake us from our dreams,
To take us back to scenes of yesterday.

## First broadcast 1 July 1982

# 10 Men of Kauri Country

The kauri bushmen of the North, remembered by
Joe Gasparich.

*Joe Gasparich was born in Dargaville in 1890. Two years later the
family moved to Kaihu, where he received his schooling – not only
within the confines of the classroom, but in a wider social sense, in
the kauri bush camps of the North.*

*His father worked for E. Mitchelson, Minister of Public Works in
the Atkinson administration, and owner of a group of stores scattered
through the Northern Wairoa district. Timber and kauri gum were also
handled by these trading establishments, and through his father's work,
and his own developing interest, Joe Gasparich came into contact with
that unique breed of men, the kauri bushmen.*

*He observed them with a keen eye – but he did not join them as
a bushman. His father had decided that Joe Gasparich would become
a teacher, and with the system then in force, this entailed the passing
of a 'Candidate's Examination', and a period spent as a probationary
teacher. Joe Gasparich taught first at Kaihu, and then at Te Kopuru.
At the age of fifteen he was in charge of a class of forty-five, some
of the pupils older than himself. He taught in various schools in the
North, fitted in a period at the then Teachers' Training College, and
was on the staff of Whangarei's Horahora School at the outbreak of
the First World War. Enlisting in the 15th North Auckland Company,
he was given the rank of sergeant: 'Seven bob a day – three bob a day
better than private's pay.'*

*He was wounded in Gallipoli, and received later wounds in France,
on the Western Front. After the war he returned to his profession,
rising to the inspectorate level.*

*Now in his nineties, Joe Gasparich still retains in extraordinary detail
the memories of life in the northern kauri bush at the turn of the
century.*

I have been in the camp at night – on still, calm, dark nights with no
moon. I've walked out the camp door and left the men sitting around
the fire; walked away from the blaze of light and the hum of voices,
some distance from the shanty itself, and stood and listened to the
silence.

I've listened, and perhaps I'd hear the trickle of water way in the
distance, of a stream rippling over the stones under the forest trees,
and every now and then the morepork would give his nightly call. I
have heard a bush rat run across the dry leaves lying on the ground,
and I've actually heard a single leaf drop on to the forest floor.

I wish I could explain that clearly . . . and I wish it were possible

The Aoroa Timber Mill of E. Mitchelson & Company in the Northern Wairoa – a view published round the turn of the century
*Auckland Institute and Museum*

for people today to experience that same thing in the great kauri forests of the North.

It was most remarkable – but it is no more.

*        *        *

I suppose I'm one of the most fortunate people living in New Zealand at this time, as far as being able to really know what a kauri stand was like.

The forests with which I was most particularly familiar were those on the slopes of the hills enclosing the Kaihu Valley, which I entered as a small boy with my parents when I was about two or three years of age – that would be away back in 1892. These forests – the kauri stands that I learned to know so well – were untouched by the hand of man, except for one that was being worked at that time on one side of the valley.

One of my first recollections is of hearing a great tree fall, and of seeing the swaying of the tree as it crashed to the ground. Later, I went down to the landings and saw the great logs where they'd been placed ready to be taken away by train. When I grew a little older, and was able to get about, like most boys I suppose, I was very inquisitive and wanted to see what was what, so it wasn't long before I was in the middle of the kauri forest itself. There I saw not only the trees before they were touched, but the whole process of taking the timber – the men who did the work, how they lived, and everything connected with it. And to me as a boy, it was all most intensely interesting and utterly absorbing in every way.

So I was brought up in an atmosphere of kauri timber, of the men who wielded axes and crosscut saws and mauls and wedges and timberjacks and so on – the crude instruments of labour of that time. I learned to know the men as they were, and I learned to marvel at their skill, their ability to improvise, their ability to master every possible situation.

*          *          *

There was just one simple great mass of trees. They were terrific. I don't know how many people are familiar with the kauri tree – a single kauri tree – but these trees usually stood up straight, absolutely straight up out of the ground. The great trunks were of varying sizes, of course, according to the age of the tree, but the biggest of them were up to sixteen, seventeen feet in diameter, and they went up in the air, some of them thirty, forty feet to the first branch. Others, more slender trees down in the bottom of the gullies, were as high as a hundred and twenty feet to the first branch, and the trunks were as clean and straight as could be, covered with a thick grey-green bark all round that gave them their distinctive appearance.

Those trees in a pure kauri stand stood in their hundreds, in thousands, packed closely together; in many cases so closely together that their branches intermingled above and almost completely obliterated

Kaihu, 1918
*Auckland Institute and Museum*

Kauri bush at Kaihu, 1918
*Auckland Institute and Museum*

the sunlight. Shut it right out, so that once you were in the forest you couldn't see the sun at all, except in places here and there where a shaft of light would come down through the branches and light up the forest. You have seen, I suppose, pictures of shafts of light coming through cathedral windows – well, it was something similar in the forest. The canopy might be fifty or sixty feet overhead, so that the whole place would be completely shut in, and once you were right in the middle of the forest you were completely isolated from the rest of the world.

Now these trees were packed so closely together that in many cases, when the bushfellers came to take the timber from a pure kauri stand, they worked the bush on a face. Right in a face, so that they went along in a continuous face until they reached the end of the job. And in some places the kauri trees were so closely packed together that there was no timber of any other type that could be used as skids and stringers and landing places, and so on. Then it would be necessary to use the smaller kauris, the young trees known as rikkers. When the job was over, these would be lifted and taken away, because they were too valuable to leave, even in those days, to lie rotting on the ground.

The men who worked them were a distinctive class, and they were extraordinary in many respects. I learned to know them very well. I knew them not only as bushmen, I knew them as members of the society in which I mixed, and I knew them subsequently quite familiarly when I went away to the 1914–18 war. They were always big strong healthy men, and they were tremendous workers.

Of course, they had to be, because they were expected to commence work in the bush at 7 a.m. They worked through without any morning break until midday – five hours – then they had a break for lunch, and a smoke, and then they started again at one and worked through until six, when they knocked off and went back to camp. They worked steadily during those ten hours; they were utterly loyal to one another and utterly loyal to their boss, their employer.

It was wholly a team job. If a man were particularly capable with an axe or a saw, and could do more work more efficiently than the man next to him, he was honoured and respected. I've known of cases where men were working out in the bush a long way back, and an accident would occur. Everybody downed tools and went to help, and I've known them walk all night and next day through a trackless bush carrying an injured man on an improvised stretcher, made of poles and sacks or anything at all that they could get. A team of eight would set out, four men at a time to the stretcher, and they would work in relays until they got the man out. They never stopped; they kept going, no matter how tired or how heavy the burden. They stuck to it – and they did exactly the same when they went to war. They were absolutely trustworthy, and I myself had the utmost confidence in them as soldiers. They could do anything at any time. They never gave in, they never grumbled, they never complained. When there was a job to do, they did it. No matter how heavy the job, how rough it was, what sacrifices it demanded, they were ready to do it, and they didn't think anything of it. It was part of the job, just as it was in the bush.

The way in which the bush people – the bushmen and their wives – stuck to one another is shown by the way they rallied round in the case of a family that was in need. A common method of raising money was called a 'basket social'. A hall would be used for the function, and the people of the district would be invited to bring along baskets. Now these baskets were made of any material at all at hand, and it was remarkable the ingenuity and workmanship shown in making them. A common material was supplejack, but anything out of the bush in the way of fernery and so on, and anything about the homes, went into the making of fancy baskets. In the basket, its maker put a supper, the food cooked at home – and of course it was always the best that could be produced.

Now on the night of the basket social, all the baskets would be handed in, and there were no names on any of them, so presumably nobody knew who was the owner of the basket. They would then be auctioned, and the purchaser of a basket would have the pleasure and the honour of having supper with the provider of the basket.

Well, some of the boys would be wheezed up beforehand, and the competition would be funny – especially when the auctioneer was a local wag or wit, specially selected for the fun he could create. Now I've seen them pay twelve or fourteen pounds in those days for a basket, just to make sure that the girl of a boy's choice saw that he really meant business. And when you come to consider that those bushmen worked all those long hours for two pounds ten or two pounds fifteen a week of fifty-eight hours, that was a considerable sum. Every penny of that would go to the family in need, and I've seen as much as a hundred and twenty pounds collected from a small community like that. Well, that was a year's wage.

Usually the men lived in a camp on the job. The preparation of the camp, and the provision of accommodation, was the responsibility of the contractor, and he'd build it in the most suitable position to enable the men to get to work quickly in the morning and to get home again. Then the camp had to be near running water and an ample supply of firewood, and that sort of thing.

It was usually made of trunks of sapling trees – that built the framework – and the walls were made from leaves of the nikau palm. When they were properly fixed to the framework, the nikau fronds were absolutely waterproof; not only that, they gave a peculiar snugness to the whole atmosphere of the place. I have slept many times in those bush camps, and I was always conscious of being very comfortable indeed.

Inside the camp, the poles were again used to provide sleeping accommodation, and that was provided down the sides of the camp. There would be two tiers along the sides of perhaps six bunks each – three above three – and at the end would be another two at least, so that there'd be say sixteen. These bunks were all made of poles cut from the bush, and the mattress was a climbing plant called mingimingi. It was a climber – it climbed up other trees – and the stems all twisted one with another. They were wiry, and particularly when they were dry, they had a springiness not unlike steel. It would be cut, dried, and placed in the bottom of the bed and covered over with sacks, and it gave a beautiful mattress on which to sleep; always airy and dry, and quite comfortable. That's where the men slept. They kept their clothes in boxes and trunks under the bunks, with others hanging from nails or pegs.

Down the middle of the camp would be a long table, with wooden seats running the full length, and up above would be the lamp. The table was either covered with what was termed 'oilcloth', or left in its natural state and scrubbed clean. Here the men had their meals and

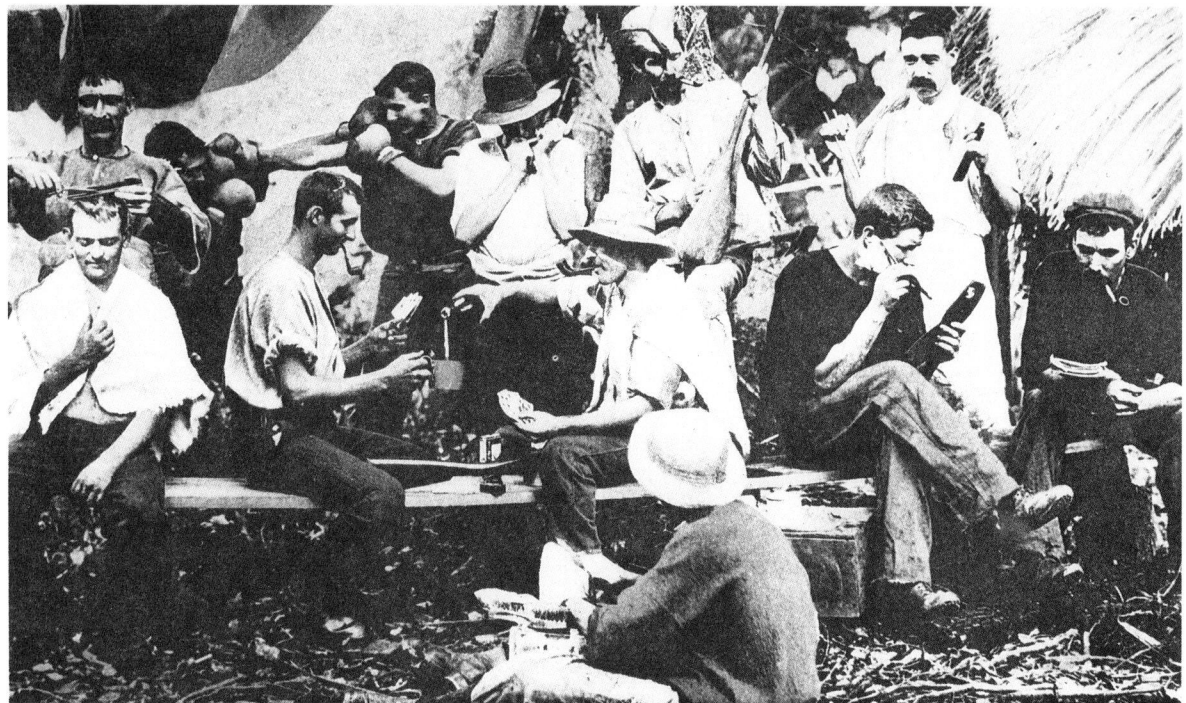

Sunday at a bush camp in the
Northern Wairoa. This carefully
posed scene was copied from
an early postcard.
*Auckland Institute and Museum*

A kauri bush camp at
Kirikopuni
*Auckland Institute and Museum*

wrote letters and played games at night under the light of the lamp. At the end of the table was usually a big block cut from kauri, like a butcher's block, and on this meats were cut up and prepared for cooking, and there the food was placed when it was dished out to the men.

At the end of the building would be a great wide chimney, usually made of corrugated iron sheets on the inside of a wooden framework, again built from poles. Right across the fireplace there would be a great beam, well above the flames. From this hung down chains with hooks, and on the hooks would hang boilers for the cooking of the food.

The fire would be on the ground, and would be made of logs five and six feet long, piled one on the other, and there was always plenty of firewood. The cook always had an offsider whose business it was to keep the fire going. On the ground in front of the fire would be the great camp ovens; these were twenty-four inches wide and eight or nine inches deep, standing on short legs. Coals of fire were shovelled under the camp oven or poured on the top to give the necessary heat, and that's where the cook did his baking. I've never eaten bread the equal of camp-oven bread, and it was famous of course to those who knew it. The cook made it from his own yeast, made in the bush.

The cook was one of the most important members of a bush gang. Indeed, a gang of bushfellers would not be able to function properly unless it was well fed, and in many cases men simply left the job if the food didn't satisfy them. So the cook had to be very carefully chosen, and indeed some cooks were so well known throughout the North that men actually sought employment in bushes and on contracts where the cook was looked on with great favour.

Now the food was always plentiful, and there was a remarkable variety, too. The meals were substantial. Breakfast had to be a good solid meal, and there was always porridge - oatmeal porridge - for those who liked it. There was always plenty of toast, great slabs cut off those tremendous loaves baked in the camp oven, with plenty of butter. There was always a meat dish of one kind or another - it could be bacon. Eggs . . . well, there were plenty of eggs, because a big mob of hens always ran around a bush camp, so there were great basins of eggs in the bush camps I frequented as a boy. There would be a meat dish - fried chops, steaks and so on - and also stews and other forms of cooked-up meats, so that the men went out early in the morning well prepared for the solid day's work.

They took their lunches with them in most cases. They also drank gallons of tea, as you can imagine, and they boiled the billy at midday and had their smoko and ate meat sandwiches, cold pies of various kinds, plus an astonishing variety of cakes. Scones and cakes. Now, bush cooks that I knew were tremendous fellows at preparing sweets of various kinds - cakes and so on. They made sponges, and the most marvellous pastry - puff pastry. The camp ovens were deep, as I say, and I've known the cook roll out his puff pastry as thin as paper and put it into the bottom of the oven, and that would literally rise right up to the lid. That was just one of the fancy things a good cook could do.

And then when the men came back in the evening, they had the main meal of the day. That is when the joints would be prepared – roast beef, wild pork occasionally, roast mutton – that kind of thing. Occasionally, some of the fowls would be prepared. And then there would be great pies of various kinds, plus vegetables.

Now here was the deficiency, because fresh vegetables – and fresh fruit incidentally – were not readily available in the bush in the North. So the vegetables with the main meal of the day were potatoes, pumpkin, swede turnips, and vegetables of that type, which could be preserved for a considerable time.

The principal sweet provided, and the most favoured by the men, was the boiled pudding with a base of suet, and there you had a great variety. I remember gorging myself as a boy on big jam rolls, but in addition there were custards of all sorts – jellies and blancmanges and things of that nature – and plenty of jam. So you can see there was a very considerable variety of food available for the men. And they deserved it, for the work that they did.

*     *     *

You know, the men weren't rough characters in the usual sense of the term. In the main, you could say they were gentlemanly men – gentlemanly by instinct. If their manners were not identical with the so-called drawing-room manners of today, it's due to the fact that if you put them in modern society they'd feel out of it altogether, and entirely clumsy. But they were always actuated by the most generous impulses altogether, and you only had to be amongst them to know that.

You could see by the way they spent their evenings. For instance, after that hard day's work it wouldn't be very long before they wanted to turn in. But before that, and after the table was cleared, some would settle down to write, and others would bring out a pack of cards. Euchre and crib were the favourite games, and occasionally they played poker. Never for very high stakes though, because the majority of them would be married men, and they wouldn't gamble much. Others again would sit in the great fireplace, particularly on the cold winter nights, with the blaze warming the whole camp, and there they would just sit around and yarn.

They read. They read a good deal. There was always a good supply of books in a camp. It wasn't what one would term classical literature, although I remember one man telling me how interested he'd become in Charles Dickens. He'd been introduced to it in a bush camp, and he said, 'My word, he's a good writer, isn't he!'

Then the *Auckland Weekly News* was read. The *Weekly News* came up regularly, and that contained a whole week's news at a time. It was almost a kind of Bible in the North.

But they were wholesome men altogether. On a Saturday, when they knocked off at four o'clock, they would tidy themselves up and dress themselves more appropriately for the weekend, then off they'd go to the nearest village. There would usually be a local pub in the township and there they'd congregate and enjoy their pints of beer. Some of them occasionally overindulged a bit, but the majority of them were very temperate in their drinking, as they were in their other habits.

In those days the customary dress was the old Blucher boots – very heavy Blucher boots – and Tairoa trousers, which were made of a kind of heavy white duck; these were tied with bowyangs below the knees. Above that they wore flannel shirts. Now these shirts were decorated with all sorts of fanciful patterns and all sorts of coloured wools, and I believe there was a considerable amount of competition among the men as to who could show the most colour and so on. These characters generally completed their outfit by wearing a hat, and this was generally broad brimmed and white in colour, and made out of bleached and finely-woven kiekie, a bush climber with flax-like leaves.

When they went away on holiday, the bushmen were especially particular about their clothing. Actually, the bush camps were a source of income to certain of the tailors living in the city. These tailors would make trips around the various bush camps every year, taking orders, and it was customary for a bushman to have a new tailormade suit once a year. And when you think of the number of times in a year he would be able to wear that, living in the bush and so on, that was quite a considerable amount of money to spend on clothes.

Generally, they would spend their holidays in the city. A man working in the bush would have his keep of course, and he would be paid about two pounds ten a week on average, so that by the end of the year he would have at least a hundred pounds coming to him. During the year, the bulk of the money earned would stay in the hands of the contractor until the bushman drew a cheque for the lot, and possibly he'd spend the greater part of it on his holiday. That applied to the single men only, of course; for the married men that wouldn't be possible.

Well, those were the bushmen of the kauri forests. Good men. Fair men and tough men. They had to be tough, because it was a strenuous business, and the bush certainly wasn't a place for weaklings, physically, or mentally either.

The job was all done under contract of course, and the contractor, who was the boss, provided everything in the way of accommodation and all that sort of thing – and all the material, the trucks and so on. But the bushmen had their personal tools, so that each man had his own particular axe, and he cared for it and it was one of his most prized possessions.

Well, you can imagine that a new job was commencing. The work of felling was in the hands of the crosscutters, and usually they were specialists at this type of work, and did it under subcontract – they were paid so much per hundred feet of timber cut. They would select a tree to be cut, and the first thing they would then do would be to examine the tree to see where the greater weight leaned. Very rarely was there a lean on the trunk of a tree. They stood straight up, but the heads quite frequently had more branches on one side than another, and that would decide which way the tree would fall. Sometimes they had to fell the tree against the lean, which was a different proposition, but fell a normal tree they would scarf the front of it; that's to say, they would first cut into the tree on the side they wanted it to fall.

They would first rig up a platform to enable them to have a flat stance, and on top of it they put trunks of punga fern, because they gave a grip to the feet, and they didn't slide. They had to be very careful about this stance. Then they would start in, one a right-handed axeman, the other a left-handed axeman. The scarf was cut like a horizontal 'V' angling into the tree, with the base of the cut horizontal, and the top slanting down at an angle of about thirty degrees.

Now the distance they went in depended upon the tree itself. They had to make sure that they went in sufficiently far to enable them to get the centre of equilibrium on the right side, so that the tree would eventually fall that way. If they didn't cut the scarf sufficiently deep, the tree would just simply sit back on the stump.

Then again there was another difficulty, especially with young trees. If they didn't scarf sufficiently deep before they started sawing the tree at the back, the tree would very likely split – and that split might run any distance from half-way to three-quarters of the way up the trunk. Then the tree would swing on the standing, uncut section and very likely swing right around before it came crashing down, and they wouldn't know where it was going. Now that was a terribly dangerous thing, and they prevented it by every means in their power, but it was very, very rarely that they were caught out, because they knew the tricks of trees.

Once the scarf had been cut, the men moved round to the back of the tree and cut off the bark, because this contained the kauri sap, which was very sticky. If that stuck to the saw, it prevented the free movement of the blade, and they always kept with them a tin containing kerosene and animal fat; this was put on the saw occasionally to counteract the effect of the gum.

At the back of the tree they would leave a couple of inches of bark and then drive an axe in to rest the saw on. Then the saw would be brought up to the horizontal and they would start crosscutting, again a left-hander and a right-hander. They would keep a steady rhythm going that looked deceptively easy and hid the power that went into each draw of the saw. And then at last the tree would begin to lift. Because of the scarf in front the weight would be well over, and presently they would see the trunk lifting and starting to move, and then there would be the call 'Before!' and it would ring right through the bush, and everybody would be ready and get out of the way, and they would pull out the saw and get back.

Cutting a scarf, preparatory to
felling a kauri. This photograph
was taken at Kirikopuni by A. N.
Breckon in 1919.
*Auckland Institute and Museum*

Kauri, scarfed and partly cut
through with a cross-cut saw
*Ted Ashby*

Not much danger normally, but sometimes these great trees came down with such a tremendous crash, such a terrific weight, that they would crash into smaller trees, and branches would come flying back at a terrific rate. If you were in the way and got a belt with one of those – well, it meant the stretcher. And then, with the tree down, they would get to work and measure off the length of log that could be handled. Again, they would cut the bark off around the circumference of the tree to prevent the saw binding with sap, and they would cut the log off. They might get one, two, or even three logs out of the one trunk, according to its length and size.

As I say, it was sometimes necessary to fell a tree against its lean, or natural bias. In that case, when they had started to put the saw in at the back of the tree, the tree would sit down on the cut. As soon as it did that, they called on the aid of wedges and mauls – they generally had a dozen or eighteen wedges on hand.

They would put the wedge into the cut and start hitting it with the maul, or sometimes two mauls one after the other, as hard as they could go. It was an astonishing thing, wedging a great tree. Heaven knows how heavy it might be, because you can imagine a tree maybe fourteen feet across the butt, towering up thirty, forty, maybe fifty feet to that great head up there. All that enormous mass was sitting back on the stump, and here was a puny man with a maul and wedges, and he had to lift that tree up.

His aim was to open the cut, lift the tree up . . . lift the tree up . . . lift the tree up, just by driving wedges into the cut. Now this was accomplished because every time the wedge was struck it sent a tremor up the trunk . . . the slightest tremor; how small, we can't calculate.

Wedging a kauri. The diameter of this tree is too great for the cross-cut saw in use, and it has been scarfed at the sides to give the sawyers room to work. Wedges keep the cut open, to allow the saw freedom of movement.
*Tudor Collins*

That tremor would go through the wood and eventually it would travel from the stump right up to the tip of the branch. Almost imperceptibly the tree would move and lift a little bit, and before it could sit back there would be another blow from the maul, and another one. The tremor would be the tiniest fraction of an inch during the first blows, but gradually it would grow, and as it swayed the cut on the stump would open. Perhaps a foot of sway on the tip would be only the merest fraction of an inch on the stump, but nevertheless that was sufficient to allow the wedge to go in. Now I've seen those trees sit back so much on the stump that the wedges were absolutely buried in the cut. I've seen a wedge driven in to its full thickness of an inch and a quarter, and the cut absolutely closed, and wood squeezed over the wedge.

Sometimes it would take hours and hours to wedge a tree up. But eventually, up it would go, and they would shift the top sufficiently far to get the centre of equilibrium over the scarf, and sooner or later she would go and the tree would crash.

*        *        *

Then of course the log had to be prepared for transport to its ultimate destination, and to start that, the log was now handed over to another gang. First of all they tapered one end, rounding the log so that it would be able to slide over impediments in its path, because it had to be dragged along the ground.

Now these men were called 'snipers', and having sniped the log, they then made two cuts, one on each side of the log opposite each other, right into the rounded part – the sniped end. That was for the purpose of holding a heavy chain which attached the log to the yoked bullocks, who would pull it out, hauling it along a rough track in the bush.

They might use fourteen, sixteen, sometimes eighteen bullocks, and these were big, strong, well-trained beasts. They were remarkable animals, and quite docile. Well-behaved, good-natured things they were, and they worked away and answered the demands of the bullocky, no trouble at all. They were yoked in pairs – the yokes were great clumsy things, and as a boy I thought them quite inadequate really for the job the bullocks were expected to do. They were made of timber, very heavy, and they had iron bands or 'bows' that went under the bullocks' necks and up through the wood of the yoke to fasten them in. Now these were put over the necks of the beasts so that the bullocks had to strain against the iron bows on their bare skin, and as a boy I always thought they were hard on the poor animals. However, the bullocks showed no sign of discomfort. They were hardy animals, and they worked with a will.

The bullocky worked them purely by word of command. He carried a long-handled whip, but at most it would reinforce a command with a touch on the flank. No bullocky ever whipped his beasts – you just couldn't work them that way.

It was particularly interesting to watch the leaders. The pair in front were the leaders; they answered commands immediately, and the bullocky could get them to do all sorts of things. At the back of the team were the 'chainers'. Now these were stocky beasts, because if you can imagine the line of pull, it sloped down from the bullock yokes to the log; consequently the configuration of a team was important. Leaders were tall, upstanding beasts, and the stockier animals were placed at the rear, to reduce the angle of pull from their yokes to the load.

The chainers had a heavier job to do than the others and theirs was the dangerous job, because if a log happened to get out of control going down a slope, they would be the first to catch it. I marvelled at the manner in which they were ready to take evasive action, because they seemed to sense somehow when a log was misbehaving itself. They would know by the strain. When they were moving they would know when they had the full strain, and when they had to put their full exertion on, but if the strain eased they would know something was wrong, and they would be ready for it.

It was astonishing the tremendous loads they could pull out of the bush along the ground – 'snigging', that was called. In many places the logs were brought out on what was called a 'cat', which was short for catamaran. A catamaran was a big heavy sledge made of bush timber – yes, everything made of bush timber. Usually the runners were the trunks of young rata trees, because they were long, could bend, and were tough. They were strong, they could be readily shaped, and the natural shape of the front of them would be curved up so that they would be able to slide over obstacles. The bushmen would build a special road for them – a corduroy road, or 'skidded' road, as we used to call it.

To make this they would cut taraire or tawa, anything up to about eight or ten or twelve inches through and about ten or twelve feet wide, and lay them horizontally across the track, like railway sleepers, and the sledge would slide over them. Usually they were helped by the bullocky's mate, or offsider, who would go along with the most evil-smelling tin of fat, which he would have melted on the fire before he went out. The stench of it would go right through the bush and the blowflies would be around in thousands, but he would go along with an old mop and spread the fat on the skids where the runners would slide, to assist the bullocks and move their load along more easily.

\*          \*          \*

Those bullockies were marvellous men. They were specialists in their own right, and some of the bullockies north of Auckland were well known throughout the whole district for their skills. The bullockies themselves didn't work all day, because the men were not able to cut enough logs ordinarily to keep a bullock team working all day. So usually the team started in the morning about ten and finished in the afternoon about five, and then the bullockies would unyoke the beasts and turn them loose in the bush.

There were some trees that were particularly liked by the animals – they enjoyed eating the leaves – and the bushmen would cut these down and allow the animals to graze on them during the night. Particularly on a winter's morning, the bullocky or his offsider would be up before daylight to collect the animals – sometimes from some distance – so that they could be yoked for the day's work. As a rule, they were assisted by a dog, or two dogs, but in order to know where the animals were they also prepared the night before, by putting metal bells around the necks of two or three of the quieter beasts. These bells would tinkle as the animals grazed, and when the bullocky and his dog came through the bush in the morning looking for the beasts, the bells would guide them.

But that was the cause of the bullockies being very unfavourably inclined to one of the loveliest birds in the bush – the tui. No bullocky ever loved a tui, for the simple reason that these birds are great imitators, and they would often lead those bullockies astray. The bullocky would follow what he thought was the sound of one of his bells, and instead, find a tui up a tree – so the bird came to be cursed in the fluent language for which bullockies were peculiarly noted. And certainly, to hear the bullocky at his best was something to be remembered.

*    *    *

Now the bullocks weren't the only method they used to get the logs out. In some cases steam engines were employed, or locomotives running on a bush railway, or 'tram'. And, of course, they also used running water. They used streams where they built dams to hold the water, and when the dams were tripped the logs would be carried down with the rush of water.

The most commonly used method of getting the logs out to a railway line or river was by means of the wooden tram, where usually draught-horses would be used. In these cases the tramlines themselves would be made of wood, and the springers and sleepers cut from the timber growing round about. The rails themselves usually came from some sawmill or other – long rails of wood, usually about four inches wide and three inches deep, and as long as it was possible to get them. Rimu was the favoured wood, because it stood up to the wear, and could be bent as needed for the shaping of the railway.

And on these were the timber trucks – special timber trucks, solidly built, with four great steel wheels, deeply flanged. The running part of the wheel occupied the full width of the rail – nearly four inches – and the flange would be at least two and a half inches deep, so that the trucks would not jump off the rails. In most of the working areas there would be a fall down to the landing – the landing would be down in the bottom of a valley. The horses would pull the empty trucks up, and when the logs were loaded they would be run down by gravity. Now the trucks were controlled, with their tremendous loads, by each truck having a wooden brake. This was worked by a handle on the side, with the operator lying full length on the truck under the log, where he could lean over and turn the handle to tighten or loosen the brakes, as required.

I remember one line in particular. They built it over watercourses and through cuttings and then gave it a straight run down to the floor of the valley, before letting the log run round the curve to a railway line, where the logs had to be loaded into railway trucks. And to maintain this steady grade, it was necessary for them to build a bush viaduct, up near the top of the hill. Now here was an astonishing thing, because, if I remember correctly, this bush viaduct would be more than fifty feet above the floor of the gully, and a hundred yards in length. All this was built on an angle of roughly twenty-five to thirty degrees, running up to the top of the hill, and it was all made of bush timber. The only equipment that those bush engineers had were the saw and axe, maul and wedges, timber jacks, adzes, and that sort of thing. For the uprights they used kauri rikkers; they calculated the lengths, the bushmen themselves; they cut them the right size, shaped them the right size, put them into the plates on the ground, set the plates firmly in the ground, put the tops on, and raised the uprights to hold the viaduct in place by means of hand winches.

Having got it up there, they anchored it firmly on wire cables, and then put on the different sets, preparatory to putting on the stringers. Then they brought the stringers down. These had all been cut ready, and somehow they got them down by means of hand winches and improvised cranes. Once again, they used kauri rikkers as cranes, and

The booms at Kaihu in the 1890s
*Auckland Institute and Museum*

ABOVE: A five-horse team hauls a kauri log on a bush tram in the Northern
Wairoa
*Auckland Institute and Museum*

BELOW: The opening of the Siberia bush tramway, Northern Wairoa – from
an early postcard
*Auckland Institute and Museum*

blocks and tackle to pull these stringers up, lower them down, and get them in position. Then they put the bush sleepers across and fixed the rails to them, working forty to fifty feet above the ground. Finally they anchored the whole lot and made it firm.

They brought out over fifty million feet of kauri over that viaduct, and there was not a single accident.

On the other side of the ridge, the line followed a bit of a stream. They had to bring the timber right down the slope to the tramline at the bottom of the gully, and that wound and twisted and turned, so instead of the tramway having a straight run, they had it curved all over the place. But the cable pulling the loaded trucks still had to be kept in the middle of the rails, otherwise they would never come up. In order to do that, they had blocks cut from trees, and they fixed these firmly in the bed of the tramline. Now, the front face of this block was on an angle of forty-five degrees, and in that face they set a special type of pulley. It would be about a foot wide, with very deep flanges to hold the wire cable, and that was bolted right through the block and through the bed of the tramline to hold it firmly.

And it's marvellous – the strain that must have been on those blocks, and on those pulleys and that rope – and yet there was never any trouble. It was an amazing piece of engineering, and it showed the versatility of these men, showed how they worked things out. They had no knowledge of mathematics or anything like that, and no university engineering skills, yet they were able to do that sort of thing. Marvellous engineers, they were.

They were a breed unto themselves. Their memorial is the houses and schools and boats, and towns even, built from the timber they felled . . . the remains of dams, or skidded roads that can still be found in the North. And of course the memories of a few like myself, who had the privilege of knowing them.

**First broadcast 31 January 1974**

# 11 Childhood at the Pass

Nancy Sutherland recalls her girlhood in French Pass, an isolated settlement on Tasman Bay, opposite D'Urville Island.

*Even in her seventies, Nancy Sutherland has lost none of the extraordinary energy which has spurred her through a full, often tumultuous life. She has a hard-earned reputation as a vociferous campaigner for many causes, particularly those concerning the health and welfare of women and children. Over the years, the correspondence columns of Canterbury newspapers have been peppered with the sharply seasoned bite of her letters, aimed mostly at what she saw as a self-satisfied Establishment, or unmoving bureaucracy. Typical of her causes was a sustained campaign for daily hospital visiting, at a time when parents were permitted only a single weekly visit to children under five years of age.*

Nancy Sutherland
*Sally Symes*

*After education in New Zealand and Australia, Nancy trained as a primary-school teacher in the 1930s, specialising in physical education. She ran a studio in Wellington, teaching physical education, dance and swimming. She also taught physical education to the inmates of the Wellington Girls' Borstal. Her interests soon widened to encompass a variety of causes and organisations – Parents' Centre, the Family Planning Association, the Family Life Education Council . . .*

*The mother of five children (including two sets of twins), she was ahead of her time as a proponent of natural childbirth and home birth, and spent some months in England attending an antenatal course run by world authorities Margaret Morris and Minnie Randall.*

*Her sporting accomplishments are no less remarkable. She represented Victoria and Otago Universities and Teachers' Colleges in swimming, tennis and hockey; she was one of the first New Zealand women to receive the Diploma of the Royal Life Saving Society, and was the first person to swim from French Pass to D'Urville Island.*

*'Tom-boy' is too prosaic a description of Nancy during her childhood at French Pass. Her attitude, often aggressive or rebellious, sprang naturally from the values and way of life of the tiny, isolated community she was born into – a community of farmers and fishermen whose survival, even in the 1900s, still depended largely on their ability to come to terms with wind, wave and weather, and cope with the demands of a life little removed from the pioneering phase.*

We lived a barbaric existence as a tribe of children at the Pass, always at odds with adults.

'We were as a band of brothers j'ined,/One in heart and one in mind' – I'll never forget that poem we learnt at primary school. But we were against all adults. I've always been *bursting* with energy, *bursting* with aggression, *bursting* with hate. Hate for everything. Hate for the System. Hate for what it's done for people, whether they like it or not. Hate for decision-makers. It started with hate for my father. I became a Labour supporter because Dad was so conservative, and yet he was a man of the most incredible integrity and hard work.

Grandad Webber had rather grandiose ideas. He was a sailor and a sea captain, and very peppery. His mother, so he said, was a descendant of French Huguenots who crossed the Channel when they had to flee. Her name was Leah, and I believe she was illiterate, but *he* seemed French. During his children's schooldays he kept a house in Nelson as well as the farm at the Pass, but he gave little attention to the Pass property; he went off in his precious sailing ships. He had a little launch which the Maoris named the *Namu,* which means 'mosquito' or 'sandfly'. She had a counter stern, and she was so little that when you went through the Pass against the tide the counter stern went under the water, you know. You were always very close to the water when you went through the Pass in the *Namu.* She was kauri-hulled, of course.

*Astrolabe* takes French Pass – a de Sainson engraving from the account of Dumont d'Urville's voyages published in Paris in 1832
*Alexander Turnbull Library*

Then, some time later, he bought the *Anaru,* and he put in – instead of the pop-pop-pop-pop petrol engine – he put in the new Twigg – the marvellous Twigg engine! That's the *Anaru*; she was kauri-hulled too, and she was a beautiful boat . . . I've got pictures of her here. And she was his pride and joy, and caused his death of course, because he was told by somebody that you can always clean your engine better when it's going, but of course Grandad was bloody careless and never did up his cuffs, and he was caught in the shaft. He should have known, because one of his best dogs got her tail caught in the shaft, and it was his quick reaction by whipping out his sheath-knife and cutting off her tail that saved the life of Gyp, who was a marvellous dog – we loved her.

But you know, Grandad was very, very dapper. He kept his body and his appearance as shipshape as he expected us to take care of the dinghies, for instance. If we took up the beach a dinghy that had been tied to an anchor or bollard or something, and took the painter and pulled it into the dinghy covered in sand, well, he'd tip us over the side, because he just didn't approve of that kind of behaviour. He coiled his ropes on the deckhouse and things . . . so that we got a kind of feeling of order from Grandad that we never got anywhere else.

But we were against all adults, as I say – except possibly our mothers. Mothers were like comfortable armchairs, and when you had a bad cut, or felt sick or anything, you knew perfectly well the place to go to was Mum. And when we wanted food, and when we wanted comfort of one kind or another, it was always Mum. But apart from that – apart from the mothers of the family – we were literally 'as a band of brothers joined', against all.

I wasn't close to my father. I was not. My family was; I was not. Mother never learnt to milk, and they never forgave her for that; her

Arthur Cruikshank Elmslie, whaler and gentleman, and George William Wallace Webber, aged five years; an 1880 photograph by W. Stuart. George Webber was Nancy's father.
*Nancy Sutherland*

The *Anaru* in French Pass
*Nancy Sutherland*

The wedding of Nancy's
parents, Ethel Amy Crump and
George William Wallace Webber,
in 1900
*Nancy Sutherland*

mother-in-law never forgave her for that. She was not a good bread-
or pastry-maker, and of course they all were. Dad was born a fortnight before Gran turned seventeen, and they were geared to be self-
sufficient, but Mother came from a rather cultured family. She played
the violin; she had golden hair; she had a lovely contralto voice; she
was one of the Crump Orchestra in Nelson – all of them Crumps. Her
brother played the cello; she played the violin; Aunt Lily played the
piano and the organ, and so on. Before the days of any outside entertainment in Nelson, the Crump Orchestra used to be asked to perform
at different functions. As a family they always practised together, and
even Uncle Tom Crump – who became a lawyer and Mayor of Eltham
– Uncle Tom played the violin. When they were young he had to super-
vise Mother's practice, and he would pay her a penny to say nothing
while he got out the window and went playing with his friends while
she went on with her practice. Darling old Uncle Tom! I think Uncle
Tom was the ugliest man I've ever seen. I liked Uncle Tom.

But Dad! Dad was self-sufficient. He told me a story after my second
pair of twins were born. He said, 'I never believed the story my mother
told me, because she was ashamed to tell it, and she only told me
because we were more like older sister and younger brother.' When
Dad was born, Gran was very inexperienced as a young mother, because
she was only a teenager really. And Gran's mother – her own mother,
and Dad's grandmother – she had sixteen children, and the youngest
was Charles, and he was born in the same week as Dad. So Gran's
youngest brother was born in the same week as her own son. Great-
grandmother Wells was a very proficient breast-feeder; you kept your
children alive by breast-feeding them. Genuinely. And so Great-
grandmama said to Gran, 'Well now, Lizzie, you're a bad breast-feeder.

Now Charles is a lusty baby and George is sickly, so we'll change babies, and I'll breast-feed George and bring him up to scratch, and Charles will bring up your milk.' So it was interesting, because those were the days when in fact breast-feeding was literally life-saving for children, because they died of diarrhoea, as they still do. Well, the thing was that this happened. Charles, Gran's own youngest brother, was brought up on his older sister's milk, and Dad thrived on his grandmother's experience as a really proficient mother.

Mother didn't fit in well at the Pass. No, no, she was very quiet. Wallace – that's my brother – and I worshipped her. We were afraid of Dad, but not all *that* afraid of Dad. You know, Dad was part of the belting males. They all belted their children, literally belted them. Of course, I came a good way down the family, and I was not particularly wanted. I was disliked – heartily disliked – by Dad when I was a child, because I disappointed him; he wanted sons. First there were daughters: Mary, who died, and then Dorothy and Gwen and Joan. And at last Wallace came, and then he thought he'd have a run of boys, but the next baby was me, so in fact there was never any basic sympathy between my father and me. I admired him – he was a great, good-looking man, a magnificent physical specimen – but I didn't *like* him, and I didn't *like* the way his family treated Mother. So of course I was always on Mother's side, and I became very mother-oriented. She got very ill after a miscarriage when I was six, and my aunt said that Wallace and I had to go away – one to Uncle Jack Crump's school at Ocean Bay, and the other one to my aunt's school at Ballarat, near Melbourne. So Wallace and I left. Well, I was literally physically ill for three months with homesickness. Ballarat's right inland, and oh, I was homesick for the Pass until I went back there.

Nancy, aged seven years, with cousin Madelene Crump, photographed in Melbourne in 1917
*Nancy Sutherland*

We were trained by our elder brothers and sisters when we were young. I'll never forget the schooling of the younger brothers and sisters by the older brothers and sisters, and I had a taste of this with my twins. I have a real feeling that the older twins were much more powerful in, for instance, the upbringing of their younger brothers and sister than even their parents were, and the point is, it was this interchange of children with children that was the first learning process. They lose this with small families today, of course.

\*     \*     \*

Well, Gran Webber, Dad's mother, told us what to expect if we used the language we used; if we stole as we stole; and if we lied as we lied. All of us, we were past *masters* at the art; it was part of our training as a young tribe against all adults. You did these things and you lied about them, and if you were caught you took your punishment, and pretty solid it was – round the legs or round the bare bottom, or knocked down or whatever – and it just proved to you that you weren't clever enough at the lying and the stealing. That stood me in tremendous stead when I left Teachers' College and went to Wellington Borstal to teach the girls. You just get this real feeling that, as the girls said to me when I asked them if they'd learnt anything, 'We learnt how not to get caught again!' And that's just about the philosophy of this tribe of children at the Pass.

We were afraid of Gran. God *might* strike us dead if we went on lying and stealing as was our habit. And so we went up the orchard gully – there was a creek, and up the orchard gully was a beautiful sun-trap where fig trees, pears, apples, plums and cherries were all planted. Well, we went up to the pear tree – an old, old pear tree with an enormous spread – and we went in by the trunk, and then one of my sisters went out to the edge, where the edge of the tree met the sky where God was, and she said in a very low voice, 'Damn you, God!' And she ran back in with us, and we waited . . . Nothing happened! We weren't struck dead. Nothing happened. The day was just as lovely, and the shade of the tree was just as lovely and secure. So she went out again, and said it louder. And she progressed and said it louder and louder, until in the end we were all dancing in the sun near the shade of the pear tree, shrieking, 'Damn you, God!' And we weren't struck dead.

Well, that was the end of my religion. I was very strictly brought up as a Methodist, I'll tell you that. I never – but never – believed in God after that. He'd let Gran down. He'd let everybody down. He'd let us down, and that was the end of it.

*          *          *

Another thing about the family, you had to learn to be very observant. You had to learn to be as quick in your reaction time as a cat, just about, in order to dodge punishment. Wallace and Joan warned me, if we'd been stealing the prunes, or stealing money from the post office (which I did, when the till was left open ... oh, I stole everywhere and lied everywhere. I'd have been jailed and jailed and *jailed* today – oh, we were delinquents, and I was the worst of them!) And so Wallace and Joan said, 'Well, if you get caught, Mum's usually sick, so I don't think she'll hit you. She'll put you in the bathroom and wait for Dad to come home, and if you howl enough, she's pretty soft, you mightn't get any punishment at all, but be told not to do it again, or to come and ask God to forgive you. If it's Dad, watch his hands.'

And, you see, this is where the belting came in; if his hands went to his belt, then you began to run. And we were faster than Dad. I honestly believe that we beat all Olympic records. There are many Olympic records that have never been recorded, and these were some of them.

And you know that the old stockyard fences were planks, set about four or five to a fence. They held the sheep in and they held the cattle in; they held everything in but deer, and your deer jumped everything of course, because we had tame deer in those days. But if Dad was after you to punish you for doing some quite impossible thing, well, then, you would run and you would put your feet on the top edge of the second plank. You'd put your ribs or belly across the top, and then you'd let go with your legs, and your legs would swing over . . . you'd be on the other side in about . . . well, in about a fifth of a second. Whereas Dad, he was a big man; he wouldn't climb the fence, he would go through the stockyard gate. He had to undo the gate, and in case the stock went through he had to close it again. And we were about half a mile away!

We'd wait for him to cool down. He had a quick temper, but he wasn't as quick-tempered as Grandad. Grandad would never wait for anything. Besides, Grandad vaulted all the gates because he was very, very fit and lithe; he wasn't as big as Dad. But Grandad would take off his seaman's cap and knock you about five yards with his cap on the side of your head, and as fast as it came out, it was over, you know. Whereas Dad would come home dog-tired from a day's slogging on the hillside and so on, and he'd have his shepherd's crook, and if one of us was waiting for punishment from him, he'd fell whatever child it was with his shepherd's crook.

I can remember one time when Jack had broken a window. The crime at the Pass was to break a window, because they all had to come back by sea, and in dirty weather the boat would arrive from Nelson or from Wellington and the window panes she'd brought us would be all smashed. Then you'd have to start again. Well, Jack – that's my younger brother – was given a cricket ball for his birthday, and he wasn't so much playing with it as learning to throw the cricket ball, and he broke the bathroom window. Well, we knew. We *knew*. I remember every window-breaking in that place in my childhood, because it was a major tragedy. And Mother said to Jack, 'Well, you're going to have to tell your father yourself, my dear, because you did it. And I know it's your birthday, but you go down when your father comes in, and you must tell him about it.' Jack knew he would have to before Dad reached the back door (which was beside the bathroom) and saw the broken window. So Dad came down the path, and we howled our eyes out because of Dad, and Dad, *dog*-tired, came in, and this mite of a boy said to him, 'I've broken the bathroom window', and Dad felled him with his crook.

And Mother – I can remember Mother running down the path and saying, 'Remember it's the child's birthday, George!' And Dad never went in the back door. He went and walked on the hill, because Jack was the apple of his eye – his youngest son, you know.

That, to me, was much more traumatic than breaking open the skulls of visiting children with stones, because we had stone battles from under the wharf and under the woolshed. And . . . Oh! There was the time when we really felt quite bad, because accidentally we killed a tuatara. And the time we cut the Gausels' launch in half.

Old Mrs Gausel had wanted a quick tea, and she sent Wilfred, one of her boys, out with the launch to get enough fish for tea. Now they had a big family, like ours – they finished up with about nine or ten of a family, and we were eight in those days. We were coming home in the launch after a muster, coming home through the Pass from the Nelson side, and on the Wellington side the lighthouse stands out and hides your view. Well, on the Wellington side, which was near our home, Wilfred was just idling the engine while they pulled in fish, because that's how you could get your fish in those days. The place was teeming with fish, especially the Pass. We didn't see his boat, the *Rita*, until the *Anaru* turned just past the lighthouse, and then it was too late, because there was a slight tide against us and so we were going fairly fast, whereas the *Rita*'s engine was idling. And so we ran her down.

I was in the cockpit then and I can remember Wallace had the *Anaru* and Wilfred Gausel had the *Rita*, which was cut in half. And Wallace called out to Wilfred to attach the bow of the launch – they had to move fast – so he went up to the bow and attached it while Wallace had his feet, one in the cockpit of the *Anaru* and the other in the cockpit of the *Rita*, and was just literally picking up Gausel children and throwing them into our cockpit. So that in the end they saved the bow and the engine. The stern sank, but the children were saved.

These are the things that leave very clear memories.

We were expected to help on the farm. Oh, it was a matter of pride to get a froth on the milk. To get a froth on the milk, it was the *peak* of one's existence. We were allowed to milk the tamest cows. I remember, I had milked a little Jersey cow – she wasn't a heifer – because she was quiet in the cow-bails. I'd been allowed to leg-rope her – I was a bit nervous about the leg-rope thing – and I got a *lovely* froth on the milk. I put the bucket over by the side of the cow-bails and I undid the stall, but I forgot to undo the leg-rope first. I'll just *never* forget it. She was frightened; she tried to get out, and her leg was held by the leg-rope, and I tried to turn her back into the cow-bail, to bail her up again so I could take the leg-rope off. On the way she had to pass the bucket of milk, and she was terrified – and she drank the milk. There was no milk to show Dad, and I came up, tears *streaming* down my face, with a bucket with about an inch of dirty milk in it. Up the path towards the farmhouse, and Dad came out to meet me, and I said, 'The cow drank the milk! I milked her and got a froth on the milk, and the cow drank the milk!' And I couldn't find out why the cow drank the milk after I'd milked it out of her, and they laughed and laughed and I howled and howled. They were so unfeeling!

*       *       *

We weren't supplied with adventure playgrounds or jungle gyms or whatever. We climbed trees, and we were forbidden. And we climbed up on the roof and fell off and broke arms, and would be forbidden. You know, forbidden, forbidden all the time, so that in fact the thing to do was really to do the thing you were forbidden to do. We were not allowed to walk on the wet beams under the wharf; we were forbidden – so we walked on the wet beams under the wharf. We dived under the wharf. My brothers prided themselves – and so did all the little boys – on walking on their hands quite as well as they walked on their feet, and they would go on their hands along the railings on the side of the wharf. And of course they could have killed themselves. This was forbidden. We were forbidden to go down to the wharf, so we went down to the wharf, and the little ones toddled along after us. That's why my brother Jack was blown off the wharf – he was far too light to be on the wharf at all.

We were forbidden to dive off the wharf when the fishing launches were in, and we were forbidden to dive off the wharf and follow-my-leader, because we might dive on one another. Well, I dived right on Jack, and realised I'd knocked him out, and he seemed to be pretty queer under the water, so I grabbed him by the hair and towed him to the steps. And before we'd got him half way up the steps he came round, and we shook the life out of him and told him we'd push him back in if he told Mum or Dad. He never told Mother or Dad anything about it until he was twenty-one. Poor Jack! When I think of it!

\*     \*     \*

Grandad ran the post office – well, he ran everything. He served the beacon light, and when service time came round, he had three days' grace to change the kerosene lamp in the beacon in the Pass. He helped build the beacon and its replacements. He helped build the lighthouse. He was the sum of all things at the Pass, and his son was his right-hand man as soon as he was eleven or twelve or thirteen.

So Grandad had to change the lamp, and he had three days to do it. He didn't like to do it on the first day. If dirty weather was coming up, he must change it on the second day, because there was no chance, no matter what the weather did, he *had* to have it changed by the third day, because then the light would run low and the ships might get wrecked in the Pass – which they very often did. So he'd have to go out in the *Namu*, and he always trailed a rope. He was a magnificent swimmer, and he always went out alone and never took his son or anyone else. He always changed the beacon's kerosene lamp alone, as far as I can remember.

He was the postmaster, and I shall never forget, when he had a lot of telegrams to put through, he had to code them – A for Arthur, B for Bob, C for Charlie, D for David, E for Edward . . . it's another of those things that made us feel we'd be much bigger in stature if we knew how to code a telegram from A to Z.

Well, when it came to Christmas, the Christmas greetings telegrams were X-M-A-S, and Grandad had to code them, because the line was very bad between French Pass and Nelson. So Grandad was coding his telegrams and he came to X, and he said 'X for . . . X for . . .

oh, X for Damnation! M for Mary, A for Arthur . . . S for Sam.'
For *years* after, in the Nelson office the code word for X was 'Damnation' – because he couldn't think what X would be for, you know.
This would be . . . I'm seventy-four, and it would be sixty-five years
ago at least. Yes. It would have been before the First World War,
because when that ended I was in Ballarat, and all the people in the
trams – the horse-drawn trams – had to wear masks, because of the
flu epidemic.

Well, because of all his interests, and all the things he could do,
Grandad was a mine of information – but he was a very peppery man.
In those days you mustered as much from the launches as you mustered
on the hills. You took your dogs along on the deckhouse, and you
followed the shoreline, because our farm was on a point running right
out, cheek-by-jowl with D'Urville Island. D'Urville Island lay off it,
and the Pass point came out, and the Pass itself is about midway along
the length of D'Urville Island. So you went in the launch, with your
dogs on the deckhouse, and then you set your dogs to bark, and you
shouted yourself, and this drove the sheep up out of the bush, and
from the cliffs, up on to the hillside where your son or your brother
or whoever was going along mustered them with the dogs along the
tops. And that was the system.

The same with the buying. The stock agents would go with Grandad
in the *Namu*. The dogs would be on the deckhouse and the men would
be in the cockpit, and they would send the sheep up and down, and
the agents would look at the condition of the sheep as the dogs sent
them up. Once Grandad was busy pointing out something up the hill
and he ran up on a rock, and he was busy about this when along came
Ole Gausel. He was the fisherman, the Norwegian fisherman, who lived
at the Pass, and his family grew up step-by-step with us. Well, along
Ole came, and he said, 'Grandad, do you want a tow off the rock?'

And Grandad turned around and said, 'Bugger that! I'm not going
to be towed off any rock by anybody. We'll wait till the tide takes
us off.'

And so the agents had to sit there with him until the tide came up
and he got off the rocks. He really was priceless.

He would go out in all sorts of weathers. He rang Deep Bay once,
when he had some ewes to take round in the *Namu*. The *Namu* was
the little launch with the counter stern. She would never go over the
waves – she always went through them. We *loved* her. Edgar Hope
had said to Grandad, 'The weather is very dirty, and it's going to get
worse, Grandad. You could leave the ewes and bring them round later.'
They were our neighbours, and his ewes had strayed on to our place
and been mustered in. You always returned ewes like that, or cattle,
or whatever it was.

And Grandad said, 'Aw, no, I've got a bit of free time. I think I'll
bring them around.' So then Dad said to Grandad, 'Well, it's pretty
dirty weather. Do you think you ought to go?'

And Grandad said, 'Well, if you don't damn-well want to come, *you'll* come, won't you ducky?' – to me. And of course any word of approval from Grandad to me was just marvellous . . . to be called 'ducky' was Grandad's one endearment. It was usually the other way.

So I went, and I can remember Mother's face, and how she wondered whether she should dispute with Grandad, but she was always brought up, 'Children should be seen and not heard', and because of her modesty, she very rarely spoke; she was very quiet. So I went. And I was frightened.

Well, we collected some more of his grandchildren – 'We're only going round to Deep Bay. There's plenty of room in the cockpit.' But she was very low in the water, because he had about six ewes in the cockpit – fat ewes – so we had to sit on the cross-seat by the engine, just under the deckhouse of the *Namu,* and Grandad was out at the tiller in the stern – there was no such thing as a wheel, or anything

The settlement at French Pass in the 1920s, with the *Anaru* moored in Elmslie Bay. The land on the skyline is D'Urville Island and the dark wooded arm reflected in the bay is Collinet Point on the mainland; the Pass itself lies between the two. In the left corner of the photo, partly obscured by the spur, is the home in which Nancy spent her childhood, the house of G. W. W. Webber. The original Webber homestead, a large building which later became a boardinghouse, and was burnt down in the 1950s, is hidden amongst the macrocarpa grove directly behind the wharf, as is the cottage of Pass pioneer Arthur Cruikshank Elmslie. At the far end of the beach can be seen the government oil store, with the white gates of the track to the lighthouse up behind. The next two buildings this way are the cottages of fishermen Ole Gausel (on the shore) and Frederick Hendricksen (behind). Adjacent are the one-roomed school and the old store. About a quarter way up the spur leading from these buildings lie the graves of Mr Elmslie and J. Brisendon (of Scott's winter stopover Antarctic expedition), who drowned off the 'old' wharf of Nancy's childhood. The remains of this wharf can be seen in the foreground at the near end of the beach and directly inland of them is the house occupied by Nancy's paternal grandparents in their old age. The 'new' wharf of this photo is still in use.
*Nancy Sutherland*

like that, in the boat; no, not in those days. And Grandad was in the stern, and as much under the water as out of it.

But I'll *never* forget it. He sang sea shanties all the way round. It was gorgeous. 'The whales and sharks will have such larks . . .' I'll *never* forget those sea shanties. And he just sang, and we forgot to be frightened. But of course he got round. He went through among the rocks; he knew every rock, you know. And so we delivered the ewes, and it was easy coming home, because the wind was with us.

*     *     *

By the time I came back from Australia, there was a school at the Pass, and then they built another one that was bigger, and they had to take land from the farm for it. Mother gave us our first education before that – Mother and the aunts, if they were there on holiday.

You had this extraordinary education system. You would have to have your children educated by having your own, and boarding two or three others, as well as an uncertificated teacher, if there were less than ten children all told. And that meant that the farmer's wife or whoever – it was usually a farmer's wife – from Monday to Friday would have to not only look after her own family and chores, but board children from the farmers' and fishermen's places round about. And board the teacher. And that was an uncertificated teacher.

My sister Dorothy went to Nelson College for Girls and matriculated and came home, and she passed what was called a 'D' Certificate, the first of the teaching certificates. (The 'C' certificate you had to go to Teachers' College for, or you had to do some teaching in some other school for.) So Dorothy was then at the Pass school, which was teetering between not having enough on the roll, and having enough, according to whether the children turned five, or went out at the top to go to secondary school – because it was a primary school. So Dorothy taught there, and she was also postmistress for the Pass at different times.

But before that, one room of a farmhouse had to be set aside, as I said. I'll tell you this. Nowadays, if you have too few children for a school, you have this *magnificent* service, the Correspondence School. Now Correspondence School teaching equals that in any primary school in the country, judging by their exam results. Scholarship holders have gone through Correspondence School. The Professor of Languages down at Otago University went through one of the earlier ones – that was Nola Leov. She won scholarship after scholarship.

Now the thing that is the driving force is the first teacher of these children. No child can work on the assignments from the Correspondence School until he or she can read. The mother is the teacher; the mother teaches the five-year-old to read and the motivation of the mother for the education of her children – there is no motivation like it. *That's* why the Correspondence School has such a name, because in fact it is initiated by the mother. It's true family-centred education, like what I'm fighting for in the hospitals today – family-centred childbirth. Because it was proved to us in the district that family-centred education was the first step, literally.

*     *     *

There were really three communities at the Pass. You had the original two: the farmers and the fishermen – all New Zealanders, Maori and European. Then, because it was a place that was absolutely teeming with fish at the time, you had assisted groups coming in who'd met some misfortune in their own country. Now these were two clear groups, and they kept apart in the most extraordinary way, and they had the original characteristics of the places from which they came. There were the Italians, and they settled on the Island Bay side of Cook Strait, near Wellington of course. Then there were the Norwegian ones, fair Nordics with gold hair and blue eyes and lovely teeth and alabaster skin. And the Italians were black-haired and black-eyed and olive-skinned, and also had lovely teeth. They were as distinct a grouping as you could ever dream of in one small district.

Stromboli blew up, and the fishermen who weren't enveloped and wiped out had to leave and go out on the coast of Italy. But they were homeless, so they were assisted immigrants, and I always remember this from my childhood, because the first boat they had they called the *Stromboli,* of course. They were down one end of D'Urville Island, and their cousins the Barnaos were opposite across Cook Strait, in Island Bay. They were the first lot who came, and it was perfect, because the fish, when it was sacked, had to be taken by boat either to its market in Nelson, or to its market in Wellington. They took it to Nelson when the boat went to Nelson, and the boat which took their fish out 'boarded' the steamer, because there were no wharves. They boarded the steamer in the middle of the night very often, from the Pass, or maybe from Waitai, or even off the Island if they couldn't get through the Pass for the weather, and had to go round D'Urville Island. They would even go from Admiralty Bay into Cook Strait with their fish. If they couldn't make the steamer for any reason, their fish would be completely wasted, but Dad built a special smokehouse, and worked with them, and they'd smoke as many as they could. Then when the boat was going from Nelson to Wellington, the fish would go across to what is still the best to my mind – and to that of many old Wellingtonians – the best fish shop in New Zealand . . . Barnao's.

There was never any conflict between the two groups, and they brought their sweethearts out as soon as they got established and had money. They were very thrifty. For instance, Nino and Vincent Moleta, the original two brothers who came out, would never buy anything with a mortgage. They waited and they worked like slaves until they got hard cash, and they kept the hard cash until they could buy a bit of land freehold. Their sons are some of the wealthiest farmers in the French Pass district today.

*     *     *

You would call us immoral as children today; we were amoral, and I believe we were quite religious really. My mother was actually quite religious, and a very strict Methodist. My father, from having grown up from about nine to eleven years at French Pass, was what I would call just a believer in nature. He had no religion except the outdoors, and always said so, but he would always go to church when the minister came on the mission launch – in those days about once every three months the mission launch would come round. We would have the service either in our sitting room or our parlour or our dining room – dining room and kitchen combined. Or we might have it in the school, or in the Hope's sitting room down at Deep Bay, or we'd have it on D'Urville Island at different times. Then about once in three months the priest would come, because of course many of the fishermen down there were Roman Catholics, and, as they hastened to say, not Irish Roman Catholics, but easy-going European Roman Catholics – a very different breed.

And Mother took Sunday School every Sunday, and we also had hymn practice, and she would play the hymns. So about the earliest music I learnt was hymns . . . 'Fight the Good Fight', and what's that one about the waves . . . 'For Those in Peril on the Sea'. They were sea hymns we would sing, because Mother was apparently preoccupied with it. She was a bad sailor. She couldn't bear the smell of those dreadful pop-pop-pop-pop petrol engines in the launches, and she'd have to sit outside, and she'd be seasick. She really was a dreadful sailor. It was an incarceration for Mother at French Pass, because you could really go nowhere, except by sea.

If they could have, Mother and Dad would have controlled our sexual morality the way they did – the way they *tried* to do – our spiritual side. But of course you can't control it. It just never is controllable. And the thing was we had dances – the dances were always in the woolshed – and we went down to each other's houses sometimes for a meal, but we'd get out behind the bushes or in the woolshed up in the loft – anywhere away from the houses. The houses were the centre of morality. And usually all that would happen, if you were playing cards or you were doing 'snakes and ladders' or something, would be that the boy beside you would slide his hand up underneath your skirt and underneath your bloomers if he could, and you would move according to whether you were afraid, or your sense of self-preservation was strong.

But I'll tell you this, that the boys who worked on the farms, and the farmers' sons and the fishermen's sons and everybody's sons – it didn't make any difference – the thing was, there was *always* this amoral sexual corresponding, and we had it in the home. I can still remember it. We inspected each other's genitals as members of the family. I was rebellious against myself and my own inadequate sex organs, because my brothers had such much more interesting ones.

Later on, when I was a teenager, I was in black rebellion against my menstrual periods. They stopped me swimming; they messed up my clothes; they sometimes gave me a bit of a pain in the pinny; and I couldn't bear it, and I was never allowed to swim, and so of course I swam. What do you say when they say, 'Aren't you going to bring your togs?' You don't say, 'No, I've got my period.' You'd die of shame. And so you make up all sorts of stupid excuses – or else you swim. And I would swim.

After a while it made my periods a bit irregular, but what was lovely was that for a whole year I didn't have a period at all. And not because I was pregnant. I just didn't have a period. I couldn't *believe* it; it was glorious. I think, as a matter of fact, it was because I was anaemic, because you know we were a very big family, and we didn't have all that much to eat, and we certainly didn't have fresh fruit and things to the same extent that outsiders did. I can remember Mother going out after a blistering southerly that had burnt everything off everything; she went hunting up around the paddocks just to get puha, because there was no greens for her children to eat. I remember that quite well. *But,* I'd have been pregnant if I hadn't had a strong sense of self-preservation . . . and the same would apply to many a girl, because we were sexually curious. We weren't sexually afraid. The tupping went on, and the mounting went on with the dogs and cattle, but usually Dad sent us away, or inside, as he did when he was killing the sheep. When he was killing the sheep we wanted to watch the killing of the sheep; when he was tailing, the girls were sent away, and I wanted to see what tailing was. I wanted to see what killing sheep was; I wanted to see what mounting was. I wanted to see men and women do it. But I didn't, and I wanted to try it. The whole thing was, we had a kind of an overall curiosity about everything to do about life, and why should this one be cut away? And it never crossed our minds that we would have a baby, as a result of sexual activity. Never. Never. And I don't believe it does today with many of these children who have experiments with sex when they're very young – twelve or thirteen – and this is when they get pregnant very often for the first time.

Now, I was tremendously keen on one of the boys from one of the neighbouring bays, and we met at dances, and Christmas parties. And after one of these get-togethers we went off along the beach, and I went along, quite cheerful. I think he was a bit older than I was – but oh, he was marvellous! He had red hair and freckles, and was gangly and God knows what, but oh, I thought he just had everything that one could dream of in a hero! And then he was in a bit too much of a hurry, and there was an old concrete well down the beach, which the water would go into at high tide, so a concrete retaining square box was put around it. He pushed me against this, and was so busy undoing my clothes, you know, that I was quite interested and went along with him quite happily. But, oh Lord, he pressed my spine against the concrete at the back, until the pain of the one completely wiped out the other, and so I slid out from under and ran like mad.

That was my main sexual pre-adolescent pre-teenage experiment. Earlier on, when I was very young, between five and seven years, some farmhand had got me up the loft and made a mess of my pants, and I disliked all that, I'll say that much. But at that time, everything to do with sex was related to the unpleasantness of it – nothing to do with babies. Just the unpleasantness of the whole messy business. As far as the adults were concerned though, it was sin. Sin, dreadful sin, it was. Now my pants were in such a mess that Mother must have found out or somebody must have found out. Maybe the teacher at the school found out, or my eldest sister, and told Mother. So that boy, who was a farm cadet – or the equivalent of a farm cadet – was sent away.

When the girls got pregnant, they usually got married. Sometimes they didn't. Sometimes they didn't believe there was a pregnancy, and then they would get married after the baby was born, very often. Mother tried to tell one little girl that she was pregnant, and she said she wasn't. She said, 'I know I'm not, Mrs Webber. I know I'm not pregnant.'

Well, of course, Mother said she was to go up to Neison, and then quite suddenly, on the boat, she needed to be alone like any animal. She was only about sixteen . . . fifteen maybe; I don't believe she was fourteen. But she had to go up on the deckhouse by herself, and it was quite bad weather off the Boulder Bank. The bows were under water as often as not, and most of the people who were going up to Nelson were under the deckhouse. And the baby was born up there on the bow. Both baby and mother were *drenched* with spray. And then, when they'd got through the bad spell and come into a bit more shelter near Nelson, one of the women in the cockpit said, 'I heard a baby cry.' But nobody gave her help with the birth. Nobody. Nobody. So baby plus placenta plus everything else were up on the bow of the boat, and there they stayed until one of the married women from the cockpit went up to see, because she'd heard the baby crying! But the girl never admitted to Mother that she was pregnant. She never at any time admitted that.

We were *grossly* ignorant. I thought for a while that to kiss you could become pregnant – just as I thought, when my menstruation started first and I was at boarding school, that I had VD, as my classmates said. I was convinced, month after month, that it was VD. In the middle of the night, because I'd stained the sheets and so on, I got up and washed those sheets, put them back, and got back into the wet bed. It wasn't until I got pneumonia that at last it was found out by the boarding-school authorities that in fact I was getting back into bed into soaking wet sheets. I was *convinced* it was VD.

And then, of course, the only time I'd been to a doctor from boarding school was when I burst my eardrum from diving, and he was an eye, ears, nose and throat man. And a lot of damned use he was, I can tell you. Because I had a detention for a month, and that was because I'd stayed away without permission, out of bounds. I'd gone and I waited and waited in that doctor's waiting-room – the only doctor

I knew. I couldn't bear to talk to him or go while there were other people, so that I was the very last person, because everybody who came in went in before me and went past before me, because I wouldn't get up and go in, because I was so ashamed. I was terrified. I had no idea what VD was. I didn't even know what the two words meant. And then at last I stood by the door, and he said, 'Well, what's the matter?' and told me his time was up and so on, and I said, 'Well . . . I want to know if I have VD.'

And he patted me on the shoulder, and pushed me away, and said, 'Don't be silly, child. Go along.'

And that was all I got, so back I went, none the wiser, to boarding school. And to an hour's detention after school every day for breaking bounds.

*         *         *

I think the most interesting person in my life at the Pass in those days was . . . yes, Ma Campbell was. She certainly was New Zealand's only woman sheep-stealer, and still is, except that she's no longer alive. She was a tremendous personality. She was in our eyes almost as powerful as a witch – somebody transcending human beings, a fearsome person – because, for one thing, she was peculiarly dressed. She had a leatherish skin, very piercing blue eyes, and untidy hair. But she always – and I heard this later – she always changed when she came to the Pass itself, because the Pass, with its post office and store, was civilisation to these people in the backblocks. And when they came over they always walked, even though she had at least six miles to walk with her daughters. I think they were half-sisters, and they joined her in her sheep-stealing exploits, because she had trained them as well as she'd trained her dogs, actually. She and the girls would stop and get out of their dungarees and their heavy boots and walking gear, and they'd get into crumpled frocks they'd carried with them, or a skirt and jumper or something, and tidy their hair, and even put on stockings and shoes in order to go down to civilisation – this little bay which held a post office and store and a few farmhouses and fishermen's cottages.

They would come down and bring whatever they had to sell. I can remember one occasion, because it made my mother the laughing stock of the district. Ma Campbell arrived with two kerosene tins. (Those were the buckets in use always at that time – square tins, kerosene or benzine, but always called 'kerosene tins'.) She arrived with them full of cherries, and she wanted to sell them at the Pass. Well, Ma Campbell was a byword in the district, with everyone knowing she would steal chickens and odd things round about whenever she got the chance – though they only *suspected* her of sheep-stealing; they didn't really have any proof at that time. But she had the cherries and Mother was so glad to see that she was trying to turn an honest penny by trying to sell the cherries that she bought some, and I've no doubt the other people did, because she sold all the cherries. Mother bought most of them, but she didn't find out until some time afterwards, when she went down to an orchard at the other end of our farm, that in fact the cherry trees were stripped. Mother had been sold her own cherries, which everyone found out about, and beautiful cherries they were. That was just one incident about this woman, who was an incredibly strong personality – physically and mentally, I believe.

My father had a neighbour whose farm adjoined his, and the boundary was partly in Admiralty Bay and partly in Pelorus Sound, and she and her two daughters lived in a bay in Pelorus Sound, called The Pines. They would come up – row, because they had no engine (besides, engines would be too noisy for what they had to do) – they would come up to a little bay right at the very end where the boundary between my father's and Dave Stewart's property was, and there they would, in absolute silence, corner a certain number of Dad's and Dave's sheep. Get them into the corner, and the dogs were trained to work in absolute silence. Not even a whistle. Nothing at all. I don't know how she did it, but it was absolutely silent, because farmers were watching for her time and time again, and there was never any easy way to tell when she was working.

The girls caught the sheep that the dogs penned up in the corner of the beach and rocks and cliff, trussed them and put them in the boat, and then rowed them back down to The Pines. There they peeled them. They sold the carcases if they could, and put the skins on the fence and got rid of all the marks and burnt whatever might be any evidence at all, and they weren't caught for years and years.

They were caught eventually, and really it was just one of those slips. In the end, Dad found she had stolen some sheep the day before, and she couldn't have had much time to get rid of every bit of evidence, so if they went to The Pines that day, or if Dad and Dave went in their launch and the police came down from Picton or from Havelock, then they'd be able to meet at The Pines beach, and they would be able to see. They'd really been in touch with the police for a while, and the police had been making enquiries at the Picton-Havelock-Blenheim end – saleyards, and so on.

So they went down there, and though there was a fire going, and there were skins – of their own sheep, they said – which had been killed and looked fairly fresh hanging on the fences, they didn't get any real evidence until they followed the creek down. They found some remains that included ear-marks, which was a common way of branding sheep in those days. Evidence of at least one of Dave Stewart's sheep, and one or two of Dad's sheep, was caught in the stones of the creek, and hadn't been washed away.

So she was caught, and she was brought to court in Blenheim. I can remember Dad coming home to the Pass very aggrieved. He and Dave had felt how unpopular they were, because in the witness box Ma Campbell put on such a good show, and looked so neat and tidy and ladylike, that she had the whole sympathy of the court with her. And Dad and Dave Stewart were hissed and booed when they went, for doing such a rotten thing against a woman. And she really was the brightest of bright sheep-stealers. Yes, we thought, she and McKenzie . . . Ma Campbell and McKenzie the sheep-stealer. There must have been more before and since, but I've never heard of a woman sheep-stealer in New Zealand, except for Ma Campbell.

*        *        *

One *enormous* excitement was when a ship came through the Pass. If we saw a yacht or a steamer had turned the Point, we knew if we ran fast enough we could get around to the lookout above the light-house-keeper's house, which was above the lighthouse. If we could get up there, we could look down and watch the fight against the tide.

Sometimes it would be a scow, and the scows had not-too-highly powered engines, and they were flat-bottomed, so that they skidded fairly easily over the currents. We'd watch them, and they'd come up with all the power they had, and if the wind was with them, some of them might have a sail up in order to catch the tide before it turned, or to get through the Pass while the tide was still not strong enough to stop them. There was a real element of competition between man and nature in this, and we could watch it happen and feel at one with the captain and crew of the yacht or boat – or the Pass, because there were plenty of times when we hoped the Pass would win, and plenty of times when the Pass *did* win.

*Penguin* takes the Pass
*Wellington Harbour Board Maritime Museum*

There was a most extraordinary thing really, because when you looked down on it, they would come up, and the tide might have just turned, and started to run against them, and every minute it was gaining power. It's an enormous concentration of solid water power, so solid that at the highest tides, neap or spring or whatever, the water piles up on one side and runs downhill towards the Wellington side of the Pass, or the other way round. And the fishermen and the farmers always know, and the seamen do also for that matter, that once you're on the 'rise' of solid water, you're through. You can win the battle. But if you can't gain the rise, and get up on it, well, the tide is strengthening, is making, is making, is making, and you're losing steadily.

Well, we used to stand there, mesmerised, and watch some part of the boat against something stationary on D'Urville Island, or against the beacon, or maybe against the reef, if the reef was out of the water. You can't watch the tide, because the tide is racing past and it looks as though the boat's getting there anyway; you've got to watch against a stationary object. And we would watch. I can remember a scow, the old *Alexander*. I can remember her so easily, with all the men on the side of the railings, looking for'ard to see if she was going to get up on the rise, or if she wasn't making it because the tide was beating her. And she would stay stationary for sometimes two minutes while they either piled on coal or they did something to get the last ounce out of the old tub. And then gradually she might lose. Still bow-on, because she must be bow-on because it's narrow water, she would begin to go back, inch by inch, and you knew she'd lost the battle.

Then you'd see the men get out their fishing lines, and they'd have two or three or four hours' fishing, before the tide turned and took them through. I'm not quite sure that the crew didn't like to be beaten by the tide, because if they got through they'd have to keep going, and not have a chance to fish, and if the weather was good it was nice to be beaten by the tide.

I can remember a handsome great yacht coming through, and Grandad said, 'Well, she's either going to come into the bay to ask for advice, or she's going to come to grief on the reef.'

She went past the point. She didn't come into the bay, and Grandad took this always as a personal affront, because the Pass was *his,* not to be trifled with – and he was quite right of course. Well, there wasn't all that much tide, but there was plenty of current, and she went into an eddy and got swung, and, sure enough, she went up on the rocks. So Grandad went up on the saddle to have a look, and he came back down and said, 'Well, it won't be long before her master will be round here asking for milk or meat, or a hand to be pulled off, or something or other.' So he said, 'Well, I know what I'll say to him – "It serves you bloody-well right, if you're going to be so busy." You don't take the Pass lightly.'

So these are the things I remember. The excitements and the

OPPOSITE: The lighthouse at French Pass today
*Lighthouse Division, Marine Dept*

lawlessness of our tribe of children. It was *dreadful,* some of the things the boys did. We couldn't do some of them, because we didn't have the strength, or else we were kept inside because we had special things to do. Girls always had to make the beds. The girls always had to clean the bath, and the chambers, because of course the lavatory was a good walk away from the house, and everybody had to have a chamber. I *hated* those jobs. And why did the girls have to do that? I still have this dreadful feeling of rebellion. I had it with my own children, when I had to clean the lavatory. Why is it the woman's job? It's extra-ordinary. Well, my sons do it. They take their turn at doing it. There's just some things that have differed about the equality of the sexes, in fact, like changing babies' nappies and so on.

But the boys at the Pass were devils. They got into the oil store once, through a broken window. The oil store is the store which belongs to the lighthouse. And it's sacrosanct. Once every three months, or six months, or whatever, the *Hinemoa* or the *Tutanekai* with old Captain Bollins, came and anchored in the bay and replenished the stores . . . the flour and paint and dried fruit, the sugar and pollard – everything – and locked the oil store and went through the Pass to the other side.

Sometimes Captain Bollins would take a tribe of us children on the *Hinemoa* or the *Tutanekai,* those beautiful ships. The *Hinemoa* was really a steam yacht. She was a *dream* of beauty, and she was Captain Bollins's pride and joy. In fact, he named his daughter Hinemoa after her, and he named his son Tutanekai, after the *Tutanekai.* He was my grandfather's greatest friend, Captain Bollins. We would go on the *Hinemoa* while she steamed through the Pass and anchored off Rock-cod Point through the Pass, in order to see that the lifeboat was properly serviced and the lighthouse itself was properly serviced and the beacon was looked after, and so on.

And do you know, the Fergussons – Sir Charles and Lady Alice Fergusson – were the first of the Governors-General to go right around New Zealand's lighthouses. I'd have sold my soul all my life – and I'm over seventy – to have been on one of those trips around every lighthouse. I would rather have done that than have gone across the world and back, which I've done again and again, and it means *nothing* to me compared with the thing I've never ever done. Really.

But these boys, they got in through a broken pane of glass, into the oil store, and they found all sorts of marvellous things. They broke a good clump of dates off the slab of dates. They got some sultanas and some prunes, and then they found the flour and the pollard. They found the sugar and golden syrup, and they found the paint, and then they thought, well, they'd mix the paint and the flour. They made a marvellous dough of the paint and flour! And it was because they were shouting with amusement and daubing paint all over the inside of the oil store that somebody found out, and told Dad and Ole Gausel.

Well, Dad was *livid,* and Wallace got the hiding of his life, on the seat of his pants, till he couldn't sit down for I don't know how long.

But Gausel took his boy out to the mooring, put him in a fish-sack, and doused him over the side. And then he picked him back in again – Dad told us this – and tipped him into the cockpit, and he didn't seem to have taken much harm from that, and he certainly didn't look as though he'd had enough punishment, so Ole put him back in the sack and again doused him over the side of the boat. When he brought him back in this time he wasn't quite so quick to move, and so Ole thought maybe he'd given him enough. Neither of the boys ever broke into the oil store again. But never.

                    *            *            *

I always wanted to go back to the Pass. Everybody who's ever grown up at the Pass has this extraordinary feeling that they must go back. It's very, very strong. Grown men still want to go back to the Pass, still must go back to the Pass. My older brother, though he was dying of leukaemia, said the one thing he wanted to do was to go back to the Pass. And this was arranged. The family flew him down there, and he died really happy, because he'd had a day at the Pass, the place that really his heart-strings were attached to.

   Now I have a feeling that the men – the farmers, the seamen, the people who are so closely involved with the risks of living and working among bush country and hilly country and dirty weather country and sea risks of all kinds – I think that bond of recall is stronger perhaps with the men than it is with the women, because they had the harder job. They took the bigger risks always . . . I would still like to go back, though.

First broadcast 16 July 1983

# 12 Doctor on the Coast

Dr Peter Anyon looks back on his introduction to general practice, in a Buller mining township.

Dr Peter Anyon
*Peter Anyon*

*The people represented in this book have come to the attention of 'Spectrum' producers through a variety of sources. In some cases it has been by word of mouth, on the recommendation of their friends or relatives. Others have been met unexpectedly, in the course of fieldwork. On still other occasions it has been a published book, or perhaps an unpublished manuscript, that has led to their door. Inevitably, years of work in this area have developed a feeling – a 'hunch' – for potentially good informants.*

*In the case of Dr Peter Anyon, the starting point was a weekly medical column he contributes to a city newspaper. It was his forthright approach that attracted the interest of 'Spectrum'. Unlike some medical men, he did not veil his craft in mystique. Unlike many more, he was not afraid to publicly criticise aspects of medical services in New Zealand, nor to admit his own past mistakes. These criticisms and admissions, however, were invariably turned to positive account, in a quiet passion – if the term is not self-contradictory – to advance his own skill and the state of medicine generally in this country.*

*Thirty years after his first experience in general practice, Dr Anyon is still a general practitioner, devoting a portion of time to his other love, paediatrics. He is a past president of the Royal New Zealand College of General Practitioners.*

Well, our first recollection of it, really, was when, having arrived by aircraft at Westport late one afternoon, we were picked up by the secretary of the Hospital Board in a large black V8 car. I'd never certainly had a car like that, but it was intimated to me that this was my car from then on, and I was suitably impressed. I was even more impressed when we left Westport and went along this magnificent two-lane highway to twenty miles north of Westport. It was very difficult for me to see why this beautifully kept highway should be there, because it appeared to go nowhere, and I was even more mystified when we went over a large overhead bridge about ten or fifteen miles out of Westport over the railway line. I passed a comment to the secretary that I thought there must be a large number of trains through the area and he said, 'Well, perhaps four a day.'

I contrasted that with McKays Crossing, north of Wellington, which in those days hadn't got an overhead bridge (and still hasn't got an overhead bridge), and the reason was of course that the one north of Westport was built in the days when the miners were all-powerful, and

The mouth of the Ngakawau
River, 1945
*John Pascoe Collection, Alexander
Turnbull Library*

they wanted a good road and that's what they got. So, we went the
twenty-odd miles north of Westport, through this Waimangaroa, which
was merely a little collection of houses with Denniston bursting out
of the cloud at the top of the hill, and then on to Granity, which again
was a very small place, and Granity merged imperceptibly almost into
Ngakawau and Hector.

Ngakawau stood on the south bank of the Ngakawau River and
Hector was on the north side of the Ngakawau River. Ngakawau and
Granity were joined by a magnificent two-laned bridge which would
be the envy of many a local authority, local body, even now. It was
a very pleasant little place, particularly on the north side, which was
more protected from the wind which howled down the Ngakawau Valley
at times. We found – and I was a keen gardener – that it was a magnificent place for growing things in. I had probably the best garden I think
I've ever had in my life there. They said, and I've got no reason to
disbelieve them, that you could grow peanuts there, and we could
certainly grow all kinds of subtropical fruits without any trouble at all.

There was a collection of, I guess, at the most 700 people in
Ngakawau-Hector. Then the secretary took me, on the same day, up
to Seddonville, which is another ten miles or so further on in a little
farming community, and waved his hand airily around and said, 'This
is all your area.' What he didn't do at that stage was take me up to
Stockton, which sat up on top of the hills. I had to discover my own
way up to Stockton somewhat later, and that really wasn't quite the

idyllic picture that you might have got from going to either Ngakawau or Hector. There weren't very many people in either Millerton or Stockton. I guess you'd call them dying townships at that stage.

Stockton was a fascinating little place. There was a big sort of square thing in the centre. I suppose you'd call it a rugby field or something. It was very rough and rugged, and I'm not sure that I ever saw anybody play rugby on it because I guess there wasn't anybody there to play rugby on it in those days. There had been. And the rest of the houses were built largely around it, and they straggled into various little gullies and up little slopes.

There was one place to which I used to go regularly to see an old man. You drove to it up a very tight drive, and he had a magnificent view of the Tasman on the days when you could see the view. But most of the people here lived, as far as I can recollect, in what seemed like a perpetual cloud of mist. I guess that was an exaggeration, but that's what it seemed like compared with the relatively good weather down on the coast a few hundred feet below.

*     *     *

The doctor before me had been there about, I guess, something like forty years. He'd become a local legend. He'd seen many people come and go on the Coast. He'd seen the rise and fall of the mines. He'd been there in the days of the Depression, and there were stories about how he used to go around on horseback, with his saddle-bags laden with corned beef and what have you, distributing to all the needy and poor up in the hills. There were stories about how he would go to Karamea, which was forty miles on through the bush, to tend the sick people, and I guess they were true, because there was nobody else in the early days when he started there to do the work. And in that sense it was an established practice. In another sense it wasn't.

Well, he was a hard act to follow, except that, over the years, vague warnings of change had hit the Coast, and some of the people had been away and got the idea that there was a bit more to medicine than what he had to offer. Really the patients fell into two classes: those who were well satisfied with the old doctor, who had done tremendous service over the years and who was what, I guess, you'd call the epitome of what people imagine the old family doctor to be . . . and the other lot, who thought he was a silly old ass, and wasn't up with the times, and they went all the way in to Westport to find their salvation. So I had a kind of dual population in the practice.

I inherited a surgery. The one at Ngakawau was close to the township itself, and not far from the bins. (The bins were where the coal came down by the ropeway from the Stockton Mine, and was held prior to being despatched by rail.) It seemed to be clouded in a perpetual shroud of coal dust, but it was when we went inside this grey building that my wife and I got a bit of a surprise. We went in the back. It consisted of three rooms in tandem. The front room was a waiting-room. It was painted in grey match-lining and it had several hard, built-in seats around. Then we went into the consulting-room, which was a respectable size, but it too was in hard grey match-lining, and in one of the corners was a colonial couch. In the middle of the colonial couch was a sack, and my wife, being of a rather curious disposition, picked up the sack to see what was underneath. Well, you soon found out, because the springs popped up! And this was the only couch on which we had to examine patients – there was no other. This didn't exactly fill me with enthusiasm, coming from Wellington Hospital, which by my standard was pretty respectable.

And then there was the dispensary at the back. The dispensary was again of grey match-lining, with a series of shelves round, to which were stuck a whole series of bottles in various shapes and sizes. They were stuck by some black gooey mess that had sort of seeped out of them over the years. I can only assume that the good doctor had various kinds of tar preparations which had sort of evaporated and swelled and done all sorts of funny things over the years and had stuck the bottles to the shelves. He'd done his own dispensing, you see. Well, I was expected to do some of my own dispensing, but this was changing, and the drugs were mostly brought out from Westport by the bus every day.

The water supply left something to be desired. There was no hot water. There was a cold-water supply from the tank on the roof, and it was filled with little black particles which, hopefully, consisted of bits of coal. (One of my friends, who had a practice up in Karamea, found the skeleton of a cat in his dispensary's rain-water tank, but I was never game to get up and look in our tank, so I didn't know, but there were certainly bits of coal floating around.)

The place, of course, wasn't the least bit soundproof. You can imagine that two layers of match-lining plonked on top of bits of four by two as studs really don't perform any soundproofing function at all, so everybody who was sitting in the waiting-room could hear exactly what happened in the consulting-room. It must have been an endless source of enjoyment to them. There were no facilities in the surgery at all such as I'd been accustomed to. No equipment of any description. I had to set to and order some, and buy some, and bludge some from the Health Department, and gradually set about the job of bringing the surgery up to something like scratch for the middle 1950s.

*          *          *

One of the problems about going into practice there was that I didn't know what general practice was about. I'd spent five years down at Dunedin, and then my sixth year in Wellington Hospital and the Hutt Hospital; two years as houseman in those two hospitals. That of course was an accepted entry into general practice in those days, but it didn't take me long to realise that while it was not completely worthless as an introduction, it was certainly largely irrelevant.

It was irrelevant because it didn't teach me anything about people. I learnt a lot about diseases in my medical course; I learnt very little about people. Today I think it's different. Our lectures in psychiatry, our course in psychiatry, consisted of six lectures delivered by a funny old man from Seacliff, and then we were taken out to Seacliff and shown all the people who were mad and were kept behind bars – and that comprised our assay into psychiatry. As for learning what normal people's emotions were about, or how they felt about things, or how they related to doctors, that was just not even considered.

So when I came down to the Coast I discovered a whole new world opened to me, and in many respects I felt very bitter about my own medical education. I had in fact acquired a very good education for hospital work. I had acquired what I think was a very poor education for general practice. I hadn't at that stage in my life decided to do general practice, but we can perhaps come to that later on. At any rate, I thought I had better start teaching myself, and to fill you in a bit about it, I am very much a self-learner. I learn a lot from people who come and see me. I write down little notes during the day on things I don't know about, and go home and look them up in the books at night, and that way I've expanded my knowledge considerably. For me, it's a very good way of learning. Maybe it isn't for everybody; for me I think it's been outstandingly successful, and it's a habit of mine that I've got into.

Well, at any rate, I thought I had better teach myself about these things they called tonics. Neither my wife nor I knew anything about tonics, except that they were something you gave to people when they came in and the people didn't have anything the matter with them and you wanted to keep them quiet. But my patients expected them, for whatever reason people wanted tonics.

Well, this old Welshman came in and said he wanted a tonic, and I examined him and couldn't find anything wrong with him, and concluded that I guess he probably *did* want a tonic. In fact I really wouldn't have known what else to do at that stage of my career other than to give him a tonic, so I told him to come back the next day and I'd make up the brew. So my wife and I went home and we looked up the books and we examined the bottles we had in the surgery, and there was some syrup of orange, and there was that miraculous tap water which had little specks in it. So I thought, well, I guess that's the way you make up a tonic, seeing there was nothing else there. So I dumped some syrup of orange in the bottom of the bottle – I can't think how much, now – and some tap water, enough to make it fairly palatable and rather strong, so that when diluted with water it really tasted quite acceptable.

Then I had twinges of conscience. I thought, 'Oh, goodness, how on earth can you give a man tap water with little bits of coal in it laced with orange?' It seemed so wrong and deceitful, so I salved my conscience by putting in some sodium bicarbonate. Sodium bicarbonate was an accepted remedy for gastric disorders, and I guess it didn't do any harm and it might have done some good, and somehow I felt a bit better about doing it.

Well, he went away with his bottle. He came and collected it next day and went away with it, and they all expected to come back a month later and see you. It was part of the accepted regime. So back he came, and he said, 'It was a mighty good bottle, Doc', and I knew then that I had succeeded. What I didn't understand, of course, and what I still feel bitter about, was that my medical school had never taught me that I was really dispensing that incredible drug, 'the Doctor'. They taught me nothing about the power that lies within the magical words 'Doctor'. They taught me nothing about reassurance therapy; they taught me nothing about understanding the emotions of people; they taught me nothing about the reasons for which people want tonics. I felt very sour about that, because it became quite obvious to me as time went on that a lot of one's work in medicine really consisted of reassurance.

In fact, as I've grown older, I've finally worked out what the purpose of medicine is. I've worked out that it's to alleviate people's suffering. It is not to cure them. It is not to make them better. It is not at all those things. Those are nice little by-products if you can get them, but the real purpose of medicine in my view is to alleviate people's suffering, and that of course was something that we weren't really taught in medical school. We were taught how to treat diseases, which is not the same thing at all. And at any rate, that's where the tonics came in – that tonic in particular came in – because it was my introduction to the management of people. The people expected the tonic, but what they really expected was a dose of the good old doctor who was there before. They expected the reassurance; they expected the recognition that there was nothing much wrong with them, but it had become a habit to dispense tonics.

Then, I hadn't dispensed tonics. Now I hardly ever dispense tonics. I've got my own way of dealing with things, and I don't know whether it suits the particular population who care to come and see me or not, but that's the way I practise and that's the way it's going to be. And so I hardly ever dispense tonics. I dispense myself in large doses. People either like it or they don't, and I guess they make their own decisions about that, but that was something that had to come years later – the realisation that what I was dispensing was myself. But that's where it all started, down on the Coast with this old Welsh miner who came in and asked for the tonic. I guess he's dead now, and I guess he doesn't realise what he taught me.

\* \* \*

I learnt other things from my patients. There was a little boy who died down there on the Coast. I'd done my spell in the children's ward of the Hutt Hospital, where, I might say, I had one of the few medical teachers, medical men, who ever actually taught me anything. Lots of medical people taught me the things I shouldn't know, but he was one of the few who taught me some of the things I *should* know. In fact, he was only one of two who taught me the things I should know about people and children and medicine in general. But this young lad died down there, and it was largely because of my lack of knowledge. I wasn't smart enough to pick up what the trouble was and so on.

That's not been an unusual experience since, of course, because over the years children have died under my care, and I've had cause to wonder about whether I . . . well I've had great cause to wonder, and to *know* at times that I could have done better. In those days it wasn't a very unusual illness that this lad had, but it was something I hadn't been trained to pick up, and I was miles from anywhere, you know – twenty miles out from Westport. Communications were slow, and he died, whereas these days he would have survived. Now I think that one of the things that medical schools should have taught me – and my years in hospital should have taught me – was my ability to recognise the trouble with this lad.

So that made a profound impression on me, did that boy's death, and I resolved, if ever I got the chance, that I would somehow make sure that the younger generation who were going to follow into general practice would know something about the things that they *should* know, because as I said earlier, it was true then that I was ill-prepared for general practice and I'm sure it's true even more so now.

They spend two years in a hospital environment, and although they get more introduction into psychology and behavioural problems, they still don't understand the problems of people that you meet out in general practice, because you don't meet the problems of people in hospital. Well, in fact you do meet them, but you choose to pass them by unless you are an exceptional sort of person. You're still obsessed with looking for diseases in hospital, because that's what the system's designed to do. Hospitals are not, as people popularly suppose, about caring for people at all; they're about caring for people with diseases.

*         *         *

One of the things I learnt down there was, as I said, about the nature of people and their behaviour. We'd been there about a year when I got a call to a house, I guess about a quarter of a mile away. It was on the outskirts of Hector, a mere two or three minutes' walk from our house. So I went down and there was an old lady – I guess she was about eighty – and she was in bed. She had contractures of her leg, so that her hips were flexed, her knees were fixed, and she was lying in bed all curled up.

And I said to the daughter, 'Well, why didn't you call me earlier?' when I discovered that she'd been in bed for a year, and she said, 'Well, Mum didn't want me to call anybody. The old doctor came and saw her the day before he left and he told her to stay in bed and wait till he came.'

And she did just that. She stayed in bed and she never moved out of bed again. We found a suitable placement for her eventually, and I don't know what happened to her . . . I presume she died. But that taught me a lot too, because here was a man who came along, saw an elderly person, and such was his power over her that he said to her, 'Stay in bed', and regardless of the fact that a new doctor appeared down the road and was only about two or three hundred yards away, there was no way that old lady would see the new doctor, for she had implicit faith in what the old doctor had said. She was to stay in bed, and no amount of coercion would make her believe that he'd gone. He just was going to come, and that was all there was to it.

*      *      *

When I went to Stockton, I discovered that there was a list of people whom I was supposed to visit regularly, i.e., once a week. This also was the same in Seddonville, but in Stockton there lived an old lady in an old miner's house. Well, she wasn't all that old – she was about sixty – but the house was filled with the paraphernalia of years. You could barely move through the corridor for chairs and tables and bric-a-brac of various descriptions, and she resided in one of the rooms there, she and her husband.

The Stockton open-cast mine, 1948
*National Publicity Studios Collection, Alexander Turnbull Library*

As I recollect, she was a whining old lady. On the first occasion I met her, she made the hair rise on the back of my neck. I just couldn't seem to get on with her. I didn't get on the wavelength. I've trained myself now, and if people can get on with me, I can get on with them, but it wasn't so in those days, and I determined in the innocence of youth that I would teach her a lesson, that there was no way I was going to see this old lady week after week when she didn't need a doctor.

My predecessor had gone there every week to see her and it was expected of me that I would do the same. So, I said that I would come and see her in a month. Well, nothing much was said, but it soon became obvious that that wasn't going to suffice, because within two days I got a call to say that she was sick and would I go and see her. I went up and couldn't see much the matter with her, and said I'd be back at the end of the month. Another two or three days went by, and I got another call, and that gave me the message, that what I had to do was go up and see her every week.

The previous doctor and she had come to a kind of collusion about things. No one had taught me about this; no one had taught me how to manage the situation; no one had taught me that I should abrogate all the principles I'd been taught in medical school and bow down to this old lady. But in fact, of course, I learnt a very valuable lesson – that life is not like it is in the hospitals, where the doctors sit on high and dispense authority and justice and drugs and God knows what else . . . but that out in the community the people also have their say. So I learnt this very valuable lesson early in the piece, that it's a two-way transaction.

\*          \*          \*

We didn't get all that many emergency calls, but there were the occasional ones when you had to go up to Seddonville at the height of a flood. In fact, my wife and I well remember one occasion when there had been a downpour and the rivers were flooded, and we had a call up to Seddonville to see some old lady who had been found dead in her house. My wife went up with me, and between us both, we laid her out and organised the family and sorted everything out and came back just in time to find that the floodwaters were lapping the road. The road was closed for a couple of days.

There was the odd call up to the mines, but in general the mine injuries were brought out, and only on the rarest of occasions did you have to go down into the mine itself. The biggest disease was 'compo-itis'. Compo-itis was a disease I soon learnt to recognise. I'm not sure that it was a disease, but that's what we called it. There were people there, miners who'd been . . . my wife and I used to reckon they'd been swinging the lead. They'd been in the grips of the System and the System was grinding to a court case, and during the time that the court case was considering being held, and while it was being held, of course, they didn't go back to work for fear some sort of damage might occur to them again, I suppose. So, they spent their time – and I'm sure they wouldn't agree with this – but they spent their time loafing around. And then in the whitebait season they'd swing the biggest whitebait nets on the river and they'd ply you with whitebait. It was very nice being supplied with whitebait, but I never really learnt to square my conscience about it all. But yes, I think compo-itis was the most striking disease. I imagine that's disappeared with the advent of Accident Compensation, but it was very striking in the mines then, very striking indeed.

*      *      *

Some of the people lived under primitive conditions. They weren't so bad in Ngakawau or Hector, but in some of the outlying little hamlets they were. There was one place – and I guess for these purposes they'd better remain anonymous – where the house was built on the side of the hill. It was a relatively modern house but it had never been painted and the people, the inhabitants, had a reputation of being rather grubby. Well, it didn't matter too much to me. I got a call up there one day and I found they had a sink which was quite reasonable really. When we went to Scotland a couple of years later we didn't have a sink in the little tenement house we inhabited, but *they* had a sink. But when I looked underneath the sink, I discovered that the water went into an enormous pit in the floor of the kitchen. It was boarded over and when one lifted up the boards there was this stinking sodden pit of water, full of filthy water underneath.

Well, I got very enthusiastic and muttered about going to the Health Department and they said they were in the process of fixing it, and it would soon be fixed. Eighteen months went by and I was a bit naive; they had no intention of fixing it whatsoever. But I learnt to accept that as part of the conditions on the Coast.

There was another man in the same area whom I went to see one day, and he was said to be in bed with pneumonia. And indeed he was, but he was also in bed with a goat. The goat was tied to the leg of his bed, and there were goat droppings around the floor and the old man had been in bed for three or four days and he hadn't been able to look after the goat. The goat had chewed up things that were inside, and the old boy had pneumonia and so we shipped him out. I don't know what we did with the goat, but it was quite an interesting experience to find a goat there.

In another place on one occasion I went in and there were three small children and they were covered in impetigo – school sores – not just like you see here, a few, but they were literally all over them. I wasn't too surprised, because when I stepped through the door, I had to step over a whole series of little piles of human excreta. It wasn't that they were fresh – far from it. They were dry and stuck to the floor, and they had been there for some days and had never been moved. I did feel moved to remonstrate with the lady of the house, and she went out and got a brush and shovel and swept them up and put them away and said, 'Oh, they must have only just happened.' But it hadn't been that way at all. They'd been there for days baking and drying in the hot West Coast sun.

\*       \*       \*

The personalities in the place were varied. There was the Manager, the District Manager of the Mines, who was a very powerful sort of man and was very much respected, and he ran the mines and he was almost in many ways like a minor god. What he said went.

There were the personalities in the miners' union. I'll tell you about one, the secretary of one of the miners' unions down there. There were a couple of miners' unions and he was the secretary of one but he, for various reasons this Saturday, came into my ken. It was a Saturday afternoon and one of my old friends had arrived on a collier from Wellington. He was a ship's engineer. He came out to stay with us, and when we got this call to go up the hill, I said to George, 'Come on', so we went up the hill and we called into the pub. This man ran the pub.

And there were a couple of burly-looking characters outside who sort of followed me into the room. Nowadays, I wouldn't have tolerated that, but I was a little naive in those days, and I didn't quite know how to handle the situation. I did know my own mind, I knew very much my own mind, but I didn't know quite how to handle that.

Well, I went in and this fellow had arrived back from Christchurch and he was drunk. Goodness knows whether he had driven back from Christchurch or not, but he was really rotten. He had an ulcer on his leg. I remonstrated with him, and said that he'd had that for some time, and it wasn't my job to come up here on Saturday afternoon, particularly when he was drunk. I was bold enough to say that he was drunk. At that, one of the heavies said, 'A guy should bloody well drop you', and the other one made menacing gestures. I wasn't the least bit deterred by this, because if he'd laid a finger, if either of them laid a finger on me, they'd have known what was going to happen. There was no way I was going to fight back because I couldn't have, but they'd have had a court case on their hands for sure.

Well, I told this fellow that he could come down to the surgery to have his leg dressed but that I didn't carry these things in my bag, which was perfectly true, and that if he'd been able to come back from Christchurch and get up the hill driving, if that's what he'd done, then he was drunk enough to come down the hill and see me. Well, I went out with a load of abuse from these fellows, and my friend saw them coming and got out of the car and prepared to do battle, but I said to him, 'Forget about it, George. We'll go.' So we went.

Subsequently, that evening, I got a ring from the local hospital to say that this fellow had been admitted to hospital and they thought I ought to know. Well, I knew full well whom I'd taken on. I'd taken on the secretary of the miners' union, and he was a man who brooked no denial. But he got his denial from me and I wasn't going to budge. Well, to cut a long story short we had an altercation. He went around saying some pretty nasty things about me, so I told him that unless he stopped doing that sort of thing there was no way I would treat him or his family ever again. Now, I'm sure – in fact, I know – I wasn't correct in doing that, but it was a piece of bravado and I thought I might get away with it. Well, his old father interceded on his behalf. His old father was a gentleman whom I very much admired and liked, but no way was I going to change my mind with this rascal saying scurrilous things about me, and I was determined he was going to change his mind. So I demanded a public apology. And I got it. And from that day on I never had any bother with the miners.

*        *        *

There were some problems in distancing yourself from people in a small community. I think that's probably true for most doctors in any community, perhaps not quite so obvious in the larger cities. It's probably a very good rule not to have your patients as friends. We certainly had learned that, but then there was hardly anybody else to talk to except another doctor in Granity, and you get a bit tired of medical conversation after a while, and we simply had to find somebody to talk to somewhere. We found a local farmer and his wife who taught us how to play euchre and we spent long hours down at their place playing euchre, and forty-fives too. He also taught us how to castrate cats.

When I got down there, it was suggested that the doctor's job was to castrate the kittens. So, they brought their kittens along, some of these people in Ngakawau, and said, 'Hey, here, Doc, castrate them' – by the way, we did quite a bit of vet work, one way and another. I thought it was humane to anaesthetize the kittens, so we got some chloroform, popped it on the kittens – and the kittens with unremitting regularity died! I discovered that the lethal dose is very close to the anaesthetic dose for kittens. I was bemoaning my fate one day to this farmer friend of mine, who said, 'That's not the way you do them.' I said, 'How?' and he said, 'Ah, come on and I'll show you.' So I got another couple of doctors – one who was up in Denniston and one who was at Granity – and we all three clustered around whilst he got an old gumboot. He shoved the kitten head-first down in the gumboot and he said, 'Here, this is what you do,' and he held up the tail and got a pair of scissors, and he went snip, snip and he said, 'That's it.' So after that I did it the farmer's way, without any trouble at all, and no deaths.

*        *        *

One day I'd been out gardening. We had a big garden, and I, being a keen gardener, tried to keep it as best I could and we supplied ourselves with vegetables and kept lovely flowers and I had a great time. I came in from the garden, and the Hospital Board had done up the house and they supplied us with a brand-new, hideous, orange-coloured suite for the main room. It was really monstrous. My wife said, 'We can't have that,' and I said, 'Oh well, we've only got to put up with it for two years,' so we put up with it. I bet it was the cheapest thing they could find in Westport.

At any rate, we had this damned thing, and I came in from the garden and I sat down on the suite. My wife, who was very house-proud, came in and said, 'You can't sit on there in those trousers.'

So I said, 'I can and I am.'

She said, 'If you do, if you sit there, I'll take those trousers off,' and I said, 'Have a go' – so she did. She got the top buttons undone and she got the fly-button undone, and I decided that discretion was the better part of valour. There was a long corridor which was perhaps six feet wide which ran the length of the house, so I grabbed my receding trousers about my waist, rushed down the corridor screaming, 'No, no, anything but that!' and opened the door – to find a patient standing there. In the turmoil we hadn't heard a knock, and I can see to this day the look of surprise, dismay, consternation, disbelief – not envy – that came over his face. I made some sort of excuse and hoped he hadn't heard all that was going on, but obviously he had, and I swear that within twenty-four hours the whole district knew about how the doctor's wife undressed him and chased him down the corridor when he had his pants off.

*      *      *

Well, these were the laughs. The problems were really concerned with my identity. I think I said earlier I emerged from the hospital well trained in various skills, well trained in the management of various diseases, but I knew nothing about people. I furthermore had decided that I would pursue an academic career, and to this end was going to England to get my higher qualifications in medicine. In those days, if you had a membership of the Royal College of Medicine in London, it was regarded as a sort of entree to anything. And I acquired that in England with one or two other little odds and ends of things, and I decided that that was going to be my life.

Well, when I went down the Coast – and nobody prepared me for this – I discovered that people were interesting. I had to set about learning this new kind of approach to medicine, and that really was what the two years down the Coast did for me. It taught me – at least the Coast taught me – how I could manage this new kind of medicine. It taught me a lot of new things that I didn't know. It taught me to think for myself and approach problems in a way that I'd never been taught before, and it taught me that people, if you manage them correctly, are a source of never-ending information and, in many respects, never-ending loyalty. I think it's marvellous how after all this length of time some people have actually been my patients for twenty-two years. It must say a hell of a lot for their stamina. It doesn't say much for mine, but it says a lot for them. And it altogether made me realise I had to change course.

And from dedicating myself, or allegedly dedicating myself, to an academic life which was going to be concerned with teaching research, I decided I'd do general practice. And I went to England as I was determined to do, and got my higher qualifications and came back and set up in general practice. And there I've remained, with a part-time hospital job, ever since. I guess I've got the best of both worlds in the present set-up. It's the eternal diversity of things that come through your door. The eternal diversity of coping, the ways of coping that you have to deal with, and the eternal challenge of the undifferentiated illness that comes through your door that's got the charm for me about general practice. And that was what the Coast taught me. It taught me to be self-reliant; it taught me to look critically at what my medical school had taught me; it taught me to unlearn a lot of what I had accepted as dogma, and it taught me, above all, to question the motives of doctors.

First broadcast 20 June 1981

# Appendix
# Oral History and its Techniques

Oral history is so subjective and personal a thing that historians are often divided in their approach to it. Some accept it as a discipline in its own right, and others reject it, on the grounds that human memory is fallible and subjective, and that cross-checking and verification is frequently difficult and often impossible. Others take a middle ground.

The very qualities that give rise to uneasiness at times in the formal historian make for wider acceptance of oral history by the public at large. This is almost certainly because it is so frequently history at a common social level, in which the shared experience of emotions, if not of actual events, engenders a sense of participation.

Much of our formal, written history outlines and analyses policies, decisions and events which have had a significant impact on our way of life. In so doing, it largely reflects the activities of legislators, statesmen, strategists and others whose exercise of power has helped shape our modern world. It goes without saying that historians must always be vitally and validly concerned with such decisive matters, but history, like a mountain, can be observed from many viewpoints, and from each, a different perspective emerges.

The necessarily broad brush of formal history will fill in the light and shade of great events, but the fine detail of the effects of such events on ordinary people is often ill-defined. The scope and depth of the political and economic dislocation caused by the Depression of the 1930s can be amply illustrated by unemployment statistics, various economic indicators, and from Hansard and press reports, but the scope and depth of the day-to-day human misery which resulted is largely implied, and viewed at a distance.

Oral history can, however, provide us with first-hand accounts of those times; personal experiences which bring into sharp and close focus ordinary individuals coping with deprivation – and perhaps even more importantly, their feelings in so doing. Oral history, then, gives back to the people their own history. It holds a mirror to our shared past, and at the same time allows the uniqueness of individual experience to be expressed.

Oral history sits uneasily with politicians, officials, and wielders of power generally. Their recollections can be guarded, often unconsciously, perhaps programmed by years of public life and the understandable desire to conceal matters which may be embarrassing to them or to others. The recollections of ordinary people rather than those of former civic officials are thus more likely to bring alive the history of a small town, for example.

Among the sources of oral history are many individuals whose background and education dissuade them from recording their memories in written form. Yet these same people frequently have an eye, ear, and memory for detail – and a narrative skill – that equips them superbly as subjects for the tape recorder.

The type of history taught in the classrooms of sixty years ago – 'battles and dates history' – has left a legacy in the minds of many. History, as they see it, is a ledger recording the debit and credit facts of past events, penned by the educated and professional classes. As an extension of this belief, they consider that only those in positions of authority are equipped to provide reliable historical evidence.

We have often found that enquiries for informants capable of bringing alive the history of a small town result in our being directed to former town officials, and a range of people respected for their prominence in community affairs. While the recollections of some of these people may be valuable, there is often a blandness and formality about them. It is often individuals whose names have not been disclosed – or indeed, those we have been warned to avoid – who have the powers of detailed observation, the narrative gifts, and perhaps the slightly eccentric perspectives which make the town's past live again.

Because oral history applies to a time period within the span of living memory, it does not follow that all the material gathered must be fifty or sixty years old. The present becomes history in an instant, and the present and the recent past should also be a focus of attention. There is little point in waiting sixty years before recording, for instance, the first-hand experiences of the social division and conflict caused by the 1981 Springbok Tour. In fact, there is much to commend recording, if not at the actual time of the event, certainly while memory is still fresh, uncoloured and unmodified by the passage of time.

One reason oral history concentrates on the early years of this century is simply a sense of urgency, the need to record information from this period while informants are still alive. The comparatively recent and widespread availability of small, cheap recorders, and the growing interest in, and acceptance of, oral history have naturally meant that the elderly have received the greatest attention.

There is, however, another strong reason for concentrating on the elderly. Despite the obvious drawbacks of failing memory, and the altering of perspectives with the passing of time, there is a well-known tendency which develops with old age – people *want* to remember their past, particularly their childhood. Early memories are intensely programmed, and many old people whose recollections of middle life are blurred and sketchy, and whose memory of recent events is even more vague, recall their childhood with a vigour, candour, and degree of accuracy rarely found in the memories of younger people.

The value of oral history is not limited to the material gathered on tape, or transcribed on paper. There are also what might be termed social benefits to the informants themselves, especially the older ones. This is because the oral historian is drawing on a living, responsive source, as opposed to the mainly inanimate documentary evidence of more formal history. And so it is not uncommon to find among people that the very process of sifting back through their lives develops an awareness of the value of their personal past, and stimulates a sense of dignity and purpose which may have been dulled with advancing years. These benefits may also be enhanced by the feeling of new friendship and mutual trust and confidence which often develops between interviewer and informant during recording. The establishing of confidence and trust will be discussed in more detail when the interview itself is considered.

In one respect, the broadcaster who employs the techniques of oral history is in a unique position. He alone is able to reach a mass audience with his material in its original form – as speech. Radio New Zealand has within its archives a recording made by Florence Nightingale – and another by a centenarian who recalled the great Wellington earthquake of 1855. In neither case is the information itself of outstanding interest, and certainly contemporaneous written accounts would furnish it in greater detail. The fascination lies in the voice, in the first-person account, from somebody who was there.

Thus, paradoxically, one of the greatest strengths of oral history is also one of its weaknesses – that in transcription to the printed page, its emotional intensity is lessened.

The purely informational content, of course, remains after transcription, and there is some compensation at least in its comparative accessibility in print.

## Recording oral history

With the popularity of the portable cassette-recorder has come a growing interest in the recording of oral history, and schools, local historical societies and individuals are becoming increasingly attracted to the work.

Because oral history relies on the entirely natural medium of speech, newcomers often overlook the very real problems involved. It appears to be a simple matter of asking a few questions, and radio probably fosters this idea, quite unwittingly. A good interview of this type on radio flows smoothly from point to point, carrying the listener along. The whole programme may seem so relaxed, so spontaneous, that its elements are completely disguised. But the informant has been carefully chosen as not only capable of telling his story, but also of telling it with a considerable degree of personality; the interviewer is highly experienced; and the programme will have been edited before it went to air. And certainly some form of research will have been undertaken beforehand.

With the exception of tape editing, these requirements can be met to an adequate extent by anyone seriously interested in recording oral history, be it a school project, family history, the oral history of a township, or the examination of an event or period in time.

# Preparation

In recording oral history for radio, the experience of thirteen years has led us to divide interviews into two groups – the 'specific' and the 'fishing'.

The 'specific' interview can be researched beforehand, but in 'fishing', the interviewer has to shape the material as it comes, searching for clues that will elicit the most telling information. 'Fishing' is often done when time precludes the vetting of an informant, or a preliminary chat. The broad outlines of an informant's life might be known – the fact perhaps that she was brought up in a West Coast coal-mining township and became the wife of a high-country sheep farmer. Under these conditions, the interviewer is forced to fossick for his material, patiently following leads and asking many questions 'on spec' – and not being too disappointed when they lead up blind alleys.

In contrast is the informant who has undergone a specific experience on which research is available. An example from this book is the late Albert Roberts's account of the wreck of the *Dundonald*. With this type of interview, research must be extensive and thorough. It is not enough to encourage the story-telling with a, 'Yes, go on . . .' The interviewer must be thoroughly conversant with the story, so that he can guide the subject through his experiences, and through his reactions to them. The interviewer provides the skeleton of the story, and the informant fleshes it out.

These, then, are the two extremes of interviews; the majority will fall part-way between them.

Ideally, the interviewer should have a reasonable knowledge of the period relating to his interview, and of the subject itself. There are obvious sources for this – libraries, newspaper files, etc. Some crafts and occupations have an idiom of their own; for example, a miner will talk of 'adits' and 'shafts' and 'drives'. A nodding acquaintance at least with the words of the trade is desirable. There are two reasons for this. The point of a story, or clues to further material, may well be lost if an interviewer is groping with the meaning of terms. More importantly, a person who has devoted a lifetime to a craft or occupation will not strike any degree of rapport with an interviewer who appears ignorant of commonplace expressions. Inevitably, there will be no depth to an interview in this situation.

It is important, whenever possible, to have a preliminary chat with the informant, and at this discussion the interviewer should clearly set out his objective – be it local history or whatever – and the end-use of the material. He will discuss the broad area he wishes to cover, at the same time keeping an alert ear open for other interesting material to follow up in the interview.

A little time is needed for two people to establish a degree of mutual confidence, so the preliminary chat should not be rushed. Most elderly people will talk readily about such traumatic events as the Depression; or an RSA badge might provide a cue to talk about the war years, and so open general conversation. Once the interviewer has established his credentials as an interested and informed listener, and the informant is relaxed, the conversation can become more specific.

Elderly people often doubt the value of their recollections, and a common response is, 'I don't know that I can remember much. I think you'd be wasting your time.' Occasionally this is indeed true, but careful questioning can very often elicit more information than the informant realised he possessed. It is worth stressing to such a person that the period he has lived through is like a jigsaw puzzle, with everybody holding one or two small but often significant pieces which might provide valuable information. Notes should be taken during the preliminary chat, and where applicable, the informant questioned about other people likely to have material of interest.

For preference, the interview should follow a few days later. Points raised in the discussion can then if necessary be checked by both parties, and the few days' gap will restore a spontaneity which might be lost should the interview follow too closely.

The 'preliminary chat' is a guideline only, and it has its exceptions. There is the occasional informant who is bursting to tell a story – possibly by pressure of recent events, possibly merely by nature. One of the stories in this book was recorded under just such circumstances. The wise oral historian keeps a tape recorder in the car even during the preliminary phase, ready for such occasions.

In dealing with Maori informants, Maori social courtesies should be strictly followed. It is customary, and certainly courteous, to be introduced to a Maori informant by another Maori. Certainly, if extensive work is to be undertaken, it will be necessary to first approach the kaumatua, the elders of the community. Their decision may take time, during which the proposal will be discussed, and very likely the qualifications of the interviewer vetted. Assurance may be sought that any material will not be used for profit – and this point is worth stressing to non-Maori informants also.

It is also customary – and gracious – to offer koha when recording in a Maori situation. This can vary from an informal offering of some small delicacy to a donation to the marae fund in a more formal setting.

Natural timidity, perhaps, inhibits many interviewers from crossing what they may feel is a cultural barrier. This is a pity, because of the richness of experience in the Maori community – as a chapter of this book bears witness. Thoughtfulness, courtesy, and a respect for Maori attitudes will in the great majority of cases open the door to a much wider appreciation of New Zealand oral history.

Maori or European, it is important in both the preliminaries and the actual recording not to tire the informant, nor disturb his normal daily pattern. Relatives can advise whether an elderly person is more alert at specific times of the day.

# Equipment

Portable cassette-recorders vary in quality, and although that quality is usually a reflection of price, most modern machines are quite adequate for oral history work. Many machines have built-in microphones, but these are usually supplemented by a socket for a separate microphone. A separate, hand-held 'mike' is much to be preferred. This is because the in-built microphone tends to pick up mechanical noise from the tape transport. It is also more difficult to get both informant and interviewer adequately on-mike when the in-built microphone is used. In that case, too, the recorder itself becomes intrusive.

We are not looking for broadcast quality in the recording, but it is necessary to have clear, intelligible speech, free from hum, noise, 'spitting', hiss, or the 'tanky' sound that results from the microphone being placed too far from the sound source. A notable feature of oral history seminars is the way participants have been converted to the use of a separate microphone after a very brief demonstration.

The advent of stereo cassette-recorders has become a complication rather than an asset to oral-history recording. They could well be effective in recording a group, although a reasonable degree of technical knowledge would be necessary in that situation. With in-built microphones, stereo-recorders suffer from the same limitations as mono machines. If a separate stereo microphone combines both microphone capsules in the one unit, there are no great difficulties; it can be simply hand-held. Frequently though, two separate microphones are used. It is impossible to comfortably hand-hold two mikes for the duration of an interview, and placing them on stands is seldom satisfactory.

In general, the mono machine is the more flexible, and perfectly adequate for oral-history recording. As suggested, it is preferable to hand-hold the microphone, and professionals almost invariably do this. Hand-holding ensures that both parties are reasonably on-mike, which would not be the case should a microphone be set up on a coffee table about sixty centimetres away.

The best seating arrangement is a couple of comfortable chairs set side by side at a slight angle, with a low table handy to carry the recorder, notes, etc. This is much better than having interviewer and informant opposite each other. It is more relaxing to both, and avoids any psychological feeling of, if not confrontation, at least formality. It also ensures that both can be kept on-mike with little or no movement of the microphone. About thirty centimetres is a good working distance for the average microphone. It should be held between the interviewer and the informant at chest level, and canted slightly to favour the person speaking at the moment. If the subject changes position, or moves back in his chair, he should be followed gently by the microphone, to maintain the working distance. It is not advisable to let the informant take the microphone himself. He will be more

An illustration of interviewing techniques. This photograph, of Jack Perkins interviewing, shows: (1) Side-by-side position. (2) Microphone position. Note turn of cable around wrist. This helps to eliminate any noise of cable movement, which can be objectionable with some microphones. (3) Right elbow rests on knee, to give support to microphone hand, and prevent tiring. (4) Eye contact between interviewer and informant. (5) Reference material handy on the table.
*Alwyn Owen*

conscious of it, and the interviewer will be unable to control the working distance.

Microphones vary in the angles between which they pick up sound – in much the same way that the angle of view seen in a camera eyepiece depends upon the lens in use. Corresponding to the telephoto lens is the 'directional' microphone, which accepts sound from a very narrow front; at the other extreme is the wide-angle lens with its counterpart, the 'omni-directional' microphone, which responds to sound from a complete 360-degree radius.

The directional microphone is too selective for general work, and the omni-directional picks up unwanted sound along with the required signal. In specifying a separate microphone for oral history work, the interviewer should ask for a 'cardioid' pattern. This type of microphone is a compromise between the two extremes. It has a heart-shaped pickup pattern that extends somewhat to the sides of the instrument, while being almost 'dead' at the back. By keeping the rear of the microphone to any unwanted noise – street noise, for instance, or washing-up in the kitchen – such noise will be considerably rejected.

Cardioid microphones of either the 'dynamic' or 'FET condenser' type (both suitable for cassette machines) are freely available at comparatively low cost.

If an in-built microphone must be used, again, care must be taken to get both people adequately on-mike. A coffee table is usually too low, and a few books or a cushion may be necessary to support the machine.

Before setting out on any recording assignment, the cassette machine should be checked. This need be no more that a brief check to ensure that the machine is recording and playing back satisfactorily, and that the batteries are adequately fresh – but it is a simple precaution that can prevent embarrassing moments. If a machine is to be left unused for more than two or three weeks, it is essential to remove the batteries. Old batteries corrode not only their own cases, but any metal with which they come in contact. As a general rule, normal 'heavy-duty' batteries will be adequate. If, however, the recorder is in constant use for recording and/or replay, 'alkaline' cells are worth considering. Although heavier and certainly more expensive, they have the advantage of greatly increased operational life.

At intervals of a month or so it will be necessary to clean the recorder's heads, which suffer from a gradual build-up of oxide, abraded from the tape. Unattended to, this degrades the signal, particularly the higher frequencies. 'Cleaning cassettes' are available from audio stores, but these can themselves pick up small dust particles and abrade the heads. A more thorough job can be done with cotton buds and a small bottle of isopropyl alcohol, obtainable from most chemists. If the machine is put into the 'play' mode, with no cassette in place, the heads move forward, and can be gently cleaned until no brown stain shows on the cotton bud. The rubber pinch-wheel should also be gently cleaned.

At no more that yearly intervals, the machine should be 'demagged' by a serviceman. This very simple operation removes any residual magnetism from the heads, so preventing the gradual buildup of hiss and noise in successive recordings.

Cassettes are designated according to their playing time in minutes – C60, C90 or C120. There is normally little point in using other than C60s, because the half-hour of recording time per side is perfectly adequate for most situations. C120 cassettes use very thin tape which can be quite easily stretched or tangled, and are not worth considering.

Above all, cassettes should be stored in their plastic cases, where they will be unaffected by dust. They should never be left loose in a car glove-box or parcel tray. Dust will not only degrade the quality of recording and playback, but will rapidly abrade the heads of the cassette recorder, which are gapped to extremely fine tolerances.

# Recording the interview

## (1) Preliminary testing

The professional interviewer invariably runs a brief test before an interview, asking his informant a question, and then playing back the recording. This is not only to check the operation of the machine, but also to determine whether the microphone placing is correct. A test like this is as important for the amateur as it is for the professional.

If, on playback, the voices are echo-y, with a lack of presence, the microphone-subject distance is too great, and the test should be repeated, with the microphone held closer. Distortion, or 'popping' of such consonants as 'Ps' and 'Ts' indicates that the microphone is too close or the recording level too high – or both. Insufficient recording level shows on playback when the volume control has to be advanced further than usual to produce an acceptable volume – and this will also bring up an undesirable amount of hiss.

Many recorders have automatic volume level, which operates quite well in the home situation. Here, of course, the operator has no control over his recording level, but working too close to or too distant from the microphone will still produce unsatisfactory recordings. Automatic control will not compensate for faulty miking.

Where a machine employs manual recording level, some form of metering is provided. Generally this takes the form of a meter, with the right-hand portion of the scale coloured red. The meter needle should just touch the red as it peaks; if it consistently swings into the red sector, the recording level is too high, and distortion will result.

Other things may well show up in the test. A weak, 'spitting' signal indicates that the batteries are nearly exhausted. Extraneous sound – street noises, for instance – not intrusive to the ear may be irritatingly loud on tape, because the microphone, unlike the ear, cannot 'discriminate', or filter out, unwanted noise. In this situation, the seating should be arranged so that the unwanted sound is at the back of the microphone. If its volume is still too high, a quieter location must be found.

Testing, then, is important, and it is essential not to begin the actual interview until a good clean signal has been obtained. The average cassette-recorder is capable of giving very good results if it is correctly handled, and there is no reason to tolerate a poor recording.

## (2) The interview

It must be remembered that an interview is a social relationship between people, with its own conventions. These must be observed to establish and preserve mutual cooperation, trust and respect.

An interview is *not* a conversation (although it can be conversational in style), nor is it a dialogue. The interviewer's task is to get the informant to talk, and to guide that talk where necessary. Accordingly, the interviewer must avoid constant interruption, yet still play the part of

APPENDIX 211

guide and helper. Thoroughness of research must never show as a parade of knowledge. Nor should the interviewer be embarrassed by silence; pauses can add meaning in the context of an interview, and allow the informant time to think.

To seek only the facts in an oral history interview is to waste the potential of the medium; we also want to discover reactions to events. It is not enough to know that a woman had to make her own and her children's underclothing from flour bags during the Depression; we want to know how she *felt* about having to do so; what it did to her human dignity; the reactions of others.

In many cases – in recording for family archives, for instance – there is a further consideration. It is necessary to record not only the recollections and reactions of an elderly relative, but to preserve also the speaker's personality on tape: to hear the speaker laughing . . . reflective . . . angry. So in some way, the interview must be controlled without any loss of spontaneity.

The most useful word in the inteviewer's vocabulary is 'why', closely followed by 'how', 'when', 'where' and 'what'.

'. . . and of course, every time she went into town she wore those black lace-up boots. All the women did.'

'*Why* was that? Was it the fashion then?'

'Good God, no! They were hideous things. But they *had* to wear them. No tar-sealing, and the streets were ankle-deep in mud.'

. . . which may well be a point you have never thought about before. Another example:

'You were wounded in France, weren't you? *How* did you get that wound?'

'Oh, that – that was nothing compared with what some of the boys got.'

No point in following up other people's ghastly wounds. The informant is pressed:

'Was it a bullet or a shell?'

'Oh, just a bullet.'

Further amplification required, so:

'But *what* happened exactly?'

'We were on patrol one night. A star shell went up, and there was a Hun patrol not twenty feet away.' (Pause.)

'*What* did you do?'

'Didn't have time to do anything. I was just bringing my rifle up, and I was suddenly bowled over. Just collapsed in a heap, and I thought, my God! I'm shot! And then . . .'

. . . and he's away at last.

In addition to the 'why', 'how', 'when', 'where' and 'what' questions, it is sometimes desirable to expand a point by means of description or comment. Phrases such as, 'Tell me about . . .', 'Can you picture for me . . .', 'Just describe . . .', 'How did you feel when . . .', 'What was your reaction to . . .' are most useful.

Questions, of course, should always be as simple as possible, and never double-barrelled. The double question will usually get only half an answer.

At times an informant will respond with an answer known to be incorrect. It is unwise in such a case to directly contradict the informant. A better approach is along the lines of, 'On the other hand, I have heard that . . .' or, 'Some people claim that . . .' This is not to suggest that the interviewer should not on occasion play the devil's advocate, but such an approach needs a certain amount of experience, and a shrewd summing-up of the informant's personality. Many subjects are upset by this technique, but when an informant is known to hold strong or aggressive views on a topic, playing the devil's advocate can on occasion highlight his attitudes.

At all times the interviewer must show interest in what is being said. This is best done by facial expression, or nod. The affirmative 'Yes' or 'Mmmm' can become intrusive with repetition, and is best avoided. Eye contact is very necessary.

Professional oral historians take pains to avoid 'leading' or 'loaded' questions, or indeed any phrasing which might suggest an answer, or persuade the informant to think in the interviewer's terms rather than in his own, e.g., 'We all know that the Model T was an utterly reliable car, which just kept on going. You'd have found this, of course.'

The exception to this rule occurs when the informant's feelings about a topic have become clear, and the interviewer is prompting for further expansion. 'Loaded' or 'leading' it might be, but this form of prompting will not redirect or modify the informant's response, but merely amplify it.

> 'I didn't like that bloke after that; too right I didn't.'
> 'You hated him?'
> 'Yes, I did. I hated him – because for years after , . .'

In a situation like this, the interviewer must be careful however to remain strictly neutral in his attitude, and not place himself in a false position by currying favour with an informant with such comments as, 'That was a rotten thing to do.'

There are several methods of extending an answer. The simplest is the direct question: 'Can you explain that more fully?'

Another technique is to echo the speaker's last words:

> '. . . a Hun patrol twenty feet away.'
> 'Twenty feet away?'
> 'Only twenty feet, as sure as I'm sitting here. And then . . .'

The use of repetition must be controlled, however. Nothing is more wearing than listening to or transcribing a tape in which the interviewer echoes the last words of each answer. This is a common fault; it is done almost unconsciously by the interviewer to give him 'think time' as he struggles with the framing of his next question.

At times an informant's memory may have slipped to the point where he finds it difficult to remember events in sequence; where he strays from the point, and rambles interminably. The value of basic research and the preliminary chat becomes very evident here, because the interviewer draws on it not only for backgrounding, but also to signpost the interview. If a person's memory is faulty, it is useless asking him, 'When did you move to Rawene?'

He is quite likely to spend ten minutes establishing a date that may already be known to the interviewer. More useful material can be gained by saying, 'In 1921 you left Kaeo and went to Rawene. Why did you move there?'

The only way to cope with a long and rambling answer is to interrupt it, gently, but firmly: 'That's interesting, and we'll get on to it later, but I'd like to get back to your move to Rawene . . .'

Despite this measure of control, many people will still tend to ramble, and a good deal of patience is necessary in handling such informants. The recording of elderly people is work that can never be hurried. No attempt should be made to push a long interview through in one session; in that way material will be lost through tiredness. Time should be allowed for a break – for a cup of tea and a stretch. It is often at such times, with the recorder switched off, that fresh leads will come to light for exploration later.

The more interesting and pleasant the recording session becomes for the informant, the better the material will be. The interviewer is not merely a sponge, soaking up information, but must be prepared to contribute, and give a little of himself – not so much during the interview, but certainly before it begins, and during breaks from recording.

## (3) The location approach

Most interviews are best conducted with only the interviewer and informant present, and preferably in the familiar surroundings of the latter's home. The presence of a third person – even a close relative or friend – can subtly inhibit or modify responses. There are occasions, however, when it is desirable to record two people at the same time. An elderly couple who have shared the same experiences may be a stimulus to each other's memory, as well as providing somewhat differing perspectives on the same events.

This stimulus of memory is constantly at the back of the oral historian's mind. Photographs, letters, diaries, etc. can be important 'triggers' to the memory, and their use should not be overlooked. One of the most potent triggers is a location connected with an informant's story. The importance of recording in the familiar security of the informant's home has been noted, but there is no reason why an active subject should not be recorded 'in situ', if he is fit enough to travel. An ex-guard at the Featherston POW camp, for example, might be able to recall the events of the tragic Japanese riot and shooting there in some detail. If he is taken over the ground again, however, his narrating of the story will take on an entirely new dimension. Some of the most intense and telling radio and television programmes have used this 'location' approach.

Wherever the interview is recorded, it is the interviewer's task to shape it. A degree of flexibility is necessary, but there should always be an overall plan in mind. A common fault with beginners is the lack of discrimination. Gratified with a flow of information, the tyro often neglects to control it, and comes away with material on half-a-dozen topics, none explored thoroughly – a state of affairs known to the professional as 'the magpie syndrome'. So a plan is necessary. It may be a strictly chronological approach, covering perhaps childhood to middle age, or it may focus on specific incidents – the 1951 waterfront dispute, the 1918 flu epidemic. Whatever the approach, a plan in the form of brief notes indicating the key areas of questioning is highly advisable. It will allow a more natural flow of questioning, and make it easier to return to the point after any digression.

The interviewer must also realise that, plan notwithstanding, he will not come away from a recording session with a tidy, nicely shaped interview like those heard from time to time on radio. Instead, his material will at times wander down blind alleys; there will be breaks during which the machine was switched off and points discussed; questions and answers may become entangled; there may be 'noises-off' from children, the sound of a washing-machine, or the intrusion of the phone ringing. But remember that the beautifully controlled radio interview has been edited, with the producer working perhaps on a three-to-one ratio – in other words, selecting thirty minutes of recorded material from an original ninety on tape. And along with the unwanted material will have gone the interruptions, the awkward questions, the 'fluffs', and the worst of the coughs and splutters.

## Storing the tapes

When the interview has been recorded, cassettes should be clearly labelled. Ideally, a card should be filled in, giving such details as name, age, address, occupation, subject of interview, time and place of interview, and any other details considered relevant. Most professional recordists preface each tape with a spoken 'ident' – an identification of informant – and this is a most useful habit to acquire. The serious oral historian will also break off the two tabs at the rear of the cassette. This prevents accidental re-recording on an archival tape. Cassettes are the cheapest item in the whole recording chain when they are set against time and travel. To lose a valuable recording through incomplete labelling or inadvertent re-use is sheer carelessness.

In research institutions, tapes are stored under conditions of strictly controlled temperature and humidity. This is not possible in the home, but cassettes will retain their information virtually indefinitely if they are kept away from extremes of heat and damp, and protected from dust in their plastic containers. A re-spooling of cassettes every six months will reduce the chances of 'print-through' – the transference of signal to adjacent turns of tape on the spool. Particularly, cassettes must be kept clear of magnetic fields. Such fields can easily erase part or all of a cassette. They are induced by anything with a high degree of magnetic flux – electric motors, transformers, etc. To place cassettes on a TV set, or adjacent to a loudspeaker, for instance, is to simply invite trouble; they should be kept well clear of any electrical apparatus.

Help is available to the amateur recordist from several sources. The use of libraries for initial research is an obvious starting point. Newspaper offices frequently hold files extending back for many years, and local historical societies are a useful source of information. If the main centres are within reach, the following all have excellent research facilities: the Auckland Public Library and that city's Institute and Museum Library; the Alexander Turnbull and General Assembly Libraries in Wellington; the Canterbury Public Library, Christchurch; the Hocken Library, Dunedin. The technical staff at local radio stations are usually happy to assist with any technical advice that might be required.

Until recently, New Zealand lacked any formal organisation devoted to the preservation of oral history. This gap has been filled with the formation of a New Zealand Oral History Archive. The archive acts as a resource, training and collection centre for oral history projects carried out by groups and individuals; it establishes standards, and files collected material in the Alexander Turnbull Library, Wellington. The archive's officers conduct seminars and workshops on oral history techniques, and undertake speaking engagements about oral history.

The NZOHA may be contacted at the address of the Administrator: Jean Harton, NZOHA, 37 Colway Street, Ngaio, Wellington (Telephone 792792).